The Unraveling of America

by Jeff Shiring

DORRANCE PUBLISHING CO., INC.
PITTSBURGH, PENNSYLVANIA 15222

ISBN-10: 0-8059-7217-X
ISBN-13: 978-0-8059-7217-7
Library of Congress Control Number: 2006921022

Printed in the United States of America

First Printing

For information or to order additional books, please write:
Dorrance Publishing Co., Inc.
701 Smithfield St.
Third Floor
Pittsburgh, PA 15222
U.S.A.
1-800-834-1803
Or visit our web site and
on-line bookstore at www..dorrancebookstore.com

Dedication

To my son, Chase, who has taught me so much about love
and responsibility.
To the Mumster and Rocko, who are my inspiration.
Most importantly, to Kimberly Hicks, who took six years of fragmented
notes and ideas and created a masterpiece.

Contents

Contents *continued*

Preface

Perhaps the sentiments contained in the following pages, are not yet sufficiently fashionable to procure them general favor; a long habit of not thinking a thing wrong, gives it a superficial appearance of being right, and raises at first a formidable outcry in defense of custom. But the tumult soon subsides. Time makes more converts than reason.

-*Thomas Paine, 1776*

In his revolutionary pamphlet *Common Sense*, Thomas Paine called upon the American people to reject the rule of the British monarchy and to follow an independent path of political, social, and economic freedom. His entreaty to discard the status quo and embrace a new vision and direction was initially considered radical and possibly even seditious. But due to his persistence and eloquence, Paine managed to influence his fellow citizens at all levels of society, living to see the realization of his ideal and becoming a patriot of the American Revolution.

While I certainly do not compare myself to Thomas Paine, I deeply believe the time has come again for a dramatic change in direction for our nation. In my own attempt to stir a reaction in the hearts of my fellow citizens, I have written *The Unraveling of America*. It is a compilation of my own efforts to observe and make sense of the often disturbing trends and events of the past several years. I have taken an honest, heartfelt, and sometimes horrified look at the current state of American society-our people, our culture, and our governing systems, both political and economic-and made an impassioned call for changes I believe are necessary to prevent the collapse of our great society and maintain our respected leadership in the world. America is teetering on the brink, and I believe it is up to ordinary citizens-as well as extraordinary ones-to embrace our nation and bring it back to a position of safety, security, and sanity.

Some readers may see this book and these ideas for change as anti-American, taking a swipe at democracy, capitalism, and freedom. For the record, I consider myself a modern-day patriot. I am a very proud American who believes in the greatness of our people and the fundamental concepts of democracy and a free market. I am prepared to make every effort to build on that foundation of our country. I am neither

Republican nor Democratic in my political beliefs; instead I lean to the moderate position which, as we will see, is more broadly capturing the values of the majority of Americans. I consider myself one voice in the growing number of the moderate majority in this country who believe it is critical to recognize our social, political, and economic strengths as well as our growing weaknesses. But I see that if we continue on our current path, we risk the loss of all that is true and good in Americana.

As an engaged member of American society, influenced as much as the next person by popular culture, the media, economic forces, and political decisions, I've learned over my lifetime how to defer accountability for my own personal actions. We've all learned this. We've all learned that we can deny the obvious truths and consequences of our actions and behavior and run from the social accountability of these actions. "I did not inhale." "I did not have sexual relations with that woman." "I did not receive a stock tip." "I am not a crook." All statements of denial. All intentional misrepresentations of the truth. These are just a few examples of literally thousands we are bombarded with from every social influence who are teaching us not to be accountable for our actions. Over the past ten years, through many trials and failures, I have learned to become conscious and accountable for my total actions and participation in our great society. This country, through its citizenry, needs to learn to admit its failures while recognizing its successes in order to grow socially, economically, democratically. The American people and those in positions of power who influence our values cannot-and should not-escape responsibility for the failures and corruption of our social life, our capital life, and our democratic life. This discourse is my way of bearing witness to and participating in the societal shift of focus to bring back accountability in our daily actions to the enormous benefit of our nation.

For the past five years, I have been accumulating information, statistics, news stories, and opinions that amount to irrefutable evidence of an erosion of American values, ethics, and accountability, driven by learned lessons from our social influences- celebrities (professional sports and Hollywood), the media, religion, the economy, and our political system. Daily examples of this erosion, coupled with growing anti-American sentiment around the world, has compelled me to research, evaluate, and understand why we are in this position and what we can do to reposition our country as an honorable, ethical, accountable superpower.

We are a great and powerful nation birthed in revolution against tyranny. I believe it is time to face another revolution today-one that involves looking directly in the mirror and recognizing that the United States, as great as it can be, is heading toward disaster on a grand and global scale. Paine wrote: "The cause of America is in a great measure the cause of all mankind. Many circumstances hath, and will arise, which are not local, but universal...." Our country wields enormous influence around the world; making changes for the better here will necessarily affect the rest of the globe, I believe, in an extraordinarily positive way. Let us meet this challenge with humility and courage, if not for our sake, then for the sake of our children and our future.

I. The Unraveling of America

I have cultivated my hysteria with delight and horror...I have received a singular warning. I have felt the wind of the wing of madness pass over me.

-Baudelaire, French poet and critic (1821-1867)

We are living in mad times: frantic, frenetic, furious times. The pace of change-technological, social, economic, political-is phenomenal. Never before in human history has there been so much achieved as in the past sixty years. Information and innovation can reach anywhere on the planet in an instant. Computer and communication technologies are obsolete almost as soon as they hit the market. Medical breakthroughs are near daily events. We have extended our life spans and enriched ourselves beyond the imaginations of just a few generations ago.

Nevertheless, it is a time of measured prosperity. We are living with war and terror. Our role models are frequently con artists and criminals. We are saturated in fats and fads. We are over our heads in debt and denial. We have become an "instant society": we have demanded and achieved immediate gratification for any and all of our urges. We are slaves to the technology we have created that gives us instant food, instant entertainment, instant information, instant money, instant power; we have the ways and means to be very complacent in our thinking and our actions. The result? A moral inertia and ethical apathy that permeates our daily life and is coupled with an expectation of entitlement. "I want something now and I am going to get it, no matter what." This attitude is both a symptom and a cause of what is a frightening disintegration of the principles and values that once gave birth to and defined America. Hard work, integrity, respect, honor, and the pioneering spirit no longer represent our country and our collective culture. Instead, we are seen (both inside and outside our borders) as lazy, arrogant, violent, greedy, and unaccountable.

Our complacency leaves us vulnerable to being overly influenced by external, superficial forces rather than the structures that traditionally gave us purpose and direction. Marriage is no longer the foundation of family and social stability-it has become an expendable commodity like so many stock options. Because of the number and the scale of scandals in recent years, many people feel that religion has lost its power to guide and heal. Our elected politicians have continually proven themselves to be corruptible and have failed to demonstrate moral and ethical leadership. Our heroes-Hollywood stars and professional athletes-are paid vast fortunes for their fame and still disappoint with unethical, irresponsible, and criminal behavior. There are so few positive role models that we no longer know how to recognize them. It has become less fashionable to report news about deserving heroes than to sell salacious stories about less-than-heroic personalities.

As a result, we drift. We are a people so scattered geographically, culturally, and socio-economically that we are unable to identify a common purpose or principle. That is not to say multiculturalism is a negative thing: America's strength lies in the diversity of its populace, but we are losing sight of the values that bridge the divisions of language and religion and culture to unite us. Without those intrinsic values-of honesty, accountability, cooperation, and acceptance-we become totally self-absorbed and vulnerable to the influence of external motivation and stimulation. Without some common galvanizing purpose, we are ripe to be controlled by popular social influence; we want to be in on "the next big thing" whether it's big business, big blockbusters, big cars, or Big Macs ("Supersize me"). Instead of raising our families, contributing to our communities, taking care of our health and well-being, and all the truly important things that require effort and intention, we allow ourselves to be diverted.

Let me entertain you…

Mikhail Bakhtin, a Russian literary theorist and philosopher, wrote extensively in the early decades of the twentieth century about our human desire for a carnival. In describing medieval carnivals, Bakhtin talked about our need to take standard social themes and institutions and stand them on their heads. At festival time, people reveled in satiric comedies that mocked the Monarchy, the Church, and the privileged elite. The more lewd and graphic the stage production, the more it was appreciated. Violence was entertainment. Unrestrained carnival behavior-gluttonous feasts, uninhibited lust, the spilling of blood-was lauded as a symbolic challenge to the authority figures who were so far removed from, but who wielded power over the masses. Those authority figures themselves encouraged carnivals at various times during the year, as they were seen to be safe and contained outlets for rebellious urges, falling short of actually overthrowing the establishment.

Joseph Goebbels, Germany's Minister of Popular Enlightenment and Propaganda, recognized this same tendency in the public psyche. He was an evil madman, but he was also a student of human nature; he advised Hitler that the best way to gain and exercise control over the masses was to give them what they wanted: a carnival. The bigger the spectacle produced, the more powerful grasp it will have on the imaginations of the viewers and participants and the more they could be influenced.

Do we not find ourselves in the midst of a carnival today? When we turn on the news to watch the events in the Middle East, we see embedded journalists, dressed as soldiers, breathlessly extolling the virtues of our latest weapons technology. We can't get enough of the coverage of bombings and carnage. When we turn the channel at a commercial break for KFC™ or Viagra™, we tune in to "reality" shows that are staged parodies of contrived circumstances with beautiful people (or ugly people turned into beautiful ones). We can't get enough of the glamour and suspense. When we turn on the radio, we listen to child pop music stars and turn them into multi-million dollar merchandising enterprises. We spend Sunday family dinnertime at McDonald's so our kids can have a Happy Meal™, complete with a toy promoting the latest hit movie or television character. We willingly submit to being told what to eat, drink, wear, watch, listen to, and think by the media and those who control it. We seem to crave the carnival in every aspect of our lives, rather than the thoughtful development of our social, economic, and political life. In the excess, we show signs of spiraling out of control.

That is essentially the crux of this discourse: we, the people of the United States of America, have allowed ourselves to be entertained to the point that we are scattered and apathetic. Our most essential values have been eroded by the overriding interference of five major influences in our society: the media, Hollywood and sports celebrities, religion, our political system, and our economy. With that said, let us begin to honestly look into an American mirror. The reflection, like in the circus funhouse, may startle you…

1. America's Youth-America's Future

Violence

Several months ago I had occasion to watch a film entitled *Thirteen*, directed by Catherine Hardwicke. The movie is about a straight-A seventh grader who, in her quest to be cool, gets involved with a popular but extremely troubled girl. She leads them into a parent's nightmare of drug abuse, sex, self-mutilation, theft, and violence. The tagline of the film is "It's happening so fast." The film is raw and bracing and all the more frightening because it was co-written by one of the adolescent stars. Born in 1988, Nikki Reid evidently knows of what she writes and portrays on the big screen.

As much as we might like to hide our heads in the safe, suburban sand and think, "That's not my kid," an Associated Press article dated March 8, 2001, described a wave of violence among children and teens across the United States within a four-day time frame:

A loaded handgun in a kindergarten class. A revolver with a sawed-off barrel in a middle school. Hit lists in high school. Even boasts that the Columbine massacre was mere child's play. Ever since Charles Andrew Williams allegedly killed two class-mates and wounded 13 others Monday at his high school in suburban San Diego, parents and educators have witnessed a rash of school-related threats.

The schools in question can be public and private. They can be elementary, middle or high. The children can be boys or girls, popular or outcast. The reports keep coming in.

In California alone, 16 students, including three teens who attend the California School for the Deaf, were detained since Tuesday for threatening teachers and students for bringing weapons on campus.

Among them was a 15-year old Perris High School student who was led off in handcuffs Wednesday when he boasted that he could outdo the massacre of 15, including two teen gunmen, at Columbine High School in Littleton, Colo., in 1999.

In Pennsylvania, a 14-year-old girl was charged with attempted homicide after allegedly shooting a class mate in the shoulder at their parochial school in Williamsport on Wednesday.

And a 12-year-old student of the Thomas Morton Elementary School in southwest Philadelphia was arrested Wednesday after a .22-caliber pistol was allegedly found in his possession.

On Monday, an 8-year-old boy armed with a loaded handgun threatened a "bloodbath" in the Henry C. Lea School in west Philadelphia before being taken into custody....[1]

In the school year 1999-2000, the most recent year for which statistics are available, 71 percent of public elementary and secondary schools experienced at least one violent incident-that is 1.5 million violent incidents in approximately 59,000 schools. Of those, 20 percent (or 61,000 incidents) were considered seriously violent: threats with weapons, assaults with weapons, sexual assault, or robberies. Bullying was determined to be the biggest problem in 29 percent of the schools, followed by acts of disrespect toward teachers (19 percent) and gang-related activities (19 percent).[2]

On March 21, 2005, the shooting rampage of a sixteen-year-old left ten people dead (including the teen) in Red Lake, Minnesota. Jeff Weise shot his grandparents before firing on school classmates, killing five students, a teacher, and a security guard. In October 2004, two Texan teens were arrested for planning to recreate the 1999 Columbine High School massacre during a pep rally at their school. The fifteen and sixteen-year-old had discussed potential targets and the wearing of trench coats to hide the weapons to which they had access, including a shotgun.[3] The day before Halloween in 2004, a twelve-year-old Baltimore girl was charged for beating to death a four-year-old family friend. The incident was just one of more than thirty youth homicides in Baltimore that year, nine victims of whom were younger than ten.[4] Another Baltimore case involved a twelve-year-old girl who was beaten into a coma at a birthday party in late February of 2004, after the boyfriend of another girl kissed her on the cheek on a dare. Several women and teenaged girls were charged with attempted murder and assault.[5] Of course, there is Columbine itself, the worst school shooting in U.S. history: on April 20, 1999, Eric Harris and Dylan Klebold shot and killed twelve students and a teacher, and injured twenty-four others, before committing suicide in the school library. The Littleton, Colorado, massacre was so shocking it will forever be recognized by a single word, much like 9/11.

While the above examples demonstrate violence among kids from various rungs on the socio-economic ladder, it is well-documented that children of poverty are at a higher risk for violence and violent crime. In the recently released annual report *America's Children in Brief: Key National Indicators of Well-Being, 2004,* the government study of seventy-three million Americans under eighteen found that more than twelve million children were living in poverty in this country in 2002, an increase from 2000 and 2001.[6] More kids than ever are at risk for becoming involved in the justice system, either as victims or aggressors. Nationally, violence by teenage boys outstrips violence by teenage girls by a ratio of four to one; ten years ago, the ratio was ten to one.[7]

Violence among children and teens is not just directed at others. The Center for Disease Control and Prevention reported 3,971 suicides of juveniles aged 15-24 in 2001, 54 percent of which were committed with firearms. Suicide is ranked as the third leading cause of death for this age group.[8]

Health and Well-Being

The physical fitness of children and adolescents is no rosier than their mental health: the number of overweight children has more than doubled since 1970, with 16 percent of kids aged 6-18 currently overweight.[9] An afternoon spent at a public swimming pool or the local mall might suggest that this number is low. Kids are too heavy and the trend is on the rise. The reasons are almost self-evident: fast food high in fat, salt, and sugar is the dietary mainstay of our youth; preferred entertainment is of the high-tech indoor variety (videogames, DVDs, MP3s, etc.); and parents chauffeur their children to activities, rather than allowing them to walk or ride their bicycles. (The argument that this practice is necessary for supervision and for ensuring children's safety from sexual deviants, abductors, and careless drivers merely emphasizes the point that our nation is in crisis.) The result is overweight children tend to become overweight adults and are at higher risk for developing chronic diseases, such as diabetes and hypertension, putting excess strain on their bodies, as well as the health care system.

At the opposite extreme is the number of teens and young adults with anorexia and bulimia. Distorted perceptions of body image seem to be the norm for American, especially female, adolescents. More than half of teenaged girls are, or think they should be, on diets.[10] Yet dieting at an early age is one of the biggest risk factors for developing an eating disorder (including compulsive overeating). While it is difficult to find reliable statistics on eating disorders (for various reasons, including lack of disclosure because of shame, ignorance of the condition, misdiagnosis, and lag time between diagnosis and treatment), it is estimated that 1 in 100 teenagers have anorexia nervosa and 4 in 100 have bulimia.[11] These numbers are significantly lower than those for obese kids, but the health ramifications are equally dire. Only 50 percent of people who develop these conditions are ever considered cured, and more serious cases-about 6 percent-result in death. The National Association of Anorexia Nervosa and Associated Disorders (ANAD) states that more than eight million Americans suffer from eating disorders (3 percent of the population) and categorizes these numbers as "epidemic."[12] Despite the media coverage of anorexic celebrities such as Mary-Kate Olsen and Lara Flynn Boyle, ANAD asserts that eating disorders afflict all echelons of society-all ages, races, and both genders.

While eating disorders are not strictly within the realm of the affluent youth of our society, another alarming trend among young women may be. The *Atlanta Journal-Constitution* recently reported the latest in high school graduation gifts for well-heeled American girls: breast implants. Despite the known health risks described by the U.S. Food and Drug Administration and the 2.35 billion dollars that Dow Corning is now paying to more than 170,000 claimants for illnesses related to silicone implants in the 1980s and 90s, American women are having breast augmentation surgery in record numbers. Both the American Society for Aesthetic Plastic Surgery and the American Society of Plastic Surgeons report a doubling of breast enlargement surgeries in the past five years, and more than 11,000 of those were performed on women under nineteen years of age.[13] Obsession about body image has reached a level where the two teens interviewed for the story compared getting implants to teeth-whitening or highlights. One girl admitted to not even having read the surgeon's information about side effects and possible complications because she "didn't want to freak herself out."

High-Risk Behavior

Beyond an alarming obsession with appearance and either too much weight or too little, our youth are also subject to other unhealthy lifestyle choices. In Monitoring the Future, a national survey by the University of Michigan's Institute for Social Research that tracks trends in substance abuse by eighth, tenth, and twelfth graders, results for 2003 were mixed. While there has been a decline in marijuana and tobacco use across grade levels since 1996 (10 percent of eighth graders and one-quarter of twelfth graders are cigarette smokers, for example), alcohol consumption was high and showed a trend toward increased binge drinking. (Binge drinking is characterized as five or more drinks in a row at least once in the previous two weeks.) By the end of twelfth grade, 77 percent of students had consumed alcohol and 50 percent reported having been drunk. One in five eighth graders reported having been drunk; 45 percent had tried alcohol before entering high school. The use of inhalants by eighth graders increased in 2003 to nearly 9 percent of students. Use of heroin, cocaine, crack, and other narcotics has remained fairly constant over the past several years: 25 to 30 percent of kids have used illicit drugs other than marijuana by the time they finish high school.[14]

Substance use among adolescents has been described and decried for many decades. Kids use drugs and alcohol for a myriad of reasons: curiosity, peer pressure, rebellion, stress, depression, sense of invincibility, and availability of the product. Perhaps another reason might be boredom. According to the National Center for Education Statistics, in October 1999, 3.8 million young adults aged 16 to 24 were not enrolled in a high school program and had not completed a high school education (11 percent of that age group). In 2003, 13 percent of this age group were neither enrolled in school nor working.[15] There was a 10 percent drop in teen employment between 2000 and 2003, pushing the job rate for this group to a fifty-five-year low.[16] If they are not working or going to school, what exactly are they doing?

Data from the CDC Youth Risk Behavior System for 2001 showed that 46.5 percent of high school students reported having had sexual intercourse (60.6 percent of twelfth graders and 34.4 percent of ninth graders).[17] According to the National Campaign to Prevent Teen Pregnancy, another 17 percent of seventh and eighth graders reported having had sex.[18] While teenage pregnancies in the U.S. have declined over the past decade to a record low, 34 percent of girls give birth before age twenty, which is the highest teen pregnancy and birth rate of the developed world.[19] Babies aside, every year there are fifteen million new cases of sexually transmitted diseases diagnosed in the U.S., one-quarter of them among teenagers.[20]

Sex and kids is an uncomfortable combination for many people, whether it is about sex-education in the school health curricula, their own extracurricular experimentation and participation, or-the worst of horrors-the adult exploitation of children. Religious values aside, most parents, educators, counselors, and others who deal with children on a regular basis would agree that kids are preoccupied with sex. "Sex on the brain" is becoming a phenomenon at younger and younger ages and, disturbingly, it is no longer teenagers who are exhibiting behaviors beyond their years. A current grade school fashion trend among eight- to thirteen-year-olds is girls wearing or boys laying claim to colorful jelly bracelets; these are secretly color-coded to represent the performance of activities ranging from kissing to oral sex to "going all the way." Shopping malls are now home to clothing stores that sell lingerie for the prepubescent customer; it is possible, and apparently acceptable, to buy a lacy, padded push-up bra in size 30AA with a matching thong panty. Popular dolls that have wiggled into the Barbie market-appropriately called "Bratz" and inappropriately wearing exaggerated heavy makeup and sexy outfits-are labeled on their boxes as "boy crazy fashion fiends"; they are marketed to little girls aged six and over.

There is little comfort in the fact that this fascination and preoccupation with sex is not hormonally induced: it is market-driven. Tweens are a twenty-five million-strong consumer group that is to merchandisers as a bell is to Pavlov's dog. They are subject to, and the driving force behind, a $335 billion market that includes their own spending, as well as their parents spending on their behalf.[21] Savvy marketers' awareness of this resource pool has inspired the industry ethos of "age compression," a strategy which capitalizes on (or creates) kids' desire to seem older, more sophisticated, and ultimately cool. Kids want to be sexy even when they don't understand the true implications of the word; worse still, even when they do.

The distinction between consumer product and pop culture is blurred to the point that kids (and their parents) can't even see it. (This is discussed further in the chapter on media.) The result, though, is an ever-growing number of kids who resemble the girls in the movie Thirteen.

Education and Attitudes

Kids who manage to avoid or survive exposure to every parent's nightmare of substance abuse, violence, and teenage parenthood, and stay in school are not necessarily staying out of trouble or demonstrating any degree of moral superiority. According to a 2002 survey of 12,000 students by the Los Angeles-based Josephson Institute for Ethics, 74 percent admitted to cheating on an exam at least once in the past year.[22] ABC *Primetime* conducted a six-month investigation of cheating by high school and college students across the country and discovered a whole new mindset. Kids see cheating and lying all around them-in business, politics, sports-and understand that since it has become the norm, they must do it too, just to stay in the game.

Plagiarism by downloading papers from the Internet is so commonplace that there are dozens of term paper clearing houses that blatantly advertise other people's written work for sale. Students who have text messaging and camera phones, personal electronic organizers, graphic calculators, and wireless mini-computers have no need to learn material in class: all of these devices can be brought into an exam with all of the information required for the test stored in digital memory. "Test Prep" companies solicit parents of high school juniors to teach their kids how to improve their SAT scores. They appeal to parents by pointing out that their child has less of a chance getting into college on his or her own academic merit than other kids who are paying upwards of one thousand dollars for their summer school services. Whether specific exam preparation such as this constitutes actual cheating is debatable, but these classes certainly are "teaching to the test" rather than emphasizing learning for understanding.

Perhaps this attitude is reflected in the ranking of the U.S. educational system among other countries in the developed world. In 2002, UNICEF conducted a study resulting in the most comprehensive look to date of how dozens of education systems function as a whole on the international level. The Innocenti Research Centre, formerly the International Child Development Centre, looked at what fourteen- and fifteen-year-old students know and what they can actually do (as opposed to what level of education they reach) and determined that the U.S. ranked eighteenth out of twenty-four countries in five measures of absolute educational disadvantage. Specifically, 39 percent of eighth graders did not reach the median of mathematics achievement for all children of all countries measured and 18 percent of fifteen-year-olds were at or below a fixed international benchmark for reading. The study found that of the many factors that determine educational success, in all of the OECD countries, it was the parents' education, occupation, and economic status that was most closely linked to student achievement.[23] Considering that 55 percent of adult male children aged 18 to 24 and 48 percent of females in the same age group are still living at home, it makes sense that parental attitudes and circumstances play a large role in the success of their offspring. [24]

Kids are doing as little as they can possibly get away with and parents are encouraging it. In many high schools across the country, graduates who have failed to complete the requirements for matriculation are allowed to don cap and gown and receive a fake diploma with their achieving classmates, so they will not be stigmatized by their failure. Without any real consequences for lack of effort or initiative, they have no motivation for success. Not only are they not reaching their potential, they don't have any idea what that potential might be. Mediocrity is the level to aim for, at best.

Apathy among youth toward academic excellence applies to the political realm as well. In the 2000 election, only 29 percent of eligible voters ages

18 to 24 (approximately 8.4 million) participated, compared with 55 percent of the general population.[25] Is it because young people feel remote from the system, their interests not being reflected in public policy? Are they disillusioned by our political leaders? Or do they feel so comfortable and privileged that they see no reason to exercise their electoral vocal chords?

The prevalence of violence in the lives of American kids, access to and widespread use of mind-altering substances, early sexual activity, poor performance in school, and a lack of interest in their own future are all indicators that we are failing to teach our children the values that will allow them to thrive and succeed in their adult years. We are not teaching them to be honorable, to respect themselves and others. We are not teaching them to achieve success through their own abilities and merit. Instead, we are teaching them the fastest possible route to making a buck, rather than encouraging them to discover the challenging journey of prosperity. America's youth are America's future: the brilliance of that future depends entirely on the polish we apply today.

2. America's Adults

It is a pan-generational experience for adults to wring their hands and bemoan the state of the younger generation: they're violent, they're lazy, they're on drugs, they're having sex too young... Youth has always been synonymous with rebellion and pushing the boundaries of what is socially acceptable. But what are the boundaries anymore? Observation of the lack of substance and moral fiber in today's society indicates that the problems of our youth are reflective of the adults-the supposed role models and guides-around them. Peering into our own funhouse mirror is just as disturbing as that of our children.

Violence and Crime
The U.S. Bureau of Alcohol, Tobacco and Firearms (BATF) reported that from 1980-1993, the most recent date for which numbers are available, 16.2 million guns were legally imported to the U.S. and another 57 million were produced for civilian use: that is an average of nearly 5 million guns per year legally available for civilian use. (The BATF doesn't know how many more are illegally imported and sold in the country.)[26]

In 1997, 42 percent of Americans said they had at least one gun in their home.[27] The National Rifle Association currently estimates that there are 60-65 million gun owners (45 percent of households) who collectively own more than 200 million firearms. The NRA claims to have 4 million card-carrying members.[28]

A 1995 FBI Uniform Crime Report determined that approximately a half-million crimes were committed in the U.S. by people with guns. In 2001, there were 20,308 homicides; more than half of them were committed with firearms.[29]   That year, homicides ranked as the thirteenth leading cause of death. (Suicide ranked eleventh).[30]   The CDC reports that 55 percent of suicides in 2001 were committed with a firearm. The CDC also claims that studies have shown the presence of a gun in the home increases residents' risk of suicide, as well as unintentional gunshot wounds among children and teens.[31] The Department of Justice reports that one-third of all female murder victims are killed by a spouse or family member and over 70 percent of all women murdered by their spouses or ex-spouses are killed with a firearm.[32]

The problem of domestic violence is so widespread that a 1996 study by the American Psychological Association found that one out of three women experienced at least one physical assault by a partner during adulthood. They also determined that 92 percent of American women rank domestic and sexual violence as one of their top priorities, even though only one in seven domestic assaults is brought to the attention of police.[33]

If we are not directly experiencing violence in our homes, we are living it vicariously through the media around us. We are inundated with violence every time we turn on the television or DVD player or X-box: kidnappings, stabbings, drive-by shootings, rapes, child molestation, bombings, and beheadings. We are so inured to slaughter and mayhem, we haven't noticed the significant increase in violence in our entertainment, including the fact that there is a higher rate of violence in animated films than in non-animated ones. The Harvard School of Public Health studied movie ratings between 1992 and 2003 and discovered a significant "ratings creep" over the decade, which translates into more violence, sex, and profanity in films rated for younger ages.[34]

Indeed, our appetites for more graphic visual content have been duly noted by filmmakers: more and more mainstream cinema is being produced with full nudity (pick one!), simulated penetration (*Basic Instinct, Original Sin*), and non-simulated oral sex (*In the Cut*). The explosion of the pornography industry is evidence of our sexual voracity. More than forty million American adults visited a pornographic website in 2003, generating twelve billion dollars for the porn industry, twice the combined revenues of ABC, CBS, and NBC.[35]   It may be argued that the Internet has added fuel to this fire: the cyberporn industry alone, with 4.2 million websites (12 percent of the total number of websites on the Internet) generated $2.5 billion in 2003.[36]

Consensual adult behavior aside, a much more alarming trend is the step beyond cybersex into child pornography and the commercial sexual exploitation of children. The U.S. Customs Service estimates there are more than one hundred thousand websites offering illegal child pornography-generating revenues between $200 million and $1 billion annually.   [37] (Child pornography possession and distribution charges filed against a national program director of the Boy Scouts of America sent a chill up the collective parental spine in March 2005. In a surreal twist of irony, sixty-one-year-old Douglas Smith of Texas served as an adviser for several years to the Scouts' Youth Protection Task Force, which taught children and adults how to detect and prevent child abuse. Smith took an early retirement when the charges were filed.[38]) While the full extent of child exploitation crimes is unknown, the most comprehensive study completed to date estimates that more than 1.7 million American children were victims of sexual harassment in 2000 and between 200,000 to 300,000 children under seventeen in the U.S. are at high risk for involvement in commercial sexual exploitation annually.[39] The U.S. State Department Bureau of Intelligence estimates that approximately 45,000 to 50,000 women and children are smuggled into the United States annually, one-third of whom are seventeen or younger; at least half of these children eventually become victims of child pornography and prostitution.[40]

Health

Adult appetites are hungry for other fare as well. The national trend toward obesity has been a regular feature on the media menu over the past few years; we are a nation obsessed with food. Two-thirds of Americans are overweight and 30 percent are considered obese.[41] The problem has become so enormous that many states have instituted (or are considering) legislation to ban junk food vending machines, mandate physical education in school, and require restaurants to post nutritional information; all this to try to rein in the soaring costs of health care from chronic obesity-related diseases, including heart disease (the number one killer), diabetes, and cancer. The CDC reported that a poor diet and lack of exercise contributed to 320,000 deaths in 2000, making obesity the second-leading cause of preventable death.[42]

The wave of popular diets, including Atkins and South Beach, may well indicate that we are trying to battle the bulge by trimming our food intake, but we are also relying heavily on prescription drugs to treat the problem (or symptoms of the problem). Five of the top ten prescription drugs sold in the U.S. in 2002 are used to treat medical problems typically related to obesity: Lipitor (2) is a cholesterol-lowering drug; Synthroid (3) is a hormone therapy for hypothyroidism often prescribed for the treatment of obesity; Atenolol (4) is a beta blocker used to treat angina and hypertension; Furosemide, also known as Lasix, (7) is also used to treat hypertension; and Norvasc (8) is a calcium channel blocker also prescribed to treat hypertension and angina.[43]

It would seem that not all Americans believe that bigger is better, and the key to staying young is a surgeon's scalpel. According to the American Society of Plastic Surgeons, 2.8 million procedures were performed by its members in 2003 on "people who took action to proactively manage signs of aging and enhance their appearance," an increase of 41 percent from the previous year alone.[44] According to ASPS spokesperson Denise Sneider, the total number of cosmetic surgeries in the U.S. performed by ASPS surgeons as well as other specialists, including ENTs (ear, nose, and throat specialists) and dermatologists, totaled 8.7 million.[45] Women going under the knife comprised 82 percent of patients, many of whom were 35 to 50 years of age. The most popular procedures were Botox injections: there were almost one million of those done by ASPS members last year. Breast augmentation ranked number two on the list: the 246,930 procedures performed in 2003 mark an increase of 657 percent from 1992-2003.

It is quite a paradox-we are obsessed with our appearance but do not necessarily translate that obsession into a healthy lifestyle. Rather than eating less and exercising more, we spend a fortune on quick fixes like surgery and drugs, including illegal ones. In 2002, 19.5 million Americans used illegal drugs; the highest rate of use was among eighteen- to twenty-five-year-olds (more than one in five).[46] That is an increase of more than two million people using illicit drugs since 2001, according to the National Survey on Drug Use and Health for those years. Workplace drug testing shows an increase in the number of employees testing positive for drugs, including marijuana, amphetamines, and opiates. The number of workers who failed drug tests in 2003 was up slightly to 4.5 percent; within that group, the number of people using methamphetamine (commonly known as ice) increased 68 percent from the year before.[47]

Why are we so unhappy with ourselves? Perhaps because the marketplace determines how we think we should look and feel, rather than focusing on actual health. In any two-hour time span of weeknight prime time television, commercial airtime is dominated by products to promote hair color, hair growth, hair removal, penile erectile dysfunction, cosmetics, anti-wrinkle solutions, upscale automobiles, beer, and convenience food. The refreshing dearth of tobacco advertisements has not deterred the estimated 46.2 million adults in the U.S. who continue to smoke cigarettes, despite the fact that the habit will result in death or disability for half of all regular smokers; it is responsible for 440,000 deaths each year.[48] In 1998, American consumers spent nearly $56 billion on cigarettes;[49] and tobacco farmers are estimated to receive $9.6 billion dollars from the U.S. government over five years under a corporate tax bill just passed by the House of Representatives.[50]

Drowning in Debt

It would seem that we spend a fortune on other things as well. A November 2003 news release of the Administrative Office of the U.S. Courts reported there were 1,661,996 bankruptcies filed in that fiscal year, a 98 percent increase from 1994. Personal (non-business) bankruptcies are at a historic high-one family files for bankruptcy every fifteen seconds-

and make up 98 percent of all filings.[51] The National Foundation for Credit Counseling advised 1.6 million households in 2003; the web-based debt management company Myvesta.org reported that their average client has six credit cards and carries $18,000 in debt.[52] According to the Federal Reserve, individual household debt (i.e., revolving home equity loans) more than doubled between 2001 and 2003 to an all-time record high of $269.9 billion as of November 2003.[53] Credit card delinquency rates (account payments more than thirty days past due) rose to an all-time high of 4.43 percent in the fourth quarter of 2003.[54] There are seventy-eight million credit card users in the U.S. and 60 percent don't pay off their monthly balance; this leaves the national credit card debt total in the range of $735 billion, eleven times more than it was in 1980.[55] Consumer debt is expected to hit $838 billion this year, an increase of nearly 7 percent from 2003 and more than double what it was ten years ago.[56]

Breaking the numbers down into age categories, Americans aged 25-34 are spending a quarter of every dollar of income on debt repayment; 18-24 year-olds are paying a nickel more. Credit card debt of the latter age group-coined "Generation Broke" in a recent report of the same name-rose more than 100 percent between 1992 and 2001.[57]

Why are we spending more than we earn? Because job growth is slow, borrowing costs are low, and living costs are high. To live comfortably in the United States-that is, affording adequate shelter, utilities, transportation, food, clothing, education, and health care-households require at least two wage-earners. According to the annual Consumer Expenditures Survey, average expenditures increased nearly 3 percent in 2002. The average consumer unit (household or family) had a before-tax income of $49,430 and spent $40,677 on living expenses.[58] Expenditures are also influenced by taxes. The average tax cut in 2004 for Americans whose household income ranked in the top 1 percent was $78,460; as for households with an average annual income of $57,000 (most likely two-income families), the tax cut was just $1,090.[59]

Some of us are spending more than we earn on what many might consider unnecessary luxuries. The Department of Transportation has determined that the number of cars in the U.S. outnumber licensed drivers in American households. Nearly three out of ten families have three cars parked in their driveways; nearly one in five new homes has a three-car garage, almost double the rate of ten years ago.[60]

On the other side of the economic fence, the number of Americans living below the poverty line increased by 1.3 million in 2003 bringing the total to 35.8 million people, or 12.5 percent of the population. (What is considered to be poor depends on the household size: a family of four is below the line if their annual income is $18,810 or less; for a two-person household, the magic number is $12,015.)[61]

Part of the debt burden on young adults can be blamed on several factors. Financial institutions target students by making it easy to apply for and receive credit cards. Students themselves go off to college expecting to maintain the same standard of living they had at home. Without budgeting skills and the ability to prioritize wants versus needs, they end up paying for necessities as well as "luxuries" with their high-limit plastic. Coupled with student loans, credit card balances leave graduates in a situation of heavy debt, starting out in the job force often with a bad credit rating and facing higher insurance premiums as a consequence of three or four years of financial mismanagement.

A critical consequence of not earning enough money, and of spending more than we earn, is illustrated in the fact that the number of Americans without health insurance is also surging. In 2003, 45 million people (15.6 percent of residents) were without adequate health coverage. With the rising costs of health care, families confronted with major illness or accidental injury without insurance face potential destitution, as do many people who have insurance through their employer. A Harvard University study released in February 2005 determined that medical bills account for nearly half of all personal bankruptcies in the U.S.; the study also found that 75 percent of those people had insurance coverage at the beginning of their illness.[62] Americans without health insurance also face huge health risks: the Institute of Medicine estimates there are eighteen thousand unnecessary deaths each year resulting from lack of access to proper medical care.[63] The United States is the only industrialized country that does not provide universal health coverage paid for by tax dollars; instead it relies heavily on employer coverage and privately purchased plans. Clearly the system is failing Americans: small and large businesses alike are struggling to afford insurance for their employees, so they are dropping plans altogether or raising employee contributions to a level that many opt out of because they are unaffordable. Many people, particularly in the service industries, work part-time and do not have the option of employee benefit plans. The reasons for the soaring costs of insurance include the increasing litigious climate and repeated health care for so many people with unhealthy lifestyles. These are probably our own fault, but the end result is that many Americans are financially hobbled by the costs of adequate health insurance or the costs of not having it when it is needed. For many of us, including the young and healthy, health care is low on the priority list of personal spending budgets.

Attitudes and Parenting

Perhaps the debt we are drowning in explains another unsavory trend: cheating on our taxes. While the vast majority of us are straight up with the IRS, 12 percent of survey respondents to a July 2003 Roper poll said "a little cheating here and there" was acceptable (the number was up 2 percent from 2002).[64] Those numbers are accurate assuming that people are answering the question honestly, but is it realistic to assume that all cheaters admit to it? Probably not. It is no wonder kids look at cheating as morally relative: if their parents think it is okay to cheat sometimes, why shouldn't they as well?

Another flagrant example of cheating recently hit the news: Elizabeth Paige Laurie, twenty-two-year-old heiress to the Wal-Mart fortune, was accused of hiring a surrogate student to complete her communication studies degree at the University of Southern California. The student, Elena Martinez, claimed Laurie paid her $20,000 over three and one-half years to write papers and complete assignments for her to graduate. Laurie's parents ostensibly donated $25 million to the University of Missouri in exchange for the right to name the school's new sports arena after her, even though Laurie was never a student there. In light of the controversy, the University opted to change the name from Paige Sports Arena to the Mizzou Arena. The family refused to comment on the allegations except to agree to the renaming and state that Laurie's academic record is "a private matter."[65]

Attitudes of parents necessarily affect those of their children, although parents of teenagers will heartily disagree. The primary influence occurs much earlier than adolescence. One-third of all school-aged children in the country are latchkey kids, and one-half of children aged 12 to 14 are home alone an average of seven hours a week.[66] The majority of American kids are growing up in one-parent households or homes with two working parents, and a great deal of what they learn necessarily comes from television and media (i.e., the Internet) and peer groups. Parents struggling to stay afloat and maintain a household simply have too little energy left at the end of the day to focus on teaching their children what should be the basics: communication skills, social etiquette, ethical behavior, community participation, budgeting, critical thinking, and how to use their imaginations. (This is essentially, how to be productive, creative, and valuable members of society.) At the other extreme are the (usually) affluent children with parents who enroll them in every activity available, chaperone their every move, fulfill their every material demand, and with the heartfelt intention of providing the best for their children, end up creating spoiled, entitled, and unaccountable adults.

Parents of every economic strata are responsible for entering more than 100,000 (some say the number is closer to 250,000) children under the age of twelve into the hundreds of beauty pageants across the country each year. According to testimonials of many parents and pageant organizers in the press and in film documentaries such as *Living Dolls: The Making of a Child Beauty Queen* (2001), there is a genuine belief that adding hair extensions to an eight-month-old's head and having false teeth inserted where a permanent tooth has not yet grown in somehow builds a child's self-esteem and prepares them for the inevitable compe-

Jeff Shiring

tition they will face in their adult years. One judge, in defending the Miss Teen USA pageant for girls aged 15 to 18, said winners are determined based on "beauty, high moral standards, community involvement and charisma."[67] Nevertheless, the contestants are still required to compete in an evening wear and swimwear parade in addition to the interview. Where exactly do high moral standards come in when teenaged bodies are being bared, examined, and scored? The Miss America organization is switching its gears to the teen scene as well, since ratings for its main pageant have plunged lower than its evening wear necklines. In Miss America's Outstanding Teen, to be held in Orlando in August 2005, the traditional swimsuit segment will be replaced by a "lifestyle and fitness" competition, with the girls appearing in leotards rather than bikinis. Organizers felt it was unfair to have thirteen-year-olds competing against seventeen-year-olds in swimsuits.[68]

Then there is the attitude of people like the management consultant who told a group of eighth grade students at a school career day in Palo Alto, California, they could earn $250,000 a year as strippers if their bust size was big enough. William Fried defended his inclusion of the profession in his list of 140 lucrative careers saying, "It's sick, but it's true. You can earn a tremendous amount of money as an exotic dancer if that's your desire."[69] It may very well be true: one can also earn a tremendous amount of money as a porn star, but is it really necessary to plant that seed in the minds of children? "Hmmm, let's see: I can pursue a career in science to find a cure for cancer, or I can take my clothes off and make lots more money...."

"The child is an ever attentive witness of grownup morality," writes Robert Coles in his book *The Moral Intelligence of Children*, which looks at the ways in which parents shape-or fail to shape-a child's behavior by their influence on his or her moral development.[70] Moral intelligence, he says, which comes directly from absorbing what is seen and heard from infancy onward, peaks during the elementary years when conscience starts to fully form. Instead of parents complaining about their lack of control and influence, and taking less and less responsibility for the behavior and attitudes of their children ("He has Attention Deficit Disorder," "She just won't listen to a word I say,") perhaps they (we!) need to take another look in that mirror and ask ourselves where we are headed and why.

The numbers in this chapter are a lot to absorb, and there is always caution to be exercised when digesting bald statistics. But they support the assertion that we are indeed in the center of a mad carnival. We are mesmerized instead by the circus entertainment around us-the lights and sounds and cotton candy-unable to focus on the health of our society and the health of our children. The entertainment is somewhat more sophisticated than the town festivals of the Middle Ages, but it is essentially the same content: violent, gluttonous, hyper-sexualized. The difference is that it is constant. As a result we have dulled our senses to the point that we are losing our ability to monitor and regulate our internal-physical, emotional, ethical-processes and have consequently lost the self-sufficiency and related values that built this great country. We are losing our drive to succeed on our own merits and have relinquished individual accountability. How did it happen? How did we find ourselves here? How do we find our way back to the carnival gates and exit the fairgrounds?

---

[1] Associated Press, "Wave of School Threats Shocks U.S.," *American Online*, March 8, 2001.

[2] U.S. Department of Education, National Center for Education Statistics, *Crime and Safety in America's Public Schools: Selected Findings for the School Survey on Crime and Safety,* NCES 2004-370, (Washington, D.C.: 2004), http://nces.ed.gov/pubs2004/2004370.pdf (retrieved July 14, 2004).

[3] Associated Press, "Texas Teens Accused in Columbine-like Plan," Oct. 6, 2004, http://www.kansascity.com/mld/kansascity/news/nation/9852712.htm?1c (retrieved Oct. 8, 2004.)

[4] Associated Press, "Girl, 12, Charged With Killing 4-Year-Old," *AOL News*, Oct. 30, 2004 (retrieved Nov. 1, 2004.

[5] Associated Press, Girl, 12, Attacked At Party After Kissing Boy," *Canadian Children's Rights Council*, March 10, 2004 http://www.canadiancrc.com/articles/AP_Girl_12_Attacked_Kiss_Boy_10MAR04.htm (retrieved Nov. 1, 2004).

[6] Jeffrey Kluger. "The Kids are All Right," *Time*, July 26, 2004. http://www.time.com/time/magazine/article/0,9171,1101040726-665068,00.html (retrieved July 25, 2004.)

[7] The CDC Public Health Law News Archive, April 27, 2004, http://www.phppo.cdc.gov/od/phlp/dailynews/default.asp?specific=194 (retrieved Nov. 1, 2004.)

[8] http://www.cdc.gov/ncipc/factsheets/suifacts.htm (retrieved July 21, 2004.)

[9] http://www.nichd.nih.gov/new/releases/americas_children.cfm (retrieved July 16, 2004.)

[10] http://www.anred.com (retrieved Aug. 2, 2004.)

[11] http://www.anred.com (Anorexia Nervosa and Related Eating Disorders, Inc. Website) (retrieved Aug. 2, 2004.)

[12] http://www.anad.org (National Association of Anorexia Nervosa and Associated Disorders) (retrieved Aug. 2, 2004.)

[13] David Wahlberg and Helena Oliviero. "Teens Not Shy About Getting Breast

Jeff Shiring

Implants," *Atlanta-Journal Constitution*. Reprinted in *The Chronicle-Herald*, Halifax, NS, Section D-1, July 27, 2004.

14 L.D. Johnston, P.M. O'Malley, J.G. Bachman, and J.E. Schulenberg (2004), *Monitoring the Future National Results on Adolescent Drug Use: Overview of Key Findings, 2003* (NIH Publication No. 04-5506). Bethesda, MD: National Institute on Drug Abuse, http://www.monitoringthefuture.org/pubs/mono-graphs/overview2003.pdf (retrieved July 14, 2004.)

15 *Highlights from the Condition of Education 2004* (National Centre for Education Statistics), http://nces.ed.gov/pubs2001/dropout (retrieved July 14, 2004.)

16 *Time*, Canadian Edition, July 12, 2004. Vol. 164, No. 2, p.8.

17 "The Truth About Adolescent Sexuality," Fall 2003. Data from CDC Youth Risk Behavior Surveillance System, http://www.siecus.org/pubs/fact/FS_truth_adolescent_sexuality.pdf (retrieved July 21, 2004.)

18 Ibid.

19 "Recent Trends in Teen Pregnancy, Sexual Activity, and Contraceptive Use," Feb. 2004, http://www.teenpregnancy.org/resources (retrieved July 21, 2004.)

20 http://www.cdc.gov/HealthyYouth/healthtopics/indes.htm (retrieved July 21, 2004.)

21 "Tweens: A Billion-Dollar Market," *CBS News.com*, Dec. 15, 2004, http://www.cbsnews.com/stories/2004/12/14/60II/printable660978.html (retrieved Jan. 2, 2005.)

22 "Cheaters Amok: A Crisis in America's Schools—How it's Done and Why it's Happening," *ABC News*, April 29, 2004, http://abcnews.go.com/sections/Primetime/US/cheating_040429-1.html (retrieved July 14, 2004.)

23 UNICEF. "A League Table of Education Disadvantage in Rich Nations," *Innocenti Report Card*. No. 2, November 2002, Innocenti Research Centre, Florence, Italy.

24 U.S. Bureau of Census. "Young Adults Living at Home, 1960-2002," June 1, 2003, http://www.infoplease.com/ipa/AO193723.html (retrieved Aug. 15, 2002.)

25 Will Lester. "Apathy Growing Among Younger Voters: Politicians Court 18-to 24-Year-Olds, but With Little Success," Associated Press (Washington, November 3, 2001), http://aolsvc.news.aol.com/news/article.

26 http://www.gunsandcrime.org/numbers.html (retrieved July 16, 2004.)

27 Ibid.

28 http://www.nra.org (retrieved July 24, 2004.)

29 Center for Disease Control and Prevention National Center for Health

Statistics, http://www.cdc.gov/nchs (retrieved July 15, 2004.)

30 Robert N. Anderson., Arialdi M. Min?no, Lois. A Fingerhut, Margaret Warner and Melissa Heinen. "Deaths: Injuries, 2001," National Vital Statistics Report, Vol. 52, Number 21, June 2, 2004, http://www.cdc.gov/nchs/data/nvsr/nvsr52/nvsr52_21.acc.pdf (retrieved July 15, 2004.)

31 CDC Injury Fact Book, 2000-2001, http://www.cdc.gov.ncipc/fact_book/26_suicide.htm (retrieved July 21, 2004.)

32 James Alan Fox and Marianne W. Zawitz. "Homicide Trends in the U.S.," U.S. Dept. of Justice. Bureau of Justice Statistics. Website (last updated November 2002): http://www.ojp.usdoj.gov/bjs/homicide/homtrnd.htm (retrieved July 21, 2004.)

33 National Coalition Against Domestic Violence, http://www.ncadv.org (retrieved July 14, 2004.)

34 "Study Finds 'Ratings Cree': Movie Ratings Categories Contain More Violence, Sex, Profanity than Decade Ago." Boston, MA: Press Release, July 13, 2004, http://www.hsph.harvard.edu/press/releases/press07132004.html (retrieved July 24, 2004.)

35 http://www.familysafemedia.com/pornography_statistics.html (retrieved Aug. 10, 2004.)

36 Ibid.

37 http://www.protectkids.com/dangers/stats.htm (Website of Donna Rice Hughes—permission required.) (retrieved July 14, 2004.)

38 Lisa Falkenberg. "Scout Official Who Ran Sex Abuse Task Force Faces Child Porn Charges," Associated Press, reprinted in *Chronicle Herald*, Halifax, NS, Canada, Wednesday, March 30, 2005, sec. A, p. 7.

39 Dr. Richard Estes and Dr. Neil A. Weiner. *The Commercial Sexual Exploitation of Children in the United States, Canada and Mexico*. The University of Pennsylvania, 2002, http://www.ecpatusa.org (retrieved Aug. 12, 2004.)

40 Ibid.

41 http://www.cdc.gov/nccdphp/dnpa/obesity (retrieved July 14, 2004.)

42 "Risk of Death from Obesity Overestimated for Americans," *CBC News Online*. Nov. 24, 2004.

43 Mark Sherman. "Are We Eating Ourselves to Death?" Washington: Associated Press, March 9, 2004.

44 Rankings from http://www.mosbysdrugconsult.com/DrugConsult/Top_200/Drugs/e0333.html. Drug descriptions from "Prescription U.S.A.: The Top 10 Prescription Drugs in the U.S." excerpted from a feature by Barbara Iozzia's article appearing in the

Jeff Shiring

Winter/Spring 2001 issue of *HealthStateMagazine*, http://www.theuniversity-hospital.com/healthlink/septoct2001/html/longs/pills.htm (retrieved July 16, 2004).

[45] "2003 Quick Facts: Cosmetic and Reconstructive Plastic Surgery Trends, " American Society of Plastic Surgeons, 2004, http://www.plasticsurgery.org/public_education/loader.cfm?url=/commonspot/security/getfile.cfm&PaperID=13526(retrieved Jan. 26, 2005.)

[46] Website: http://www.plasticsurgery.org/public_education/loader.cfm?url=/commonspot/security/getfile.cfm&PaperID=13619 (retrieved Jan. 26, 2005. Telephone conversation with Denise Sneider at ASPS on February 14, 2005 to confirm conflicting statistics on two virtually identical published fact sheets.

[47] U.S. Department of Health and Human Services. National Survey on Drug Use and Health (2002) Website: http://www.oas.samhsa.gov/NHSDA/2K2NSDUH/Results/2K2results.htm#chap2 (retrieved July 25, 2004.)

[48] Associated Press, "Tests Detect Surge in Methamphetamine Use," New York, July 23, 2004.

[49] *Targeting Tobacco Use: the Nation's Leading Cause of Death, 2004*. CDC At a Glance Report, http://www.cdc.gov/nccdphp/aag/aag_osh.htm (retrieved Aug. 14, 2004.)

[50] H. Frederick Gale, Jr., Linda Foreman and Thomas Capehart. Tobacco and the Economy: Farms, Jobs and Communities. Economic Research Service, U.S. Dept. of Agriculture, http://www.ers.usda.gov/publications/aer789/aer789a.pdf (retrieved Aug. 10, 2004.)

[51] *Time*, Canadian Edition, July 12, 2004, Vol. 164, No. 2, p. 8.

[52] Karen Redmond. "Personal Bankruptcies Continue to Rise in Fiscal Year 2003," Administrative Office of the U.S. Courts; news release, Nov. 14, 2004, http://www.uscourts.gov/Press_Releases/fy03bk.pdf (retrieved July 25, 2004.)

[53] http://smartmoney.com/debt/advice/index.cfm?story=debtdrowning. Oct. 7, 2004.

[54] Robert Folsom. "As Fed Expands Credit, Consumers Drown in Debt," Fox News, Nov. 26, 2003, http://www.foxnews.com (retrieved July 14, 2004.)

[55] Jeannine Aversa. "Credit Card Delinquency Hits Record High," Washington, March 23, 2004, http://aolsvc.news.aol.com/news/article.adp?id=20040323 (retrieved March 23, 2004.)

[56] http://www.socialistworker.org/2004-1/486/486-06Debt.shtml. Feb. 13, 2004 (retrieved Oct. 7, 2004.)

[57] Jathon Sapsford. "As Cash Fades, America Becomes a Plastic Nation," *Wall Street Journal* (on-line), July 23, 2004.

[58] Sturgeon, Julie. "Younger Americans Going Deeper Into Debt."

Bankrate.com, Jan. 26, 2005,
http://pf.channel.aol.com/bankrate/credit/youngdebt.

[59] U.S. Dept. of Labor. Bureau of Labor Statistics. "Consumer Expenditures in 2002," Washington, Nov. 23, 2003,
http://www.bls.gov/news.release/pdf/cesan.pdf (retrieved Aug. 16, 2004.)

[60] "Numbers," *Time*, Canadian Edition, Aug. 23, 2004, p. 11.

[61] Keith Naughton. "Three for the Road," *Newsweek*, Dec. 1, 2003, p. 49.

[62] Associated Press, "More Americans in Poverty," *CNN.com*, August 26, 2004.

[63] "Medical Bills Spark 46% of U.S. Personal Bankruptcies: Study," *CBC News online*, Feb. 2, 2005, http://www.cbc.ca/story/world/national/2005/02/02/medical-bankrupt050202.html (retrieved Feb. 3, 2005.)

[64] Julie Appleby. "45 Million Americans Have No Health Insurance," *USA Today.com*, Aug. 27, 2004.

[65] Jeanne Sahadi and Leslie Haggin Geary. "Do You Cheat on Your Taxes?" *CNN Money*, March 26, 2004, http://money.cnn.com/2004/03/24/pf/taxes/taxcheats/index.htm (retrieved April 4, 2004.)

[66] Kelly Weise. "Missouri Removes Name of Wal-Mart Heiress," *Associated Press*, Nov. 25, 2004, http://msn.foxsports.com/story/3192130 (retrieved Nov. 30, 2004.)

[67] Kemper Alston, Frances. "Latch Key Children," NYU Child Study Center, http://www.aboutourkids.org/aboutour/articles/latchkey.html (retrieved Nov. 30, 2004.) Lauren Bishop. "Teen Competes for Beauty Title," Article appeared on *Cincinnati.com*, July 27, 2004,
http://www.enquirer.com/editions/2004/07/27/tem_tem1beaut.htm (retrieved August 21, 2004.)

[68] "Miss America Plans Teen Spinoff," *CBC.ca Arts*, March 22, 2005, http://www.cbc.ca/story/arts/national/2005/03/22/Arts/missamerica050322.html ?print (retrieved March 22, 2005.)

[69] "Stripping can be Lucrative, Students Told at Career Day," *CBC News Online*. Jan. 14, 2005, http://www.cbc.ca/story/world/national/2005/01/14/stripping-050114.html (retrieved Jan. 14, 2005.)

[70] Robert Coles. "On Raising Moral Children," Excerpt from his book, *The Moral Intelligence of Children*, Random House, 1997. Printed in *Time*, January 20, 1997.

II. Under the Influence

1. The Media Ether

What the mass media offers is not popular art, but entertainment which is intended to be consumed like food, forgotten, and replaced by a new dish.

-W.H. Auden, (1907-73)

Media is communication in all its forms. It is television, radio, cinema, books, newspapers, magazines, billboards, signs, packaging, marketing materials, brands and logos, videogames, the Internet...it is anything and everything that broadcasts a message and constructs a reality in the perceiver. Media is everywhere-it is part of our conscious and unconscious experience. From the second our clock radio (or our programmed home entertainment system) wakes us in the morning until we switch off the late night news, we are deliberately or inadvertently absorbing media inputs. Just try to extract yourself from any media influence for one day-eliminate all print, audio, video, windows (to avoid seeing the U-Haul truck pull up to the neighbor's), phone (to avoid answering a call from a telemarketer advertising a product or service), and computer device of any kind...I submit that unless you live on Saturn, it is impossible to avoid the reach of the media on a daily basis. We like it that way. It keeps us entertained and, we like to think, informed.

Unfortunately, the information that bombards us is not necessarily fact or truth. The media, particularly journalistic media, has become a big business propaganda machine, telling us what and how to think. What is real-current events, for example-is contrived, or at least slanted to reflect the opinion or purpose of the person or controlling interest presenting the information. What is covered by news outlets is selectively determined by individuals, corporations, or government officials with their own opinions, biases, and agendas. Someone makes the decision to offer five broadcast minutes to the Laci Peterson murder case on the evening news rather than the genocide in Sudan. The reasons include the fact that Americans are morbidly titillated by a pregnant woman's mysterious murder in California, but we are either horrified by or numb to the rape and

The Unraveling of America

slaughter of tens of thousands of Africans in Darfur; we will invariably tune in to the former and turn off the latter. Media producers know this: it is all about ratings. Essentially we are not receiving news; we are being fed sensational, profitable, controlled propaganda. Even in the most balanced journalism, there is always a subjective element: information has been selected and edited to present a story, which reflects an agenda or opinion of the presenter. Even if all sides of a story are presented equally and fairly, most issues are too complex to present in a thirty-second or two-minute clip, so they get watered down or sensationalized in order to keep viewers tuned in and interested. If the presentation is skillful-that is, provides drama and provokes an emotion or a response in the audience-then they will stay involved. That is entertainment: an engaging diversion, something that is produced or performed for an audience. That is also propaganda: the spreading of ideas, information, or rumor for the purpose of helping or injuring an institution, a cause, or a person. Truth or reality is not a necessary element, so long as an experience is conveyed, typically manipulating your thoughts and emotions in the process.

The line between what is news and what is entertainment is increasingly blurred by programs such as *Inside Edition* and *Entertainment Tonight* that provide the inside scoop on the entertainment industry. Even investigative news programs such as *Dateline: NBC* frequently delve into the lives of entertainers and end up becoming hour-long infomercials for the industry. They unabashedly self-promote their own industry and package it all up to look like news. Talk radio and talk television are daytime media staples, filling endless hours with streams of conversation-opinions and rumors and half-truths about what is going on in the world-manipulating audiences into believing it is all legitimate reportage. If it airs on TV, then it must be true. (How often does someone say, "It's true, I saw it on Oprah"?)

This may seem somewhat cynical an analysis, but the current wave of reality shows on television illustrates the point. Not including daytime and late-night talk shows (*Dr. Phil* and *Larry King Live* to name but two of dozens of top-rated talk television programs) and news broadcasts (news channels such as CNN or network news hours), there were nearly two hundred "reality" shows on the television line-up for the fall season of 2004.[71] They include every possible life scenario: from being stranded on a deserted island with a group of strangers (*Survivor*); to families switching mothers for a week (*Wife Swap*); to a funeral home series (*Family Plots*).

Reality television is programming designed to capture real people, i.e., not actors, and their behavior in particular circumstances, creating a supposedly authentic but entertaining viewing experience. It is ostensibly unscripted and unrehearsed, but it is very definitely manufactured-often with elaborate sets, huge monetary rewards, and careful editing to

Jeff Shiring

ensure maximum ratings value. It incorporates all the major film genres-drama, action, comedy, romance, horror, documentary-condensed into a one-hour episode, adding the key ingredients of money and/or fame.

Television audiences cannot get enough of it, and the media has been only too happy to provide a ceaseless supply since the successful release of early films such as *The Truman Show* (1998) and *EdTV* (1999) satirizing what was to quickly become a completely new entertainment industry. Why are we so hooked?

1. We are so bored with our own lives that we need to be distracted and live vicariously through the contrived situations and experiences of others (*Dream Job, Fear Factor, American Idol*).

2. We seek cheap and safe titillation by watching other people eat pig uteruses and log roll naked?

3. We are thrilled by the possibility that average people like ourselves can still get their big break (*Average Joe, Joe Millionaire, Joe Schmo*).

4. We are so unhappy with ourselves that we are obsessed by the transformation of others (*The Swan, Extreme Makeover, America's Next Top Model*).

5. Our penchant for voyeurism is so overwhelming that we can't tear ourselves away from the mindless minutiae of a camera lens (*Big Brother, The Newlyweds, A Simple Life*).

6. We thrive on the humiliation and disappointments of the losers in these contests because other people's letdowns make our own weaknesses and misfortunes easier to accept and rationalize.

Perhaps the answer is "all of the above."

We are indeed in the midst of a carnival-we want it, we need it, and we feed on it like so much cotton candy at the fair. Instead of focusing on our own realities-our families, our work, our personal goals, all things that require sustained effort-we respond instead to external realities beyond our front door. Realities that are, paradoxically, not real: they are created and contrived by other people for our entertainment pleasure. Instead of taking on the challenges that real life has in store, we passively cheer other people on the tube as they endure what are arguably pointless and meaningless difficulties. We look for external fulfillment (relief?) in the same way that Aldous Huxley described it in *Brave New World*; the citizenry of his satiric utopia regularly attended "the feelies" and gobbled "soma" to take regular and continuous holidays from their empty daily existence.

Many would say this national pastime is harmless entertainment, but that is just the point. Entertainment is the experience, but it is not necessarily harmless. We are becoming a nation of spectators instead of participants. We have made voting for our favorite teen idol an act of participation more important in our daily consciousness than voting for our president: 54 percent of all eligible voters in the U.S. turned out in the

2000 presidential election (about 100 million people) to select their national leader for a four-year term. To compare, 24 million votes were recorded for the 2003 season finale of Fox TV's *American Idol*. However, Verizon and SBC reported that their daily call volumes the same night increased by 116 million and 115 million respectively.[72] The speculation that more Americans-albeit many below voting age-at least attempted to cast a vote for their favorite American Idol than cast a vote for president is worthy of note.

Media As Political Instrument

The media, via print, broadcasting, and advertising, is responsible for creating and propagating social and political trends as well as reporting them. The current trend in book publishing, for example, parallels the political debate leading up to the 2004 presidential election. Bookstore shelves are overflowing with books critical of the Bush government (i.e., Graydon Carter's *What We've Lost: Americans Under the Bush Administration*) as well as the conservative backlash (i.e., David T. Hardy's *Michael Moore Is a Big Fat Stupid White Man*) demonstrating an opposition of political viewpoints that reflects American public opinion leading up to the polls. One would think that so much discussion would be a positive sign of democracy operating to the fullest extent; however, the plethora of critical analysis is cause for concern for some politicians, including Senator John McCain (R-AZ) who says, "These books are a symptom of the extreme political polarization in this country, and I don't think it's healthy."[73]

He is absolutely correct: it is not healthy to have just two sides of debate split along partisan lines. In a truly healthy democracy, there would be many diverse points of view given equal time and attention in the media. Massachusetts Institute of Technology linguistics professor and noted author Noam Chomsky explains why the mainstream American media remains largely two-sided:

> There is a complex system of filters in the media and educational institutions which ends up ensuring that dissident perspectives are weeded out, or marginalized in one way or another. And the end result is in fact quite similar: what are called opinions "on the left" and "on the right" in the media represent only a limited spectrum of debate, which reflects the range of needs of private power-but there's essentially nothing beyond those "acceptable" positions...and then [the media] present a range of debate within that framework-so the debate only enhances the strength of the assumptions ingraining them in people's mind as the entire possible spectrum of opinion there is.[74]

Chomsky's theory of the structure of the media maintains that large media outlets are conglomerates that have agendas based on a product and a market: "the product is audiences, the market is advertisers. So the economic structure of a newspaper is that it sells readers to other businesses." The political point of view of a newspaper or any other organ of the media to a large degree reflects the agenda of the controlling company or institution, which in the United States tends to be either conservative (Republican) or liberal (Democrat).

The problem is that the media, as a two-sided political instrument, is out of control. Facts, which the media has a responsibility to unearth and present to the public to enable us to make informed opinions, which in turn guide our behavior, are distorted and misrepresented so continually by both sides of the political spectrum as to be nothing more than propaganda. This may be blamed on the repeal of the Fairness Doctrine by the Federal Communications Commission in 1987. The Fairness Doctrine was initially put in place to ensure that broadcast licensees met their obligation of presenting issues in the public interest in a fair and balanced way, but with deregulation and the surge of cable channels in the 1980s, the FCC decided the policy was too limiting for real debate to take place. The demise of the doctrine effectively ended the standard for balanced coverage of politics, and realized the trend of talk radio and TV. "The television universe splintered between the old networks and the new cable gladiators in which opinion was more entertaining than information and cheaper to produce as well." The result has been an increasingly blurred line between news and opinion, political advocacy and advertising. We don't know who or what to believe, which leaves us unable to make educated decisions and vulnerable to manipulation by whoever beats the loudest drum, waves the biggest flag, or flashes the brightest smile for the camera.

In her book *Dark Age Ahead*, Jane Jacob discusses the media and its use as a tool by people in power to influence those not: "False image making has become a very big business throughout North America and is a staple of the U.S. government… Spin doctors, virtuosos of deceptive image making and damage control, have become authoritative spokespersons in political campaigns and troubled institutions, able not only to disconnect reality but to construct a new reality."[76] The government spins reality on a regular basis. In August, the U.S. Census Bureau released data on poverty levels and health insurance coverage of Americans a full month before the figures are annually published. While the numbers were indicative of a stagnant economy and the dire financial situations of millions of Americans, the government issued the information with a positive slant: that despite the number of people who lost health insurance in 2003, more Americans currently have health coverage than at any other time in the country's history. Democrats countered with accusations that the information was deliberately released early so it would not be as fresh in voters' minds in November.

Further evidence of the perpetual motion propaganda machine abounds in the lead up to the presidential election. As various partisan groups hurled accusations at both John Kerry and President Bush for their historical shortcomings, whether real or imaginary, CBS also embroiled itself in the dogfight. On September 8, 2004, CBS aired the contents of documents alleging that the President had shirked his duty in the Air National Guard thirty years ago. While it was subsequently determined that the documents were manufactured, the fact that Bush has never adequately addressed questions about his service history (suggested from other bona fide records) was lost in the flurry of accusations that Dan Rather was a liberal extremist trying to undermine the current administration. The real issue underlying the whole controversy is that the media in general, and journalism in particular, has become derelict in its duty to present true and incontrovertible facts-through vetting of sources and fact-checking-without comment or influence from either mainstream political camp. (CBS addressed the problem in-house on January 10, 2005, by firing three executives and a producer over the *60 Minutes* broadcast.) As it stands now, facts only have merit if they support one side or the other; politicians, as well as the media, are masterful at spinning them in whatever direction they chose. Regardless of what is uttered by anyone of influence, whether it is fact, fiction, opinion, or slander, all of it will be in the news the next day for readers, viewers, listeners, and bloggers to digest.

Take, for example, the presidential debates. In the second televised debate when the candidates discussed their platforms on domestic issues, both Kerry and Bush frequently spouted incorrect statistics, contradicted earlier on-the-record statements, and misrepresented information to the national (and international) television audience. In one instance, Kerry accused the Bush administration of overseeing the loss of 1.6 million jobs during his tenure, ignoring the fact that increased public sector jobs actually cut the overall job loss number in half. On the other side, Bush, had previously acknowledged the findings of the Duelfer's Iraq Survey Group report that Saddam Hussein did not have weapons of mass destruction when the U.S. invaded. Yet he claimed during the debate that Saddam was a threat to the U.S. because he could have given weapons of mass destruction to enemy terrorists.[77]

Do our leaders not know what is fact, or are they choosing to ignore it or misrepresent it to suit their purposes? Either way, the electorate seeking information to determine a qualified leader is severely disadvantaged. We are caught in a perpetual spin cycle of misinformation and distraction. The day after the Duelfer Report was released, Republicans and the Democrats both leaped upon it as definitive proof of their respective positions on the Iraq war. Magically, the same information supported opposing ideologies and bolstered both campaigns. The Democrats said the report proved the administration was wrong in invading Iraq because there were no WMDs, which had been the government's initial justification for a pre-emptive strike; the Republicans spun the findings as proof the invasion was the right thing to do because Saddam had intent to build WMDs and was undermining the U.N. oil-for-food program.[78] Despite the fact that the report's conclusions effectively eliminated the administration's stated case for going to war, the public relations experts in the White House were still able to present a game face to the American public and essentially say, "Well, even though we didn't have exactly the right information, we were still right in going there. See?"

While this kind of propaganda is an integral part of the political game, where the presidential competitors roll the media dice and hop around the board in a race to the Win square, we should be alarmed by the more blatant acts of manipulation by those in power. In the fall of 2004, a group called the People for the American Way accessed records through the Freedom of Information Act that showed the government hired a public relations firm with public funds to create a video news release for the Education Department. The firm, Ketchum, allegedly received $700,000 for the video, which was crafted to look like a news story and was sent to television stations to promote the government's education laws drafted in the No Child Left Behind Act. The Health and Human Services Department used the same format earlier in the year to promote the new Medicare law, but it was found to be covert propaganda and in violation of federal law by the Government Accountability Office.

More documents obtained through the Freedom of Information Act in January 2005, revealed that the Education Department, also through Ketchum, paid $240,000 to a prominent, conservative television and radio commentator to regularly promote the No Child Left Behind Act in his broadcasts. Armstrong Williams, a former aide to U.S. Supreme Court Justice Clarence Thomas, admitted to accepting the contract to incur support for the law among black families and asserted he did nothing wrong because he believed in the policy. It is clear to most observers, however, that the entire exercise was pure propaganda financed by taxpayers.[79] Because U.S. communications law says that broadcasters and journalists must publicly disclose paid sponsorship, the FCC launched an investigation in January 2005. Some members of the Senate have requested the GAO look into whether the Bush administration has paid other journalists to advertise government policies. Armstrong has refused to return the money.

Ketchum's public relations services also included creating a system that ranks individual reporters based on how positively or negatively they portray the education law in their coverage.[80] Such a "report(er) card," along with the Williams affair, suggests that the government extends preferential treatment for those in the media who are favorable to the administration's policies, further alienating and marginalizing dissenting and inquiring opinion. The public and the wider media might probe the question more deeply (but only if they know about it in the first place).

Enter stage right, film director Michael Moore who has assumed the role of Chief Probe and Propaganda-buster for Americans. Moore has been widely criticized by conservatives and liberals alike for his guerrilla style of film-making: he has a penchant for ambushing powerful people and asking them uncomfortable questions, and he carefully edits his footage of speeches and news segments for maximum emotional impact. Many critics accuse Moore of overt manipulation of his audience by featuring events and statements out of context, but his research is stringent and he has never been found guilty of defamation or libel despite several highly provocative films: *Roger and Me* (1989), *The Big One* (1997), *Bowling for Columbine* (2002); and *Fahrenheit 9/11* (2004). Moore is a master of the documentary genre, creating his own brand of liberal propaganda that effectively inflames the sensibilities of his audience regardless of their political bent. What is refreshing and unusual about Moore is that his agenda is blatant. His express purpose for making the film *Fahrenheit 9/11* was to rally Americans to vote Bush out of office in the coming election. We are not used to witnessing so bold an attack on the existing power structure, and the skillful use of the usual media tools to achieve that was a shock to the movie-going, voting public.

The 2004 distribution of *Fahrenheit 9/11* is a prime example of corporate conglomerates controlling-or attempting to control-media content and political comment. As the theatrical release date approached, the Walt Disney entertainment group refused to distribute the film despite Moore's contract with Disney's subsidiary, Miramax Films, to produce and distribute it. Disney exercises veto power over Miramax under certain circumstances (such as an NC-17 film rating) but the circumstances surrounding the blacklisting of Moore's film remain nebulous. Accusations were made (and denied) that Disney CEO Michael Eisner told Moore's lawyer that backing the film would negatively affect tax rebates for Disney theme parks received from the state of Florida (whose governor is Jeb Bush). The controversy only served to heighten publicity; the result was the film became the first documentary ever to debut as Hollywood's top weekend box office draw.

The film was released almost immediately on DVD and home video in early October, the timing calculated to reach even more audiences right before the election. Detractors called Moore's directorial dissension over the U.S. political system and current administration "unpatriotic," while supporters counter that his refusal to tone down his approach is testament to his deep sense of patriotism by exercising the American democratic ideal of free speech.

The negative furor and the label of "anti-American" that results when the current administration is taken to task over policy by activists such as Michael Moore is ironic in a country that so cherishes its freedoms. It is not surprising; freedom of speech and freedom of the press are sometimes sacrificed to higher priorities, such as national security. In May of 2004 the International Press Institute, a body of editors, journalists, and media executives that acts as a global press watchdog, accused the United States of violating that freedom by shutting down the weekly newspaper of Iraqi Shi'ite cleric Muqtada al-Sadr. IPI also cited Washington for interfering with the independent media at home; it requested to CBS to delay airing photographs depicting the abuse of Iraqi prisoners at the hands of U.S. soldiers. The network acquiesced and aired the story on 60 Minutes II two weeks later.[81] The White House justified the actions saying that the weekly newspaper incited hatred and endangered American troops in Iraq, and publicity about the abuse would have inflamed tensions even further. Saddam Hussein's iron control over the Iraq media has been a sticking point for the U.S. since 1968 and the cause of much rhetoric about liberating the Iraqi people; the Iraqi state television station in Baghdad was destroyed by a U.S. missile attack five days into the war. Not long after, three journalists were killed in nearly simultaneous U.S. missile attacks on the Baghdad television headquarters of the Abu Dhabi and Al-Jazeera networks and the Palestine Hotel, where most foreign journalists were staying at the outset of the war. The government seems willing to censor the foreign and domestic press when it is deemed expedient, and the mainstream media appears more and more willing to allow it.

During Operation Iraqi Freedom, the behavior of the U.S. press was called into question by some analysts. In a May 2003 discussion with Noam Chomsky, interviewer Michael Albert asked about the role of the American media establishment in the war. Chomsky replied, "The media uncritically relayed government propaganda about the threat to U.S. security posed by Iraq, its involvement in 9/11 and other terror, etc. Some amplified the message on their own. Others simply relayed it. The effects in the polls were striking, as often before. Discussion was, as usual, restricted to 'pragmatic grounds': will the U.S. government get away with its plans at a cost acceptable at home? Once the war began it became a shameful exercise of cheering for the home team, appalling much of the world." [82] In the early fall of 2002, when the National Security Strategy was announced, the majority of Americans believed that Saddam Hussein had weapons of mass destruction, that Iraq was involved somehow in the 9/11 attacks, and that Iraq posed an imminent danger to U.S. security. These declarations by the government were continually reported by the popular press. Along with frequent issuance of terror alerts that sustained a sense of perpetual threat, this successfully generated and maintained national public support for the invasion. Very few people recalled the intelligence reports of the previous two years that determined Iraq did not have WMDs, and because of the decade of economic sanctions against the country Saddam Hussein posed little or no threat to the U.S. at all. Even fewer brought up the fact that the U.S. supplied vast stores of weapons and cash to Iraq prior to the first Gulf War when Iran was the enemy of the day. As George Orwell wrote in *1984*, "the past not only changed, but changed continuously."

The mainstream media went further in ceding its independence to the government and the invasion of Iraq by literally beating the war drum. Nightly television news segments were introduced with dramatic military-style music, with the Stars and Stripes displayed prominently on the screen. Anchors delivered the latest updates using value-laden language such as "our heroes in the desert" versus "the enemy" and "rebel attackers" and extolled the virtues of the latest weapons technology. Reporters themselves became virtual paramilitaries, with more than six hundred American journalists dressed in camouflage and embedded with the troops. This idea may have stemmed from both the desire for protection as well as a first-hand look at the realities of war using the most advanced communications technology ever available. Videophones and satellite links allowed for greater and more immediate coverage of events in the field; however, the result was that those reports were heavily censored to avoid revealing information to the enemy. In essence, war correspondents became public relations representatives for the military, and those traveling under cover of military troops were as much at risk as those covering the war independently. In 2003, as a result of the Iraq conflict, nineteen journalists were killed by landmines, enemy fire, suicide bombings, or friendly fire (fourteen during the war, five in the aftermath, with two missing and presumed dead).[83]

The mainstream press was perhaps less obvious in its effort to promote popular support of the war, but equally guilty. *The New York Times*, for example, ran a series of articles, including a front page piece, that described biological, chemical, and nuclear weapons facilities in Iraq based on dubious and unsubstantiated information from Iraqi exile and "intelligence source" Ahmad Chalabi. In May 2004, the paper ran a back page apology of sorts, openly acknowledging where the paper fell short of journalistic standards and excusing itself by saying "...it looks as if we, along with the administration, were taken in..." by misinformation. The editors did not, however, overtly apologize to its readership or demonstrate that the responsible reporters or editors would be held accountable in any way.[84]

To keep up momentum for an action that was becoming less and less popular, either because of or despite of the lack of real information about what was happening in Iraq, the major U.S. media organizations were compelled to provide continuous coverage of the conflict even if was devoted to non-news. There were endless hours of interviews with experts, ranging from ex-military officials to university lecturers, discussing their opinions about the events in the Middle East; and then counter-comments on the first person's remarks. Within this range of debate, there was a curious lack of criticism of the government's decision to invade Iraq-when it did appear, comments were given cursory attention or the commentators were discredited, a fact which gives credence to Chomsky's theory and is echoed by other observers of the propaganda machine.

The U.S. media ceded much of its power to the government at a time when it should have been the most critical. In the name of liberating Iraq and creating democratic freedom in the Middle East, the American "free press" was forbidden by the Department of Defense to broadcast photos or footage of American soldiers killed in action, including their flag-draped coffins returning to American soil. It is open to debate whether the reason for this blackout was to respect the grieving families or to prevent waning morale of active duty soldiers and the American public. Similarly, while the most blatant examples of civilian carnage were reported (i.e., dozens of Iraqi men, women, and children mortared at a wedding celebration), for the most part, non-military casualties were downplayed. When called to task for obvious strategic errors, the U.S. military sidestepped responsibility saying their intelligence was incomplete or that collateral damage was inevitable during conflict. The purpose was to sanitize the human cost of the war in the psyche of the American public, resulting in a national complacency and lack of accountability for our actions.

For this reason, the administration and the mainstream media was highly critical-virulently so-of the Qatar-based Arab news network Al Jazeera for broadcasting photos and video footage of the war that included dead American and Iraqi soldiers, POWs on both sides, and civilian casualties: men, women, and children; journalists; aid workers; and other innocent victims. For their part, Al Jazeera's stated mandate was to document the war and inform the world, something that the U.S. media was loathe to do lest it seem they were being unpatriotic. While George Bush called Al Jazeera "the mouthpiece for Osama bin Laden," the network gained the respect of many Americans in Iraq for its honest and fair war coverage, including correspondents Tom Mintier (CNN) and David Shuster (NBC), U.S. State Department spokesman Nabeel Khoury, and Central Command Press Officer, Josh Rushing. In the 2004 documentary *Control Room*, Samir Khader, a senior producer with Al Jazeera said, "The message of Al Jazeera is to educate the Arab masses in something called democracy, a respect of the other opinion, free debate with no taboos. We want to shake up the religious societies and say, 'Wake up to the world around you!'" With an audience of forty million Arabs in the Middle East, the network was successful in raising the hackles of both sides of the conflict. Ironically, there is film footage of the Iraqi Information Minister Saeed Al-Sahaf yelling into a camera, "I warn Al Jazeera-stop your American propaganda!"

While the western media was persistent in portraying Al Jazeera as a fanatical media wing of terrorist supporters, in the film there is an interesting exchange between a BBC journalist and the Al Jazeera journalist and producer Hassan Ibrahim. The two men meet at the media operations center at U.S. Central Command headquarters and realize they know each other. When the BBC reporter asks Ibrahim what he's doing now and is told he is with Al Jazeera, the Briton says, "Of course." Ibrahim asks, "Why of course?" The BBC reporter answers, "Everyone who works for BBC eventually works for Al Jazeera."

While this tidbit of information is certainly not bandied about in the mainstream media, perhaps it is well known among the "paramedia"- bloggers, radio talk shows, university presses, and others outside of the big media bubble-who have been responsible for debunking some of the most glaring and widely reported myths of the election campaign. Some observers believe the public has become so disillusioned with the media that it is losing its credibility and its relevance. Canadian journalist and author Ira Basen writes, "Traditional reporting operates on the principle that both sides have a right to have their stories told, but too often in the context of the modern political campaign, that puts reporters in a position of acting not as filters for truth but as stenographers for spin..." Every comment and accusation gets air-time whether it is valid or not. He suggests that modern media must evaluate the news it reports much like the paramedia does, giving readers and viewers an honest interpretation of what is being said and why.[85]

Journalists themselves are beginning to realize they have not been doing a proper job. In October 2004, a national journalism organization found nearly 70 percent of their surveyed members were dissatisfied with the presidential campaign coverage, giving it a C, D, or F grade. The group from Committee for Concerned Journalists cited an excessive media preoccupation with trivial issues as one of the biggest problems, as well as an increasing lack of impartiality, particularly in television journalism.[86] While changes in the performance of the mainstream media may be emerging from within the industry, the degree of change and the rapidity will only be determined by the public as consumers of the product. We need to examine our daily media fare, determine what is acceptable and what is not, and act accordingly.

Big Media, Big Money

More examples of the tightly woven fabric of media and the government come from the entertainment industry. During the 2005 Super Bowl, watched by 86.1 million Americans, the average cost of a thirty-second commercial spot was $2.4 million (or $80,000 per second).[87] Despite the advertising price tag, big companies spend fortunes to create new and edgy commercials for the most-watched television event of the year, often dumping the bulk of their annual ad budget into the Super Bowl. Controversial content is a preferred staple; even if the ad is rejected by the network, the free publicity surrounding it is invaluable. Technology has enhanced the lucrative pay-offs for advertisers: the product that enjoyed the most website hits on 2004 game day was Cialis™. The vague ad for the erectile dysfunction drug was aired during the game and prompted curious viewers to increase traffic on the site by 240 percent.[88]

Although the 2005 game was broadcast by Fox, it marked the one-year anniversary of "Nipplegate," which has haunted CBS ever since the less-than-a-second-long glimpse of Janet Jackson's breast was flashed into American living rooms. CBS and MTV, which produced the half-time show, exercised control over the advertising lineup of the 2004 broadcast. It included the perennial appearances of beer (Anheuser-Busch), soft drinks (Pepsi), and major automotive companies (Dodge, Ford, Cadillac). Some advertisers such as MoveOn, a non-profit advocacy group for social and political responsibility, were unsuccessful in securing a spot on game day. CBS refused to sell MoveOn's thirty-second segment, which was critical of the rising national debt, saying the content of their ad was too controversial. It was a weak excuse considering the fact that the Office of National Drug Control Policy was allowed to air a government-sponsored ad during the 2003 Super Bowl that linked marijuana use to terrorism.[89]

It would seem to be in the best interests of CBS and Viacom to avoid criticism of the White House because CBS apparently spent four million dollars over the past four years lobbying Congress in support of the Federal Communications Commission's efforts to extend media ownership rights. (Viacom is the media giant that owns both CBS and MTV.) The FCC proposed to end the ban in most cities of cross-ownership of television stations and newspapers, allowing media conglomerates (like Viacom and AOL Time Warner) to further monopolize local news outlets and control roughly half of American viewing and listening audiences. In June 2004, in what was considered by many media watchdogs to be a strike in defense of democracy, the U.S. Court of Appeals ruled against the FCC, rejecting the claim that the industry was not deregulated enough. The Third Circuit Court sided with public interest advocates in what is known at the "Prometheus Decision," allowing local media organizations to maintain what little diversity is left in print over the airwaves.[90]

For skeptics who are not convinced of the corporate grasp on the sleeve of the media, the Columbia Journalism Review maintains a convincing, up-to-date listing of the major corporations with ties to media. For example, General Electric owns 80 percent of NBC Universal, which comprises fourteen NBC and Telemundo stations nationwide, MSNBC, CNBC, Universal film and television studios, and Universal Parks and Resorts. At the same time, GE also owns subsidiary companies in the following industries: aircraft engines, consumer products, commercial finance, industrial systems, medical systems, insurance, plastics, power systems, transportation systems, and specialty materials. How much of the commercial interests of the parent company spill over into the programming of the media offshoots, whether through advertising alone or through broadcasting and production decisions?

Another example of corporate interests shaping our cultural evolution is demonstrated by the influence of mass merchandisers such as Wal-Mart and Costco on the literary and musical diets of Americans. Big discount chains account for more than 40 percent of sales of best-selling books and 50 percent of best-selling albums.[91] When a new release is mass-marketed on the scale that large chains can sustain, it has a greater chance of becoming widely purchased and reaching best-seller status. At the same time, if a new release is considered controversial or less-than-conservative by the buyers for these chains, it doesn't get placed on the shelves. Critics argue that this is essentially censorship determined by the agenda of the retailer, the result of which is the homogenization of popular culture. Mainstream literature and music abounds in quantity but selection remains limited, reinforcing the status quo. Consumers buy what is available and the retailers carry what people are buying.

The monopolization of the media by a few corporate super-entities necessarily limits the choices and access of the public to information that, ironically, is theoretically widely and instantly available thanks to modern technology. Even the highly respected National Public Radio (NPR) is not immune from charges of corporate and partisan bias. The private, not-for-profit corporation, widely regarded as one of the most balanced sources of news, analysis, and quality cultural programming in the country, has been the subject of a report by the media watch group, Fairness and Accuracy in Reporting (FAIR). FAIR studied every on-air source quoted in June 2003 on four NPR news shows, a total of 804 stories and 2,334 quoted sources, and discovered that of all partisan sources quoted, Republicans outnumbered Democrats 61 percent to 38 percent. They also found that other journalists made up 7 percent of NPR's sources, 83 percent of whom were employed by commercial U.S. media outlets.[92] NPR's twenty-two million U.S. weekly listeners are apparently getting the same information from the same sources as the mainstream corporately and politically influenced commercial media.

Another example of media distortion of information involves a January 11, 2005, broadcast of ABC's "A Closer Look" segment of the *World News Tonight.* In the show, anchor Peter Jennings was discussing the Bush administration's plans to privatize Social Security. Jennings made the statement that "there's no question that baby boomers will place great strain on Social Security as they retire," leading viewers to believe just that: there is no question. He mentioned that "by some measures, the system may not have enough cash to pay full benefits" by 2042. The show went on to say that money currently paid into Social Security is spent by the government, leaving IOUs instead of cash in the national account. FAIR issued a critique of the program pointing out the inaccuracies in the segment. For one, although Social Securities trustees predict that the current system won't have enough money to support retirees by 2042, the non-partisan Congressional Budget Office forecasts full benefit payments until 2052 (when the oldest boomers will be 106 and the youngest 88 years old). FAIR also corrected the IOU statement, stating that money put into Social Security is actually held in U.S. government bonds and the government has never defaulted on a bond. Additionally, they mentioned, some economists predict that if future economic growth remains healthy, the system may never run out of cash.[93] Clearly, despite mainstream media assertions to the contrary, there is most definitely a question (or two) surrounding the debate.

Despite a deluge of news and entertainment sources available to us through every imaginable media format, we are sadly limited in our ability to access true and factual information. It is in our best interests, therefore, to carefully evaluate our media diet and ask these questions: "Where is this coming from? Who is funding it? What else is out there?" More importantly, we need to teach our children to do the same.

Media Influence on Children and Youth

What we experience through media-images, sounds, emotions-has the potential effect of dulling our senses and perceptions of real, firsthand experience. When you can freeze the frame of an image of dewdrops on a perfect rose across a four-foot plasma screen, how affected are you going to be by the real thing? When you can go on safari in the Serengeti from your La-Z-Boy, why would you ever bother to go to Kenya and experience it first hand? Children today are prime examples of this effect of media saturation: they are extremely hard to impress and are variously labeled "sophisticated," "urbane" and "tech-savvy." A nine-year-old I know summarily dismissed my photo-filled program of a Cirque de Soleil performance I wanted to share with her, saying, "Oh, yeah. Whatever. I've already seen that on TV-we get 558 channels."

Media is the most powerful substitute for actual events and experiences because it provides its own reality; it is so pervasive and omnipresent that the possibilities for those alternate realities are virtually limitless. You can switch on the satellite dish or go online and find any "reality" you want. For kids trying to discover who they are in relation to what they know about the world, this has an irresistible appeal. It also has risks. Some psychologists, such as author and family therapist Dr. Ron Taffel, believe that kids are more and more disengaged from societal structures because of media and pop culture. In his book, *The Second Family,* Taffel bluntly and quite frighteningly explores "Planet Youth," described as the "materialistic, kid-centered universe where instant gratification reigns" and where kids demonstrate a disconnection from their families, schools, and moral values that used to be a major influence on their development. In an effort to help parents deal with the inexplicable anger and defiance and often outrageous behavior of their teens (and grade school-aged children), he poses the theory that the combination of peer groups and pop culture form "the second family," which meets their primary need of self-indulgence. By adolescence, the key motivator for kids is not rebellion, but rather comfort. "They value comfort above all and worship celebrity" and are slaves to the "tyranny of cool," which influences kids as young as five and six via the ubiquitous power of the media and peer groups. Taffel describes teens' sliding moral scale as an "elastic sense of morality" that determines their code of conduct; it is not recognizable to most parents.[94]

It is hard to ignore the influence of the media on children, and much has been studied and written on the subject since the advent of the television. A detailed analysis of the research is beyond this scope of this book, but there are some statistics worth thinking about. For example:

- 65 percent of American children have televisions in their bedrooms;
- the average seventh grader watches three hours of television a day;
- by age eighteen, the average American child has watched 16,000 murders on television;
- in 2001, teens aged 12-18 spent $172 billion;
- 87 percent of school-aged kids own videogame equipment
- 40 percent of American families "almost always" watch television during dinner.[95]

Clearly, television watching takes up a significant amount of a child's day. In the text of the Telecommunications Act of 1996, the FCC wrote that the average American child watches twenty-five hours of television each week and some as much as eleven hours a day.[96] In the face of this exposure to mass entertainment, which includes thousands of depictions of violent acts, sexual exploitation, product pitches, and contrived reality, there is merit in the theory that kids are bound to be negatively affected in some way. Are they becoming programmed any more than you or I were by growing up with television in our lives? The answer is probably, because for the current youth generation, media is their life. Today's

"Millennials" (the generation currently under twenty-four) are the entertainment generation: they have grown up not just with television but with satellite television offering hundreds of channels at the click of a button. There are also videogames, CDs, DVDs, MP3s, the Internet, text-messaging, and camera cell phones; all these combine to produce total multimedia saturation.

Millennials are the key demographic for advertising because they are immersed in cultural and commercial convergence: they watch a popular character on a television show or music video who becomes an instant idol. The idol is then marketed via products such as dolls, games, toys, and clothing (á la Mary Kate and Ashley Olsen and Hilary Duff) and other products branded with that idol's name and face to create an entire image package that is coveted and copied by millions of youth. The public appearances and performances of that idol (no longer a person, but a celebrity icon) are frequently staged in shopping malls (Avril Lavigne), which further buttresses the link between entertainment and spending; this captures a wider demographic audience than a typical concert venue where box office tickets can be beyond the allowance of many pre-teens.

The process begins in infancy. Programs such as *Teletubbies* are specifically and successfully created for the twelve- to eighteen-month-old set, who are completely vulnerable to sensory stimulation. Infants and toddlers watch the brightly-colored, unintelligible but singsongy "tubbies" from their exersaucers, entranced by the combination of color, tinkling music, and hypnotic voice-over narration. Parents reinforce their attraction for the show by buying them a Po doll to cuddle in their crib; then they get a Teletubbies book to color or read; then they are dressed in their favorite Teletubby costume for Halloween. The connections between what is seen on the screen and the materialization (and consumption) of the character or brand or product are complete long before the child can talk. Advertising capitalizes on this phenomenon by promoting the "I want" mentality of children who are too young to process the message as separate from the product; consequently, they become voracious consumers because what they are pitched is always the new cool trend, whether it's breakfast cereal, toys, clothes, music, or celebrities. The chicken and egg phenomenon of the demand for and supply of "bubblegum" food, music, and fashion for kids is so entrenched as to be almost invisible to the uncritical eye.

In an interesting feature article entitled "Can We Save These Kids?" author Hal Niedzviecki wrote, "When entertainment is made solely for profit and entertainment monopolies are allowed to rule our brain space complete with increasingly embedded product placements, opportunities for creativity and play shrink."[97] Despite the trend toward interactive games and activities, much of children's exposure to media invites reaction rather than interaction, or worse, passivity. Even television channels like PBS, which broadcast quality children's programming on their *PBS Kids* segments, advertise sponsors such as Chuck-E-Cheese. Their shows are linked to URLs where kids can go online and play pre-formulated computer games to enhance their total viewing experience, rather than encouraging them to go outside and explore their environment or build a go-cart and have a neighborhood race. Kids are staying indoors, remaining physically inactive and isolated from any social interaction beyond that of the family. There is no requirement to be creative or imaginative (much less read!) because they can be entertained effortlessly by the television, the computer, the GameBoy™, or the X-Box™.

Much research has been done on the effects of mass entertainment-particularly violence on television-on children's brains. Dr. John Murray, a professor of developmental psychology at Kansas State University, has written extensively on the subject of children and television since the early 1970s. His 2001 study looked at the effects of watching violent scenes compared with nonviolent ones on the brains of children aged 8 to 13. MRIs showed there were actual physiological changes in areas of the brain responsible for long-term memory of emotional perceptions, suggesting that kids retrieve the violent images when their emotional buttons are pushed and use them as a guide for social behavior. [98]

Violence in video games is another hot button issue for many parents and educators and another stimulus for mountains of research. There are many claims that video games promote addictive behavior and program young minds to become inured to the graphic violence characteristic of many of the top games (dismemberment, decapitation, shootings, stabbings, rape, arson, etc.). Manufacturers, advertisers, and gamers themselves laud the development of skills acquired from playing video games; they claim these skills are necessary for specific professions and are generally beneficial to kids by teaching them to multi-task and become completely at ease with technology. Some research has shown that early game playing develops nerve pathways useful in careers that require sharp reflexes, eye-hand coordination, 2-D and 3-D conceptualization and peripheral. These include laparoscopic surgeons, pilots, soldiers, race car drivers and, of course, video game programmers and designers. Video games are becoming the fastest growing segment of the entertainment industry, with worldwide annual revenues estimated at twenty-eight billion dollars last year alone. Americans will spend more time-an average of seventy-five hours-gaming this year than watching rented movies.[99] More than half of U.S. households have at least one video console, a number that does not take into account video games for home computers or those played on the Internet. Sixty percent of the market is comprised of six- to fourteen-year-old boys, a statistic compelling enough to prompt the development of post-secondary programs in video game design. The DigiPen Institute in Redmond, Washington (the home of Microsoft founder Bill Gates) offers a four-year bachelor of science degree in real time interactive simulation, which essentially prepares graduates to design, program, and animate video games.[100]

Pop culture and entertainment cannot be avoided, and it is difficult to even marginally limit children's exposure to it, despite parents' best efforts. Many would agree, however, that it is critical to teach children the skills required to navigate the media so they will not be hopelessly manipulated in their adolescence and adulthood. Media literacy is as necessary in our age as literacy in reading and mathematics. If we want children to be able to make their own decisions and form their own opinions, they need to be able to recognize and understand both the surface messages and the underlying meanings and intents of the words, sounds, and images they encounter every day. They need to be able to analyze the persuasive language, sexual and cultural stereotypes, context, bias, credibility, imagery, and symbolism, and their own emotional responses to all of it. A Wal-Mart television commercial is a prime (time) example of the mixed messages aimed at the youth demographic. Several teens are shown standing in separate frames, each dressed in the fashion uniform of the day: low-rise jeans, hooded sweaters, t-shirts, and the requisite hairstyles and facial piercings. Each teen is echoing the same statements: I would never wear something because I heard it was cool; I'm not afraid to be who I am; If I stand out...whatever; I am me. Despite the mantra of individualism and freedom of choice and expression, each teen looks like they have been plucked from any school hallway or mall concourse in Conformityville, USA. The message is: It's okay to be different, as long as you look like everyone else and buy your clothes at the biggest retail chain in the United States. How many kids would be able to critically interpret that advertisement and, more importantly, choose to reject it by exercising their spending power elsewhere?

Media literacy programs in U.S. public schools are proliferating; individual teachers incorporate lessons into the mainstream language arts curriculum, and some states such as New Mexico have instituted ML as a standard curriculum subject. The New Mexico Media Literacy Project broke ground in this area in 1993. They are largest independent media literacy project in the country and one of the few that does not accept any funding from the media industry. The NMMLP mission is to lead "a cultural revolution in the health of our children and the health of our democracy."[101] Their goal is to give youth greater freedom and choice, not only by teaching them how to analyze and evaluate media influences but also how to produce media tools. By creating and utilizing media to convey a convincing message, kids learn the power of those tools and are better equipped to use various modes of media for social activism and education rather than commercialism. The hope is that active, conscious exploration of media influences will lead to changes in attitude and behavior over time. Indeed, critical thinking skills are necessary for full and informed participation in a democratic society. One media critic summarized the point this way in an online article entitled "Reality Television: What It Is and What It Means": "We as a society cannot continue to value entertainment which purposefully seeks to not inform. The purpose of mass communication must shift to be one of entertainment coupled with enlightenment, else we are headed for an ignorant renaissance in which ratings and advertising are the only currency."[102]

Media Accountability

There has been a lot of finger-pointing by media analysts and critics (including this writer) at the government and corporate powerhouses for the shortcomings of the mainstream media; but regardless of who sits on the board of directors of any media organization, or what advertiser provides the bulk of the production budget, it is still the responsibility of the individuals within those organizations to be accountable for their actions and the decisions that have an impact on the viewing and listening public.

The Motion Picture Association of America is one example. A recent study by the Harvard School of Public Health found that the amount of violence, sex, and profanity in movies increased significantly between 1992 and 2003 and suggested that the MPAA has become much more lenient in assigning its voluntary, non-standardized age-based film ratings. What was considered to warrant an R (Restricted-Under 17 requires accompanying parent or adult guardian) rating a decade ago is now typically rated as PG-13 (Parents Strongly Cautioned-Some material may be inappropriate for children under 13). Researchers also found a higher amount of violence in G-rated (General-All ages admitted) animated films than non-animated ones, and calculated that 51 percent of G-rated films studied depicted the use of tobacco, alcohol, or drugs.[103]

It would seem the film industry has lowered the bar of acceptable content for viewers of all ages, which has resulted in significant "ratings creep." Obviously, parents need to be tuned in to what their children are viewing on the big screen, but as it is highly unlikely that many have the time or money to preview every box office release, most rely on the ratings for guidance. While the MPAA might argue that they do promote responsible media production and distribution by voluntarily assigning ratings in the first place, it is in their fiscal interest to assign particular ratings to films. The Harvard study correlated movie content with reported revenues and found that the film industry receives higher gross revenues for PG-13 and R-rated films that received a rating only for violence compared to those films that were rated as PG.

Equally problematic is the lack of standardized rating system for other media formats, especially in light of increasing media convergence and cross-marketing. For example, the movie *Spider-Man 2* was rated by the

MPAA as PG-13, but the Spider-Man console video games are rated as T (Teen) and the PC and hand-held video games are rated E (Everyone) by the Entertainment Software Rating Board. The ESRB is a separate, self-regulating body created in 1994 that assigns age-based ratings to video games, which are then labeled on the boxes along with the descriptions; however, the ESRB ratings have been found to be lacking in accurate disclosure as well. In a separate Harvard study, two researchers randomly chose eighty-one video games rated T and played them each for an hour. They analyzed the content of each game to that point and found that 48 percent of the games depicted violence, sexual themes, profanity, substance use, and gambling, but none of them had warnings on the box.[104] It is even less likely that a parent will be able to navigate the multiple levels and layers of every video game to determine the amount of slashing and flashing it contains. Even in a household where parental vigilance is acute-limits on television viewing and internet controls-it is virtually impossible to monitor all of the disturbing and potentially harmful images to which kids are exposed. Prohibiting access altogether just encourages children to go and find it elsewhere without parental knowledge and supervision.

More recent research has determined that children aged 12 to 17 who watched a lot of television with sexual content were about twice as likely to start having intercourse during the subsequent year as those with little exposure to television sex.[105] Researchers from the Rand Corporation point out that while both depictions of and allusions to sex are pervasive on television, it rarely deals with negative consequences of sex, such as unwanted pregnancies, STDs, and AIDS. As a sidebar to this finding, I watched one of the early episodes of the prime time television drama *Nip/Tuck*, which not only graphically depicted the realistic-looking gore of cosmetic surgery, but also a several-minute long sequence of a sexual threesome. Prior to engaging in the act, however, one of the naked male characters was shown pulling a condom out of his toiletry kit and tossing it at his friend. Perhaps portraying what many would categorize as pornography on a network television station at 10:00 P.M., when many teens still channel surfing, is appropriate as long as there is a nod to safe sex. Have the networks not figured out that announcing "Viewer discretion is advised" is an invitation to people to tune in, rather than turn off?

Having pointed out where the media has penetrated the often gauzy garments of broadcasting decency, it would be remiss not to discuss the recent uncomfortable cinching of the corset of censorship. In the enlightening article "Can a Nipple Change the World?" Vinay Menon calls 2004 "The Year of Outrage," which began as "a tempest in a C-cup" immediately following the 2004 Super Bowl halftime show. Since the FCC slapped CBS with a $550,000 indecency fine (perhaps to reflect one dollar for each of the half-million complaints the commission received?), network hosts of live awards shows and sporting events have instituted tape delays and have cancelled broadcasts of such programming as the *Victoria's Secret Fashion Show* and *Saving Private Ryan*. Sixty-six affiliates of ABC opted not to air the film on Veteran's Day for fear of reprisals over extensive profanity.[106]

Non-cable broadcasters have been extra nervous since the FCC slapped each of Fox TV's 169 stations with fines totaling a record $1.2 million in October 2004. The stations aired an episode of a since-cancelled reality show called *Married by America*, in which sexually suggestive behavior at bachelor and bachelorette parties was shown. A reporter, Jeff Jarvis, later discovered through a Freedom of Information Act request that instead of the 159 complaints the FCC claimed they had received about the show, there were actually ninety letters received from twenty-three people and most were copies of the same letter. According to an analysis of the complaints by Jarvis, the final number of individual complaints amounted to three.[107] In another precedent setting move, Viacom agreed, in December 2004, to pay the FCC $3.5 million to settle a series of indecency complaints (excluding the Super Bowl fine, which the media giant is appealing). In the settlement, which ensures that outstanding complaints won't be held against Viacom when its various properties come up for licensing renewal, the company promised to introduce measures to prevent future broadcasting of indecent material.[108]

The circulation of the First Amendment has been cut off with a girdle of conservative pressure, even at PBS. The network announced it would not distribute an episode of its animated children's program *Postcards from Buster* in which Buster visits a Vermont farm where two lesbian couples and their children make maple sugar. The series was designed to teach children about tolerance and cultural diversity; however, newly appointed Secretary of Education Margaret Spellings sent a letter to PBS expressing her dissatisfaction that public funding was being used to promote alternative lifestyles. She suggested PBS consider returning the funding it received for the series through the government's Ready-to-Learn program. As many as 27 of the 349 PBS stations across the U.S. have vowed to air the show anyway on March 23, 2005.[109] The CEO of the network, Pat Mitchell, has announced she will step down when her contract expires in June 2006. FAIR pointed out the hypocrisy of the Education Department in condemning the program, since their own terms of allocating grants require that funded programs:

> "appeal to all of the children of America by providing them with content and characters with which they can identify. Diversity will be incorporated into the fabric of the series to help children understand and respect differences and learn to live in a multicultural society. The series will avoid stereotypical images of all kinds and show modern multi-ethnic/lingual/cultural families

Jeff Shiring

and children."[110]

Similarly, in a December 2004 *New York Times* column, Frank Rich described several media "non-events" that blow a chilling breeze through the halls of free speech, all in the name of moral values. Three weeks after the 2004 election, New York's public station WNET dropped a spot for the biograpahical film *Kinsey*, about the American zoologist whose research on human sexuality gained him infamy in the late 1940s. A public radio station in North Carolina told an international women's rights organization they were not allowed to use the words "reproductive rights" on the air. In Los Angeles, five channels refused to broadcast a public service announcement about syphilis created by the public health department.[111]

Between the pervasiveness of arguably inappropriate sex and violence in the mainstream media and the extreme (and inconsistent) reactions of the FCC, there must lay a demilitarized zone of common sense. Activist groups, such as the Parents Television Council, play a justifiable role in trying to protect children from inappropriate television viewing; however, the nearly one million members of PTC make up a minute fraction of the U.S. population, yet they are responsible for nearly 100 percent of the decency complaints to the FCC.[112] For its part, the FCC does not censor programs; it initiates indecency proceedings based on complaints. Consequently, the PTC's power to dictate what should and should not be available for public viewing seems stunningly disproportionate. That power seems to be getting stronger as the U.S. House of Representatives passed a new bill on February 16, 2005, increasing the penalties for indecent programming to $500,000 for either a company or an individual entertainer. (Previously, companies could be fined a maximum of $32,500 and individuals $11,000.) The FCC will now also be able to revoke a broadcaster's license after three indecency violations.

Personally, I find that turning off the television when I am disturbed by something is an effective way to protect myself and my family from what I deem to be inappropriate content, which I am aware may not be offensive to my neighbor. While it is fair and necessary to want to protect children from graphic sex, violence, profanity, and other undesirable behavior, it is also fair to expect parents to exercise reasonable judgment with regard to the television remote. Concerned citizens have the right to voice their opinions-we are talking about free speech here-and media makers similarly have the right to produce and distribute text, film, audio, and computer bytes, even if they risk offending someone (and they most surely will). It is hoped that above the cacophony, a cloud of reason will form that will rain good judgment upon the heads of those who influence and are influenced by the flood of entertainment media in our daily lives.

Although entertainment media should be subject to reasonable standards of decency, what is reasonable is extremely subjective. What is fun for one person may be filth to another; therefore, the standards should be as broad as possible to ensure no one's rights are being trampled. News media, however, needs to be more strictly regulated. Free, unbiased, and accessible information is the key to an informed and productive society, which is why most journalists accept the general creed of the profession to always seek the truth and act in the best interests of the public. Not all journalists, however, are immune to lapses in judgment and questionable conduct. Considering that most individual journalists hold themselves to high standards of accuracy, several highly publicized scandals have rocked the print media in recent years, and have served to undermine respect for people who investigate and report the news.

Jack Kelley, a respected foreign correspondent, resigned from his twenty-one-year position with *USA Today* in January 2004 after an internal investigation into the accuracy of several of his stories. Kelley was asked to produce a translator he had used in an interview in Belgrade in 1999; when he couldn't find her, he asked someone else to impersonate her.[113]

Jayson Blair, a twenty-seven-year-old reporter for the New York Times, resigned his position in May 2003, when it was discovered he had fabricated information and interviews and plagiarized other reporters' stories in his published articles. One article in particular brought what had been a recurring internal disciplinary issue to a flashpoint and precipitated Blair's resignation from the *New York Times*. In a profile written about a soldier fighting in Iraq, Blair quoted the soldier's mother and described details about her home. When checked out, it became apparent that Blair had appropriated all of this information from an article that had run in the *San Antonio Express-News*, and the soldier's mother made it known that she had never met Blair.

This one incident was not the exception, but the rule. Dating back to 1998, Blair had a consistent correction rate well above the professional standard the Times had quantified as its threshold. These correction rates were enough to warrant citations from his immediate supervisors. More evidence of Blair's penchant for literary license was found in various articles: inventing an interview with Jessica Lynch's father, copying information from an article that appeared in a Washington newspaper, and fabricating information about Lee Boyd Malvo's (the younger convicted "Washington Sniper") case.[114]

Janet Cooke was a reporter for the Washington Post during the early 1980s who wrote a story about an eight-year-old heroin addict living in Washington, D.C. The story about the boy garnered critical attention and was awarded the Pulitzer Prize in 1981. Unfortunately, Cooke admitted she had never actually interviewed the subject, or any boy for that matter, and that she had made up the story. As a result, the *Washington Post* returned the Pulitzer Prize and Cooke resigned her position from the newspaper.[115]

Jay Forman contributed an article to the online magazine *Slate*, in June 2001, that detailed an excursion he took in 1996 to fish for monkeys. He described, with vivid examples, a ride on a boat through the Florida Keys in search of an island inhabited by castaway monkeys; they were purported to have been abandoned by a pharmaceutical company and were, at that time, a recreational and environmental nuisance. Although the substance of the article was substantiated, most of the details were fabricated. *Slate* published an apology and called the article a journalistic fraud.[116]

Stephen Glass was an accomplished reporter by the age of twenty-five and was expected to become a great journalist. His stories in the late 1990s for The *New Republic, Rolling Stone*, and *Harper's* brought him acclaim and demand for more of his articles, which were almost entirely false. His assertions of the Monicondom, a condom designed specifically for oral sex and named for Monica Lewinsky, along with such tales as those describing an all-night, drug-soaked orgy of young Republicans in Washington, were complete inventions. In an attempt to cover up these lies and provide sources for his stories, Glass constructed an elaborate network of voice-mailboxes, fake websites, and e-mail addresses.

His cover was blown when the online version of *Forbes* magazine wanted to do a follow-up story on an earlier story Glass had written about teenaged website hackers. *Forbes* contacted the editor of *The New Republic* to discuss the lack of verifiable facts in the story, who then confronted Glass about the allegations. Initially Glass dove right into more lies in an attempt to cover himself, but eventually he was exposed and fired. Glass has recently published a book, *The Fabulist*, based on his escapades.[117]

Patricia Smith was a front-page columnist in the Metro section of the *Boston Globe* when it was discovered she had embellished and falsified certain quotes and references in some of her articles. These inventions were uncovered in June 1998, and shortly thereafter the Pulitzer Prize-nominated columnist resigned her position at the paper. Although she did use imaginary sources and quotes in some of her pieces, it was noted that her work that was nominated for the Pulitzer was not tarnished by falsifications. Nonetheless, it had an impact on her candidacy for the coveted prize.[118]

These are just some of the examples of the fallible and morally suspect representatives of the media, which illustrates that what we see and hear and read everyday is not necessarily true. Even when outright lies are not being presented as fact, frequently the spin of the story is quite different from the actual event, or the headline misrepresents the content of the story. The purpose of mass media is no longer to inform, but rather to sell products and services, opinions and ideology. There is an argument to be made that human beings are incapable of being unbiased, either in relaying the news or interpreting it. There will always be some measure of opinion or interest that creeps in to the delivery or receipt of information;

however, it is incumbent on both the media and its consumers to consciously recognize when that is happening and take steps to minimize it as much as possible. We as taxpayers have an obligation to fund a national, independent media entity, similar in purpose to NPR, but uninfluenced by corporate and government interests and contributions; free of ratings-driven programming decisions and subject to strict standards of accuracy and balanced reporting. Such a body may seem to be an unreachable ideal, but it is one I believe to be worth the effort.

In the meantime, the media and information menu is determined primarily by corporate interests; what we are served is as intellectually and morally substantial as the nutrition of a hot dog. Auden, with great foresight, described media offerings as entertainment for endless consumption. We are growing fat on it.

---

[71] http://www.realitytvworld.com/realitytvworld/allshows.shtml. All reality shows airing or scheduled to air on US networks, complete with news updates and ratings (retrieved Aug. 25, 2004).

[72] Associated Press, "American Idol Voters Cheated?" *CBS News.com*, May 16, 2004.
http://www.cbsnews.com/stories/2004/05/16/entertainment/main617696.shtml (retrieved Feb. 15, 2005).

[73] David Kronke. "Culture War Raging as American Electorate Polarized," *Los Angeles Daily News*, (reprinted in the *Chronicle-Herald*, Halifax, Nova Scotia, Monday, Aug. 16, 2004).

[74] Noam Chomsky. "The Media: An Instiutional Analysis," in *Understanding Power* (New York: The New Press, 2002), p. 13.

[75] Nancy Gibbs. "Blue Truth, Red Truth." *Time*, Canadian Edition, Sept. 27, 2004, p. 18.

[76] Jane Jacobs. *Dark Age Ahead*, (Toronto: Random House Canada, 2004), p. 137.

[77] Calvin Woodward. "Bush, Kerry Mangle Facts on Taxes, Jobs," *AOL News*, Oct. 9, 2004.

[78] "Iraq WMD Report Enters Political Fray." *CNN.com*, Oct. 7, 2004.

[79] Greg, Toppo. "Bush Administration Paid Commentator to Promote Law," *USA Today.com*, Jan. 7, 2005,
http://aolsvc.news.aol.com/news/article.adp?id=20050107071709990018.

[80] Ben Feller. "Bush Ad Portrays Itself as News Story on Schools," *AOL News Online*, Oct. 12, 2004.

[81] Vanessa Gera. "U.S. Accused of Violating Press Freedom," *AOL News*, May 19, 2004.

82 Noam Chomsky, interview by Michael Albert, *Z Magazine*, Znet.com, May 9, 2003.

83 *World Press Freedom Review 2003*. International Press Institute Press release, Vienna, March 10, 2004.

84 Greg Mitchell. "The *New York Times*, in Editor's Note, Finds Much to Fault in its WMD Coverage," originally published May 29, 2004 in *Editor and Publisher*, (Reprinted on website http://www.commondreams.org/head-lines04/0526-09.htm (retrieved Oct. 29, 2004).

85 Ira Basen. "The Campaign's First Loser Declared: It's Big Media," *CBC News Online*, Oct. 30, 2004, http://www.cbc.ca/news/viewpoint/vp_basen/20041030.html (retrieved Nov. 1, 2004).

86 Committee for Concerned Journalists Survey, "Journalists Not Satisfied with Their Performance in the Campaign," *Journalism.org*, Oct. 2004, http://www.journalism.org/resources/research/reports/campaign2004/ccj-camp2004/default2.asp (retrieved Nov. 2, 2004).

87 "Rating the Super Bowl Ads," *CBS News.com, The Early Show*: Feb. 7, 2005, http://www.cbsnews.com/stories/2005/02/07/earlyshow/main672016.shtml (retrieved Feb. 15, 2005).

88 "Super Bowl Advertisements and Publicity Stunts Score Online," press release of internet ratings analysis company, *comScore.com*, Reston, VA, Feb. 5, 2004, http://www.comscore.com/press/release.asp?press=420 (retrieved September 13, 2004).

89 Veda Renfrow. "Free Speech? Free Media? CBS, MoveOn and the Super Bowl Half-time Show," The State of Media Education, Newsletter of the New Mexico Media Literacy Project, Spring 2004, http://www.nmmlp.org/newviews.htm (retrieved Aug. 24, 2004).

90 "Court Rejects FCC Media Ownership Rules," *Media Alliance*, June 24, 2004: http://www.media-alliance.org (retrieved Aug. 24, 2004).

94 David Kirkpatrick. "Shaping Cultural Tastes at Big Retail Chains," *NYTimes.com*, May 21, 2003.

92 Steve Rendell and Daniel Butterworth, "How Public is Public Radio?" *Extra!* June 2004, http://www.fair.org/extra/0405/npr-study.html (retrieved Oct. 29, 2004).

93 Fairness and Accuracy in Reporting, "Action Alert: ABC Muddles the Social Security Debate, Not Everyone Agrees With Distorted Claims," press release, January 14, 2005, http://www.commondreams.org/cgi-bin/newsprint.cgi?file=news2005/0114-15.htm (retrieved Feb. 1, 2005).

94 Ron Taffel and Melinda Blau, *The Second Family: Dealing with Peer Power, Pop Culture, the Wall of Silence—and Other Challenges of Raising*

Today's Teens (New York: St. Martin's Press, 2001).

95 http://www.pbs.org/teachersource/media_lit/quiz.shtm (retrieved Aug. 24, 2004).

96 http://www.fcc.gov/vchip/legislation.html (retrieved Aug. 24, 2004).

97 Hal Niedzviecki. "Can We Save These Kids?" *Globe and Mail*, June 5, 2004.

98 John Murray. "Children's Brain Response to television Violence: Functional Magnetic Resonance Imaging (FMRI) of Video Viewing in 8-13 Year-Old Boys and Girls," abstract of presentation at biennial meeting of the Society for Research in Child Development, Minneapolis, Minnesota, April 19-22, 2001, http://www.johnmurray.org/srcd.htm (retrieved Sept. 1, 2004).

99 Daniel Rubin. "Video Game Skills May Give Edge in Life." May 7, 2004, http://www.smh.com.au/articles/2004/05/06 (retrieved Sept. 1, 2004).

100 http://www.teachingtools.com/GoFigure/VideoUniversity.htm (retrieved Sept. 1, 2004).

101 The New Mexico Media Literacy Project, http://www.nhmmlp.org/medialiteracy.htm (retrieved: Aug. 24, 2004).

102 Logan A. Ayliffe. "Reality Television: What it is and What it Means." November 2002, http://www.geocities.com/occamstoothbrush/realitytv (retrieved Sept. 1, 2004).

103 "Study Finds Ratings Creep: Movie Rating Categories Contain More Violence, Sex, Profanity than Decade Ago," Press release of the Kids Risk Project at the Harvard School of Public Health, July 13, 2004, http://www.kidsrisk.harvard.edu (retrieved Aug. 24, 2004). Ratings descriptions from the Motion Picture Association of America, (http://www.mpaa.org/movieratings/ (retrieved Sept. 10, 2004).

104 L. Brent Bozell, III. "Lazy Cops on the Video Game Beat," February 26, 2004, http://www.parentstv.org/PTC/publications/llbcolumns/2004/0226.asp (retrieved Sept. 10, 2004).

105 Lindsay Tanner. "High Exposure to television Sex Affects Teens." *AOL News*, Sept. 7, 2004.

106 Vinay Menon. "Can a Nipple Change the World?" *Toronto Star*, February 6, 2005, sec. C p. 14.

107 Jeff Jarvis. "The Shocking Truth About the FCC: Censorship by the Tyranny of the Few," *BuzzMachine*, November 15, 2004, http://www.buzzmachine.com/archives/2004_11_15.html#008481 (retrieved Feb. 15, 2005).

108 Todd Shield. "Viacom Agrees to Pay Feds $3.5 Million," *Mediaweek.com*, November 24, 2004, http://www.mediaweek.com/mediaweek/search/article_display.jsp?schema=&vnu_content_id=1000726041 (retrieved February 16, 2005).

[109] Associated Press, "PBS Stations Will Air Cartoon Depicting Lesbians." *Chronicle Herald*, Halifax, Canada, February 3, 2005, Sec. D p. 11.

[110] Action Alert: PBS Censors Postcards from Buster: episode Featuring Lesbian Moms Deemed Not 'Appropriate.'" *Fairness and Accuracy in Reporting*, New York, January 31, 2005, http://www.fair.org/activism/pbs-buster.html (retrieved February 16, 2005).

[111] Frank Rich. "The Plot Against Sex in America," *New York Times*, December 12, 2004 (reproduced in a pamphlet distributed by Fox Searchlight Pictures at various theatres showing the movie *Kinsey*, acquired in Houston, January 2005).

[112] Todd Shields. "Activists Dominate Content Complaints," *Mediaweek.com*, December 6, 2004, http://www.mediaweek.com/mediaweek/headlines/article_display.jsp?vnu_content_id=1000731656 (retrieved Feb. 16, 2005).

[113] "*USA Today* Reporter Admits Deception in Probe," *AOL News*, January 11, 2004.

[114] Howard Kurtz. "More Reporting by Times Reporter Called Suspect," May 8, 2003, http://www.washington post.com (retrieved December 18, 2003). Also: Shafer, Jack, "The Jayson Blair Project: How Did He Bamboozle the *New York Times*?" May 8, 2003, http://slate.msn.com/id/2082741 (retrieved December 18, 2003).

[115] Alex Boese. "Janet Cook and Jimmy's World," http://www.museumofhoaxes.com/day/04_17_2001 (retrieved January 13, 2004).

[116] Michael Kinsley. "Monkeyfishing: Slate Apologizes," June 25, 2001, http://slate.msn.com/id/110932/ (retrieved January 13, 2004).

[117] Steve Kroft. "Stephen Glass: I Lied for Esteem, *CBS News*, August 17, 2003. http://www.cbsnews.com/stores/2003/05/07/60minutes/main552819.shtml (retrieved January 16, 2004).

[118] "Boston Globe Columnist Resigns, Accused of Fabrications. *CNN*, June 19, 1998, http://www.cnn.com/US/9806/19/globe.columnist.resigns (retrieved January 16, 2004).

2. Crazy about Celebrity

Fame is a fickle food / Upon a shifting plate...

-Emily Dickinson (1830-1886)

There is a certain chicken-and-egg relationship between the ubiquity of the media and the undeniable American infatuation with fame and celebrity. Do we love our stars because of the publicity they receive-we see them all the time so they are the objects of our attention-or do they become famous because of our fascination and adoration? We have always loved our idols, but it is fair to say that at no other time in history have our celebrity figures been so public, so accessible, and consequently wield so much influence on our collective social being. The in-your-face influence of fame is so pronounced that it has become a highly destructive force among youth and adults alike. We so crave knowledge of our idols, and are so willing to pay to satisfy it, that the media, for its own survival, must offer it to us. The paparazzi (or rather, the "stalker-azzi") provide whatever information they can gather or fabricate and serve it up as a feast; and we gorge realizing that our social norms and expectations are being eroded by our fixation on negative role models and their pronounced influence on our lives.

Dickinson nicely echoes the sentiments of Auden: celebrity, like the media, is a consumable product. Sports heroes and Hollywood stars typically become the flavor of the month. The palette is highly fickle: celebrity and fame generally have a "best before date" and if the flavor gets a little stale, we spit it out and move on to the next dish. The flavor is often fleeting, but it is intense; the aftertaste stays with us long enough to influence our attitudes and behaviors significantly. There have always been a select few who have an extra measure of preservative and have managed to replace fame with infamy. Elvis, Ali, and Marilyn still resonate many decades after their careers and/or lives ended, despite the fact that their personal travails pale in comparison to today's celebrity role models. I suspect that future generations will be more familiar with OJ, Jacko, and Martha because of their very public failings, and yet we currently laud them as role models to whose fame and fortune we aspire.

Our idols are many and although the flame of our adoration often flickers briefly, it burns hot. Our culture has become one in which we use the word hero so freely that it has become a synonym for idol. The label of hero (or heroine) is no longer reserved for those who display great strength, courage, achievement, or noble character; it is equally, or more frequently, used to describe the objects of our affection. Soldiers, fire fighters, nurses and Good Samaritans are still granted hero status, often short-lived and given short shrift, but most of our attention and adulation is showered on the rich and famous-professional athletes, film actors, singers, and musicians-who have talents and gifts we celebrate, but whose money and power we revere. Our heroes are primarily celebrities with attitudes and agents instead of leaders with vision and virtue. Daniel J. Boorstin, American social historian and educator noted, "Celebrity-worship and hero-worship should not be confused. Yet we confuse them every day, and by doing so we come dangerously close to depriving ourselves of all real models. We lose sight of the men and women who do not simply seem great because they are famous but are famous because they are great. We come closer and closer to degrading all fame into notoriety." Notoriety is certainly the main ingredient in the recipe of how to make an instant celebrity.

Sports Celebrities

Ask any child on a playground, "Who is your hero?" Chances are the answer will be that of a professional athlete: Shaquille O'Neal, Tiger Woods, Serena and Venus Williams, Mia Hamm, Michael Jordan. Children barely big enough to dribble a basketball watch the NBA's finest on television and dream of reaching that level of the sport (any sport). Top athletes epitomize sporting excellence, which has been lauded and appreciated by humans since the dawn of civilization. We have been sitting in arenas for millennia, cheering on the elite who demonstrate the most skill, strength, stamina, and speed. For many the arena has been condensed into a television screen, but watching others is still our favorite entertainment: 44 percent of U.S. households watched the 2004 Super Bowl, with 63 percent tuning in to the game at some point, the biggest audience ever recorded for the annual event.[119] Indeed, the top ten most watched programs in television history were all Super Bowls.[120]

The select few whose skills meet the highest standard are handsomely rewarded. Golfer Tiger Woods made close to $80 million in 2003, the bulk of which came from endorsements rather than competition winnings. Tennis players Serena and Venus Williams made $10 million and $9 million respectively.[121] In exchange for their remuneration, these sports stars are subject to intense pressure-from fans, coaches, agents, sponsors, and the media- to continue to perform as the best. They have grueling training sessions; strict diets; exhausting travel, promotion, and competition schedules; and run the continual risk of permanent injury. They tend to have short careers and no job security. They are also expected to live up to their status as "hero" and the attending scrutiny by behaving in socially and morally acceptable ways at all times.

In a perfect world, one might say that top professional athletes earn every cent of their salary. They provide a model of performance excellence and determination to which the rest of us can only aspire. They bring in much more money than they actually pocket, which then goes to their sponsors, media outlets, owners, trainers, and others in their entourages, so they deserve a fair share; but the worthiness of their hero status and their paychecks become a bit more difficult to justify when those same athletes display less-than-heroic sides.

For example, take the recent statistic that 40 percent of NBA players have police records.[122] One high profile example is Philadelphia 76er Allen Iverson, who hit the news in 2002 after being charged with fourteen felony and misdemeanor charges including assault, making threats, and weapons offenses. All charges were later dropped. More recently, Iverson was fined $10,000 in March of 2005 for arguing heatedly with a game referee. Iverson currently leads the NBA in scoring and made $13.5 million in the 2003-04 season. He stands to earn $90 million in league salary alone by the end of his six-year contract.[123]

Los Angeles Lakers' star Kobe Bryant is another famous player who has been embroiled in criminal proceedings. In December 2003, he was charged with sexually assaulting a nineteen-year-old hotel worker. The criminal case was dropped in September when the accuser refused to participate in the trial; she sued the basketball player in civil court and the two reached an undisclosed settlement in early March of 2005. Bryant is in the second year of a seven-year, $136 million contract with the Lakers. In 2003, he signed a $45 million endorsement deal with Nike, but has not appeared in any of their ads since the scandal.[124]

Former Utah Jazz center Olden Polynice was convicted of a misdemeanor assault in July 2002 after hitting a twenty-one-year-old man on a golf course. When the man tried to apologize for an errant ball that hit Polynice in the arm, Polynice pushed him, then punched him in the face and kidney and spit in his eye.[125]

Milwaukee Bucks' forward Glenn Robinson was also arrested in 2002 and charged with domestic battery, assault, and unlawful possession of a firearm. When interviewed in his hometown about the charges, he declined to comment. The basketball player did, however, say, "The people who know Glenn Robinson, the people in the city of Gary, I'm a role model in the city of Gary. God has blessed me with that. It's something that will never be taken away."[126] Robinson has a previous arrest record for disorderly conduct in 1999.

The reputation of NBA players was further tarnished by the violence demonstrated during the November 19, 2004, game between the Indiana Pacers and the Detroit Pistons in Auburn Hills, Michigan. The Pacers' Ron Artest fouled Pistons' Ben Wallace who took exception and shoved Artest in the face. Both teams came off their benches and a free-for-all started when fans started throwing drinks and ice at the players. Several fans were punched in the face by players, specifically Artest, and several more fans tossed beer, popcorn, and a chair at players; the game was halted and players were herded into their dressing rooms. The NBA quickly condemned the actions of the public and the players, suspending Artest for the rest of the season, and tossing teammates for various lengths of time: Stephen Jackson (thirty games); Jermaine O'Neal (twenty-five games); and Anthony Johnson (five games). Wallace was suspended for six games and four other Pistons had to miss one game each. NBA Commissioner David Stern commented, "We must...not allow our sport to be debased by what seem to be declining expectations for behavior of fans and athletes alike."[127]

Unfortunately, the punishments meted out do not appear to have the expected deterrent factor and many players maintain their pattern of belligerent and childish behavior even after being sanctioned. Minnesota Timberwolves' Latrell Sprewell was given a one-game suspension in December 2004 for yelling a vulgarity at a female fan that was picked up by a broadcast microphone. A year earlier, he was fined $25,000 for cursing and screaming at the New York Knicks' chairman and the team's bench. In 1999 he was fined $10,000 for uttering profanity at fans during a game, and in 1997 he was suspended for sixty-eight games for choking a coach at a practice.[128] Clearly this player has not received the message that the NBA doesn't tolerate bad behavior, perhaps because he is still allowed on the court.

Criminal and juvenile behavior among athletes is not confined to the NBA. There are daily media accounts of assault, drunk driving, domestic abuse, drug use, adultery and general bad behavior by sports figures. Former NHL player Mike Danton was sentenced in early November 2004 to seven and one-half years in prison for conspiring to have his agent murdered. Baseball player Frank Francisco of the Texas Rangers was arrested in California after a game with the Oakland Athletics in September 2004 after throwing a chair that broke a female fan's nose. New York Giants' rookie Jeremy Shockey was fined $10,000 in July 2003 for giving heckling fans the middle finger salute and tossing a cup of ice over his shoulder, which hit two young children. He came under fire a few months later for calling Dallas Cowboys' coach Bill Parcells a "homo" in an interview for New York magazine, a statement he later said he could not recall uttering. Baltimore Orioles' pitcher Scott Erickson was charged in 2002 with second-degree assault after a domestic dispute with his girlfriend. The charges were later dropped. Olympic swimmer Michael Phelps, who won six gold medals at the Athens Olympics, was pulled over near Baltimore for drunk driving in November 2004. The nineteen-year-old pleaded guilty to driving while impaired in exchange for dropped charges of underage drinking, driving under the influence, and running a stop sign. Phelps was given eighteen months probation and ordered to pay a $250 fine, $55 in court costs, attend a M.A.D.D. meeting, and give three speeches at local schools about the dangers of alcohol.[129] Considering his youth, hometown-hero status, and pocketbook after signing endorsement deals with high profile corporations such as Visa, McDonalds, AT&T Wireless, and Speedo, the leniency of the punishment does not seem to fit the gravity of the crime.

Clearly, the bar has been lowered for standards of behavior by athletes, both on the job and in their personal lives, which is reflected by the behavior and attitudes of their fans. After the Pacers-Pistons melee, some sports-bar loungers told television reporters they thought such contact in the NBA was laudable. One enthusiastic fan said, "Yeah, I think it's great. We have fighting in the NHL, so why not all the pro-sports? It makes the games more exciting." Apparently, some people think it is acceptable to throw objects and fluids at players, and it's even better when they retaliate with punches.

Sports Stars and the Cheating Culture

Drug use and abuse is a systemic problem among pro-sports that no one wants to talk about. Sky-high salaries and advancements in pharmaceutical science make it easy for athletes to procure and use recreational as well as performance-enhancing drugs. When so many top athletes use drugs to reach their peak performance (and the corresponding salaries that go with being the best), teammates and competitors naturally feel they are at a disadvantage unless they use them also. While drug use has come under more scrutiny in recent years, athletes continue to use them to try to get an edge, hoping that the next generation of steroid or hormone will be undetectable. Steroids are illegal in the U.S. unless prescribed for a medical condition; they hold the allure of producing undeniable and quick results in performance and are the drug of choice for many athletes. Both the NFL and the NBA test and ban athletes for steroid use-the NHL does not. Major league baseball only instituted a policy in 2004, which has been widely criticized for being too lenient and inconsistently applied. Tests are done in the minor leagues, but typically there is no punishment or incentive for players to stop using them, beyond the unpleasant and frequently dangerous physical side effects that accompany long-term steroid use.

Several high profile Major League Baseball players have popped the lid on steroid use in recent years, particularly since Mark McGwire admitted to using a natural steroid-mimicking supplement called androstenedione to help him break Roger Maris' home run record. In 2002, *Sports*

Illustrated magazine did an in-depth investigation into drug use in the major leagues. Jason Giambi of the New York Yankees testified to a grand jury that he had used steroids for at least three seasons and had injected himself with human growth hormone, contradicting his earlier public denials about using performance-enhancing drugs. He said he got the drugs from Greg Anderson, Barry Bonds' personal trainer.[130] Bonds has repeatedly denied using steroids despite an obvious surge in the forty-year-old's performance (seventy-three home runs) and physique over the past few years. Former star Jose Canseco, accused of steroid use himself, estimated that 85 percent of Major League Baseball players use them. He released a tell-all book in February 2005 entitled *Juiced: Wild Times, Rampant 'Roids, Smash Hits and How Baseball Got Big*; it named several high-profile players as steroid users, including Mark McGwire and Rafael Palmeiro. Another former player, Ken Caminiti, more conservatively estimated that half of the league uses steroids, amphetamines, Ritalin, HGH (human growth hormone), or some variety of the stimulant Ephedra to get the edge required to hit further, pitch harder, and run faster, all of which translate into lucrative contracts and fan appreciation.

Former outfielder Chad Curtis, commenting on the public's response to blatant steroid use in baseball, said, "If you polled the fans, I think they'd tell you they don't care about illegal steroids. I'd rather see a guy hit the ball a mile or throw 105 miles an hour." Echoed Caminiti, "They come to the arena to watch gladiators...They want to see warriors."[131] Caminiti, who had a history of drug and alcohol addiction and was sentenced to three years probation for cocaine possession in 2001, died in October 2004 at the age of forty-one from heart failure induced by an overdose of cocaine and opiates. He had breached his probation by testing positive for cocaine a month before his death.[132]

In order to address the reluctance of the baseball players' union to voluntarily accept and institute a comprehensive drug testing plan, Senator John McCain (R-AZ) threatened the league with legislation in March of 2004. That threat, coupled with extensive negative media coverage, prompted the league and the players' union to draft a new policy, announced in January 2005. Under the new rules, players will now submit to year-round random testing, rather than just one scheduled test during the regular playing season; they will face immediate suspension of up to ten days for their first positive test, and a one-year suspension after their fourth offense. (Players used to have five chances.) Previously acceptable substances, such as human growth hormone, ephedra, and androstenedione, are now banned.[133] While the new policy is an improvement over the old, many critics believe it still falls short: amphetamines and other stimulants are not considered banned substances. (Apparently, steroids are out, but it's still okay to play pro baseball on speed.)

Senator McCain may have been appeased by the new MLB rules, but the U.S. Congress was not. A House Government Reform Committee hearing on March 17, 2005, called many major leaguers to testify about their own alleged steroid use, as well as general use within the league. Mark McGwire refused to answer direct questions about his own use saying (with a straight face), he was not going to go into the past or talk about his past. Instead, he expressed a willingness to clean up professional baseball's reputation for youth. Sammy Sosa and Rafael Palmeiro denied ever using steroids and said that Canseco's accusations were lies.

The dirty secret of steroid abuse is now so open that it can no longer be condoned or ignored. Despite the long-standing culture of denial, media coverage has forced athletes, managers, and the public at large to address the issue, perhaps most notably through the BALCO scandal. The Bay Area Laboratory Co-operative, a California nutritional supplement company owned by Victor Conte, has come under intense scrutiny over the past year. Conte has been investigated for money laundering, Medicare fraud, and steroid-trafficking in a case that has involved the grand jury testimonies of more than forty athletes. Conte, indicted for conspiracy to possess and distribute anabolic steroids and human growth hormone, settled a civil lawsuit with the government in October 2004, agreeing to pay $60,000 in fines for having allegedly made $1.8 million in false Medicare claims.[134] Conte has accused dozens of high-profile athletes of steroid use, including sprinter Marion Jones, who filed a defamation suit against Conte in December. Jones, a gold medalist in the Sydney Olympics, has consistently denied ever having taken steroids, despite allegations by her ex-husband that they did so together for various competitions. As a result of the BALCO investigations, the U.S. Anti-Doping Agency has slapped sanctions on at least thirteen athletes, including Michelle Collins, former world indoor 200 meter sprinting champion. Collins was given an eight-year ban and forced to forfeit both her 2003 world indoor title and her U.S. 200 meter title without having tested positive for banned substances. The USADA based its case on BALCO documents and test samples over a period of years; Collins is appealing the ruling to the Court of Arbitration for Sport.[135]

Drug use is not solely a phenomenon in professional athletics; it is increasingly affecting high school and college-level athletes. Although a positive drug test results in a one-year loss of eligibility from the National Collegiate Athletic Association (NCAA), the relentless pressure on young athletes to perform-from parents, teammates, coaches, and college and league recruiters-drives more and more students to steroid use. While pure anabolic steroids are a controlled substance, they are not regulated when they are an ingredient in dietary supplements. These supplements are easy to get either over-the-counter or over the Internet, particularly for older of age alumni, who are not an official part of college athletes. They are perhaps the primary generators of abuses among young athletes. Coaches are typically tightly governed within their athletic departments, but alumni are not; their self-imposed prerogative to act as team benefactor often extends beyond financial donations and includes getting the players whatever they need or want to win the game.

Many teens say they don't want to use drugs, but they feel steroid use is their only option in order to stay competitive with those who have no such qualms. Studies show steroids are used by up to 11 percent of teenage male athletes, but female athletes are the fastest growing group using the drug.[136] The University of Michigan's Institute for Social Research survey, Monitoring the Future, reports that more than 300,000 students between eighth and twelfth grade used steroids last year and as many as one-third of them were girls. Despite significant side effects in most users, kids believe they are invincible: the number of seniors who consider steroid use a serious risk to their health dropped from 68 percent to 55 percent over the past five years. Many don't even consider performance-enhancing substances as drugs, since they don't result in a typical drug high, and many, such as creatine, are found in unregulated nutritional supplements that can be purchased at the health food store.

Steroid use is such a non-issue for teens that a popular videogame called "Duke Nukem: Total Meltdown" has an option to allow the main character to take steroids when he is tired, advising gamers that "Steroids give Duke a super adrenaline rush."[138] The game doesn't mention the shrunken testicles, male pattern baldness, breast development, extreme acne, and "roid rage" related to Duke's steroid-induced energy boost. Nor does it point out the double-edged sword of steroid use in teens: frequently they sustain crippling injuries of joints and ligaments that are not able to handle the added bulk of muscle and the corresponding stress of increased performance. Kids who have taken steroids to get into professional sports often miss their opportunity because they have wrecked their bodies before leaving high school.

Performance-enhancing drug use has increasingly become a problem in the bastion of amateur sport, the Olympics. Despite the fact that the World Anti-Doping Association (WADA) has led the charge on cleaning up the dope-soaked games, athletes continue to try to improve their performance with drugs and other measures as drastic as blood transfusions. At the 2004 Athens Olympic and Paralympic Games, WADA introduced the expansive World Anti-Doping Code, the first document to harmonize anti-doping regulations for all sports and all countries. Despite the announcement that athletes would be tested for previously undetectable substances, such as THG (tetrahydragestrinone, a synthetic designer steroid) and HGH, two dozen of the world's elite were caught with those and other performance-enhancing substances in their bloodstreams and were disqualified from their events and/or stripped of their medals. A total of twenty-four athletes were caught for drug-test violations-thirteen more than at the 2000 Sydney Games-and several more were suspected, including Greek sprinters Kostas Kenteris and Katerina Thanou, who failed to appear at their drug tests amid curious circumstances. Half of those caught cheating were weightlifters who, as punishment from the International Weightlifting Federation, are now banned from competing at the 2008 Beijing Olympics.

American cyclist Tyler Hamilton has been at the center of Olympic controversy since he won the gold medal for time trials in Athens. An initial drug test seemed to show evidence that he had a blood transfusion to boost his performance, but the International Olympic Committee (IOC) dropped its investigation in September because a second blood sample was mistakenly frozen. This damaged the red blood cells and left too few to analyze in a second test. Hamilton denied any wrong doing, but the Russian Olympic Committee filed an Appeal with the Court of Arbitration of Sport (CAS). Hamilton retained his gold medal but has since been given a two-year suspension from the sport for another infraction. Under the current rules, an athlete is only considered guilty of doping after two positive blood samples.[139]

Other U.S. athletes on the docket of the CAS include several of the U.S. men's relay team. The International Association of Athletics Federations (IAAF), the governing body of track and field, wants to strip the entire 2000 squad of their Sydney gold medal, because member Jerome Young tested positive for the steroid nandrolone in 1999. Young has already been divested of his medal and USA Track and Field has been accused of trying to cover up the results of his test prior to clearing him for competition in the 2000 Games.[140] Other sprinters on the team have since been handed suspensions for doping violations; Alvin Harrison was recently handed a four-year suspension after admitting to using "numerous undetectable performance-enhancing substances," and his brother Calvin is already serving a two-year suspension.[141]

WADA is so determined to rid the Olympic Games of the drug problem, President Richard Pound convened an executive meeting less than one month after Athens to draft the 2005 Banned Substances and Methods list.[142] Within the year there will undoubtedly be more, hard-to-detect designer hormones or procedures available to give those athletes the edge they desire. Indeed, they are willing to risk their health, reputations, and careers for this edge. Pound, a Montreal lawyer and former Olympic swimmer, is passionate about cleaning up sports in general, despite the reluctance from professional leagues to adopt the strict WADA code. He believes that professional athletes have such an enormous influence on the public, and youth in particular, that they have an obligation to demonstrate a respect for rules as well as self-respect. In a January 2003 interview, Pound described his philosophy about doping in sports. "It's a completely antithetical view to what sport should have been in the first place. It's essentially a humanistic endeavour to see how far you can go on your own talent...(Sports are) a precursor to how you're going to behave in other aspects of social intercourse."[143]

The once-glorified reputation of the Olympic organization has suffered from other cheating scandals beyond doping. In 2002, Sandra Baldwin, President of the U.S. Olympic Committee resigned after it was discovered she had lied about her academic credentials. Also that year, several International Olympic Committee members were forced to resign when it was discovered they had accepted bribes ("gifts") to vote for Salt Lake City to host the Winter Games. The same games were plagued with further evidence that judging in the figure skating event was rigged: a French judge admitted she had been pressured to vote for the Russian team over the Canadian pair Jamie Sale and David Pelletier, even though the Canadian team had skated an almost flawless routine. Sale and Pelletier were eventually awarded the gold along with the Russian team.

Cashing In

Another subject of debate involving the Olympics revolves around the fact that the games are no longer reserved for amateur athletes. The American basketball team, for example, is comprised primarily of professional NBA players who make enormous salaries and earn even more from endorsements. The reasoning behind allowing them to compete on the Olympic stage is ostensibly to raise the profile of the games and increase television ratings commensurate with an increased level of play. Isn't it enough for LeBron James to earn $18.5 million over four years (in addition to his $35 million in endorsements) that he must compete for an Olympic medal as well?

Other American Olympians are cashing in on their physical gifts in a different way. High jumper Amy Acuff posed for *Playboy* and *FHM* magazines shortly before the Athens Olympic Games. Her practical justification was, "I did it for the financial aspect. It's really hard to make that kind of money in the real world."[144] Other Team USA athletes who appeared in bikinis on the September cover of *FHM* include volleyball player Logan Tom; swimmers Amanda Beard and Haley Cope; and hurdler Jenny Adams. Cope and pole vaulter Mary Sauer both posed nude for *Playboy* as well. U.S. Olympic Committee spokesman, Darryl Seibel, has stated that the USOC aggressively markets its athletes to consumer-oriented publications and broadcast outlets, but the decision to appear partially or completely unclad in men's magazines is entirely that of the individual athletes.[145] Sports and sex has always been a lucrative combination (*Sports Illustrated*'s annual sell-out swimsuit edition is one indicator) and the Olympics are no exception. Beach volleyball competitors wear bikinis; other non-water sports, such as pole vaulting and sprinting, also have form-fitting bikini bottoms and "tankini" top uniforms. People will always watch the Olympics for the sport, but they will probably tune in more often and for longer periods of time if they can enjoy some eye candy at the same time. When athletes reap more financial rewards from their skin than their sweat, many are willing to oblige.

Perhaps the poor attendance at the 2004 Olympic Games is an indicator that the world is becoming jaded over the Olympics. It has become a media-fest primarily because of the expectation (and delivery) of scandal and controversy: there were 11,100 athletes in Athens and 21,500 media representatives.[146] Although organizers claim that over three million tickets were sold for all of the events, spectator attendance was markedly absent of both Greek residents and tourists. Tens of thousands of seats were empty every day-except for swimming and men's basketball-and the venues were devoid of the typical celebratory atmosphere of most games.[147] For many, the energy and emotion of the Olympics has been overshadowed by the problems associated with the transformation of the Olympics Games into another enormous corporate enterprise. The two-hour spectacle of the opening ceremonies has become the highlight of the games, replacing the pride and perseverance of the athletes that used to define the Olympic ideal and galvanize the globe for a few weeks every four years. What was once an institution of pure amateur sport and excellence has become a ridiculously expensive arena of corruption, scandal, drugs, and politics. (It has also became a security nightmare: Greece spent more than $1.5 billion on security in and around Athens for the 2004 games.) The evolution of the Olympics to its modern form precludes any immediate return to the original vision of Pierre de Coubertin, but changes need to be made. The suggestion of placing restrictions on Olympic participants-more thoroughly defined "amateur" status; a limit to the number of times an athlete can participate; and lifetime bans for doping-is just the tip of Mount Olympus in reforming what was once the pinnacle of athletics.

The commercialization of sport is nothing new. Corporate sponsorship has been a part of athletics throughout my lifetime, but it is reaching greater heights than ever. Product placement banners are not just papered along the walls of the outfield and rink boards anymore; entire arenas and stadiums are now named for sponsoring companies rather than the historical icons of excellence who used to be honored: the Houston Astros play in Minute Maid Park (formerly known as Enron Field); the Buffalo Bills touchdown in HSBC Arena; the Colorado Avalanche skate in the Pepsi Center. Corporate naming rights are just one of the many perks that multi-million dollar sponsorship brings. FedEx pays the Washington Redskins $7.6 million a year to have their name on the stadium. The New York Yankees, the richest team in Major League Baseball, earned $223 million in revenues in 2002: 13 percent from corporate sponsors that include Adidas, Anheuser-Busch and JP Morgan

Chase. In 2001, $58 million of the Yankees earnings came from television contracts alone.[148]

Professional sports is one more link in the entertainment/big business chain. The current lockout of National Hockey League players is another telling example of how pro sports have everything to do with money and little to do with actual sport (that is, athleticism, healthy competition, sportsmanship, and dedication). Despite the fact the average hockey player's salary (not the superstars, just the middle-of-the-ice guys) has grown from $733,000 a year in 1994-95 to $1.83 million last season, the six hundred member of the NHL Players' Association balked at any hint of team owners trying to institute a salary cap during the final days of their collective bargaining agreement. The NHLPA's last ditch counter proposal to the league was refused, and hockey fans are remembering the 2004 season that wasn't. The players' union argues that the owners make far more money on their backs than they do, but when the median salary of the players on the New York Rangers was $2.8 million last season, it makes it somewhat difficult to feel their pain. Nonetheless, die-hard fans will be adrift until the NHL can get its economic house in order and return to the ice for another season of hockey.

Bad Attitudes

The examples of opportunistic, cheating, and criminal behavior in sports are many, but there are even more examples of seemingly more minor attitudinal shifts that have lowered the bar in terms of how our athlete role models behave. Former Los Angeles Lakers' star Shaquille O'Neal was suspended without pay for one game in February 2004, after using profane language on television and publicly criticizing game officials. The punishment by the NBA was considered "rather severe and childish in some ways" by indignant Lakers' coach Phil Jackson. After all, it deprived fans of seeing O'Neal play against the Indiana Pacers and it cost the player $295,000. (Considering his $26.5 million dollar salary in the 2003-4 season, it probably wasn't all that much of a hardship.) Larry Bird, former NBA star and current president of the Indiana Pacers, and Bill Parcells, head coach of the Dallas Cowboys, two respected figures of authority within their leagues, have both been tripped up by the media for making racist comments on the air.

Profanity and bad behavior at sporting events is not confined to players. Fans are responsible (or irresponsible?) for their fair share of petulance and potty language. One shining example is Matt Starr, who achieved his fifteen minutes of fame at a Texas Rangers baseball game in June 2004); he snatched a fly ball away from four-year-old Nick O'Brien when it landed at his feet in the stands. National outrage at his bullish behavior eventually compelled Starr to apologize and give the ball back to the child, but only after team members presented the young fan with two bats and four baseballs, including one signed by former Ranger Nolan Ryan.

Coarse behavior has become common place among fans in arenas around the country, particularly at college sporting events. Hundreds of University of Maryland students were broadcast shouting obscenities at rival Duke University during coverage of a January 2004 basketball game. Despite widespread complaints about the language, students and university officials maintained a university is a public institution that promotes and protects free speech and as such is unable to prohibit profanity (either spoken or written on clothing, faces, or placards), nor should they eject verbally abusive fans from the venue.[149] The debate rages between defending the First Amendment right to free speech and protecting the interests of others in a public facility, ensuring their right to a safe and non-offensive setting. Students themselves are defiant in their choice of words: "It's a free country," and "We're in college; you're not my mother and no one can tell me what to do." They don't seem to realize or care that their behavior embarrasses their team and their school or that their language is not appreciated by families who bring their children to games. It doesn't occur to them that they attend institutions of higher learning and ostensibly represent an educated "higher standard." Instead, parents in the stands get to say, "Look honey, you can grow up to be just like that swearing student over there." (Parents, that is, who are above the ilk of Thomas Junta, who was convicted of manslaughter in the 2000 beating death of forty-year-old hockey dad Michael Costin during a fight at their sons' hockey practice in Reading, Massachusetts.)

Bad attitudes at the college level extend to players as well as fans. In September 2004, Virginia Tech quarterback Marcus Vick was suspended from the football team for the season after pleading no contest to three misdemeanor charges of contributing to the delinquency of a minor. Vick and two teammates were arrested after a night of drinking with fourteen- and fifteen-year-old girls in his apartment. In a plea agreement, Vick received a thirty-day suspended sentence, was fined $100, and was ordered to perform twenty-four hours of community service. A month prior to this incident, Vick had pleaded guilty to reckless driving and no contest to marijuana possession.[150]

The University of Colorado football team has been at the center of scandal and controversy since 1997, when a high school student accused a player of rape. Since then, there have been nine allegations of sexual assault against Colorado players, including one in 2002 by a woman who accused two players of having drugged and sodomized her. The bartender at the bar where the woman met the players refused to testify as a witness, telling police, "They're on scholarships. I can't do that to them."[151] Another rape allegation came from the only woman to have ever played at The University of Colorado. Katie Hnida said she was raped by a player, as well as repeatedly harassed verbally and sexually, while she was a place kicker on the team in 1999. An additional accusation that recruits were lured to Boulder with strippers, sex, and alcohol, amounted to a scandal that prompted an NCAA task force and congressional hearings into recruiting practices. Coach Gary Barnett was put on paid leave in February 2004, because he called Hnida a terrible player just hours after she came forward with her story; but he was reinstated in May after the university investigative commission found that he had not knowingly sanctioned any of the spurious activities of the players.[152]

It's not all bad. Despite the high profile instances of abuse of privilege, law-breaking, and the poor examples of many athletes, there are those who are actually deserving of the title hero. Cyclist Lance Armstrong overcame testicular, brain, and lung cancer in 1996 to become the only cyclist to ever win the grueling Tour de France six consecutive times; he also established a non-profit organization to raise money for cancer research. [Note: In January 2005, Armstrong was notified that French authorities were opening an investigation into allegations he used performance enhancing drugs over the course of his many Tour de France wins. The cyclist denied ever having done so.] Tiger Woods was the youngest person to complete the professional golf Grand Slam (the Masters, the U.S. Open, and the British Open) in one year; only five other golfers have ever won all three events, in the same year. He was also the first major championship winner of African or Asian heritage, breaking the racial barriers of the "social club" for which the sport has been traditionally known. Despite the intense media pressure, Woods is invariably described as having nearly superhuman dedication, and he comports himself as a gentleman.

Billie Jean King was the best tennis player of her time as well as an activist: she fought for and won prize money equal to male players during her career. Her public victory over Bobby Riggs made the sports world sit up and take notice of female athletes. Mary Lou Retton was the first American woman to win an Olympic gold medal in all-around gymnastics in 1984. Her five-medal haul in Los Angeles was the most of any athlete of those Olympic Games. Ten years after being named Sportswoman of the Year by *Sports Illustrated*, Retton was named the Most Popular Athlete in America based on an Associated Press national survey. Speedskater Bonnie Blair was the first woman in Olympic history to win consecutive gold medals in speedskating and the first American woman to win consecutive Winter Olympic golds. She is the most decorated winter athlete in the U.S. and the record holder for most gold medals (five) won by an American woman in any sport. Blair is also a noted cyclist, skier (water and snow), golfer, and softball player.

Indeed many sports figures-those with celebrity status and without-contribute their time and money to making the world a better place.

Many sponsor and act as representatives for various charities, using their high profiles and influence to greater purpose than filling arenas. Brett Favre is one example that comes to mind: in 1996, he and his wife Deanna established the Brett Favre Forward Foundation, which has raised $1.5 million for charities for disadvantaged or disabled children who live in Wisconsin or Favre's home state of Mississippi.[153] Similarly, several NFL teams, tennis players, and Major League Baseball teams have raised and donated more than one million dollars for the South Asia tsunami disaster relief effort. The media does a poor job reporting on the positive contributions of celebrity sports stars, because they are less newsworthy (read: tabloid fodder). It is much more interesting to cover the salacious details of rape trials than the charity golf tournaments.

Celebrity Performers

Image has become the hallmark of our culture; it is even more revered than talent in terms of a marketable asset. Those who have it-beauty, sex appeal, style-become overnight sensations and instant icons. We adore them, emulate them, and raise them to heroic heights. We pay homage literally and figuratively. Cameron Diaz reportedly makes $25 million a movie and was listed in the *Guinness Book of World Records* as the highest paid actress in 2004 based on her 2001 earnings of $42.1 million. Adam Sandler was currently the highest paid actor for earning $42.9 million in 2001.[154] Actor/director Mel Gibson was Forbes Magazine's top power celebrity for 2004, bringing in $210 million that year.[155] Other film stars who command $25 million a movie include Tom Cruise, Jim Carrey, Julia Roberts, Tom Hanks, Will Smith, and Harrison Ford.

Pop and rock stars stand to make even more money than Hollywood stars. According to *Rolling Stone* magazine, Prince was the highest earning musician in 2004, raking in $56.4 million from records and concert tickets. Madonna's haul was next at $54.9 million; R & B sensation Usher was number sixteen on the list earning $25.8 million in his breakthrough year; and the ubiquitous Beyoncé trailed at $16.1 million, despite several high profile endorsement deals and her work with Destiny's Child. Rapper R. Kelly, despite child pornography charges, earned $11.5 million and ranked forty-second on the top fifty list.[156]

Yet, as someone once famously said, "Hero worship is mostly idol gossip." Our insatiable appetite for glamour, rumor, and scandal is schizophrenic: we love watching the beautiful people, but we love watching them crawl in the dirt even more. One essayist on pop culture recently wrote, "While it seems silly to believe a star's foibles can offer fans a sort of redemption, it nevertheless appears to be the guiding principle behind celebrity worship. Their public faults mirror our private fears."[157] We deify otherwise normal people and then watch, riveted, when they fall from grace, unable to hold the religious office of celebrity for long: fame and fortune requires the forfeiture of freedom. In exchange for the adoration and wealth, stars are wed to the media, for better or worse, in sickness and in health. Every detail of their lives is seized, recorded, exaggerated, and offered up for public consumption. We are gluttons for our daily bread of scandal and gossip.

It all makes money; hence the credo that no matter how bad the publicity, it's better than none at all. Television networks are saturated with entertainment news shows, celebrity biographies, and interviews with the stars. We, the market, want to know everything there is to know and the more salacious the better. If it isn't salacious enough, then someone somewhere will spin it that way.

False reality is an oxymoron that aptly describes our popular culture and our obsession with celebrity. In our continued hunger for the next larger-than-life figure, we confuse the persona with the person. Someone may be an incredible singer or a gifted actor, which gives him/her the persona of "Invincible Star"; but the person may be, and often is, totally unprepared to carry the weight of the expectation-and the wealth-their persona creates. The consequence for many is a slide down Mount Hollywood into a gully of drug use, serial infidelity, violence, drunk driving, and other destructive (or self-destructive) behaviors. As witnesses, we cannot help but be influenced by their lapses. The repeated patterns of excess serve to lower the bar of what we expect from our idols, as well as distracting us from being entertained by their art to being entertained by their scandal. "The tabloidification of culture makes an artist's work secondary to their biography."[158]

It is reaching the point of absurdity: the hottest new reality television concept is several upcoming series about famous former and soon-to-be convicts, including Bobby Brown and Lizzie Grubman. Even Martha Stewart has signed on with Mark Burnett, producer of the immensely popular *Survivor* and *Apprentice* shows, to do a tell-all show. Since her trial and conviction for insider trading, Stewart has become even more of a media commodity than she already was. The curiosity factor is high; media executives (and Stewart, herself) are ready to cash in, and we as viewers are ready to buy in to the whole disgraceful parade. We are part of the "cultural equation that rewards someone with the big wet kiss of TV visibility for being associated with a crime."[159] It is surreal that so many disgraced stars are willing to drag their dirty laundry out to the front yard and hawk it piece by piece to so many willing consumers. Money is the ultimate motivator for them; overwhelming voyeurism drives us.

A Compendium of Controversy

The following is an alphabetical listing of some of the most flagrant misconduct-ethical, moral, criminal-of many famed sport and Hollywood celebrities in recent years. So much for role models....

- A -
MARV ALBERT - sexual assault
Noted sportscaster Marv Albert was put on trial for assault and battery related to forcible sodomy in September 1997. Accusations against Albert included biting the alleged victim on her back and forcing her to perform oral sex on him. During the trial, it was revealed that the woman had maintained a ten-year sexual relationship with Albert that included rough and unconventional sex, including a penchant for multiple sexual partners at the same time. One of the witnesses testified that Albert had attempted to seduce her while wearing women's underwear.

Albert pleaded guilty to a misdemeanor of assault and battery and received a suspended twelve-month sentence; if he did not commit any crimes for twelve months, the charges would be expunged from his record.[160]

- B -
CHARLES BARKLEY - assault
Named one of the fifty greatest NBA players of all time, Charles Barkley has been accused of aggravated battery, assault, and resisting arrest in at least three altercations since 1991. Criminal charges were filed in two of the cases; a third resulted in a civil lawsuit against Barkley. In December 1991, Barkley allegedly punched a bar patron in Milwaukee and was charged with assault; he was subsequently acquitted. In 1992, he was accused of being in a bar fight in Chicago, but the charges were later dropped. In October 1997, he threw a man through a plate glass window in Orlando and was charged with aggravated battery and resisting arrest. The civil lawsuit was precipitated by Barkley punching a man in the nose in Cleveland in July 1996. The victim sought $550,000 in damages, but the suit was rejected by the jury.[161]

HALLE BERRY - leaving the scene of a crime
Oscar winner Halle Berry was charged with a misdemeanor count of leaving the scene of a crime after a collision in Los Angeles in February 2000 left a woman with a broken wrist. Berry ran a red light and ran her truck into a car. She was sentenced to a three-year probation plus $14,000 in fines and court fees and two hundred hours of community service. In 1998, Berry was sued, but not criminally charged, for allegedly having struck a Volkswagen with her Range Rover while driving on Sunset Boulevard.[162]

ROBERT BLAKE - murder and solicitation of murder
Known for his title role on 1970s television show *Baretta*, Robert Blake

is currently awaiting trial for the murder of his wife, Bonny Lee Bakley, who was killed in Los Angeles in May 2001. Bakley was shot twice while sitting in Blake's car after dinner with her husband at a restaurant in Los Angeles. Blake is also charged with solicitation of murder as he sought someone willing to murder his wife.[163] (Blake was acquitted on March 16, 2005.)

KOBE BRYANT - accused of rape

Los Angeles Lakers' star Kobe Bryant was accused of sexual assault in December 2003. A nineteen-year-old hotel clerk accused the basketball player of raping her in a Colorado hotel resort in Eagle County, Colorado, in July 2003. He denied the allegations, insisting the sexual encounter was consensual. The criminal case was brought to trial, but the felony charge was dropped when the accuser refused to participate in the trial because a publication ban was breached and her name was splashed over the Internet.[164] Bryant, who is married with a daughter, settled the civil suit against him out of court for an undisclosed amount in March 2005.

- C -

JENNIFER CAPRIATI - drug use

Jennifer Capriati was, at age thirteen, the youngest player to win Junior titles at the French Open, the U.S. Open, and then an Olympic Gold Medal in 1992. Unfortunately, her early successes were followed by bouts of illegal activities. In 1993, Capriati was detained by Tampa police for shoplifting an inexpensive piece of jewelry and was later arrested in a Coral Gables motel for drug possession. Capriati was able to straighten up and made a comeback to the professional women's tour that culminated with Grand Slam titles in the Australian Open (2001, 2002) and the French Open (2001).[165]

RAE CARRUTH - convicted of conspiracy of murder

Former Carolina Panthers' football player, Carruth was sentenced to nineteen years in prison for his role in the November 1999 shooting death of his girlfriend, Cherica Adams, in Charlotte, North Carolina. Carruth was charged and convicted of conspiracy of murder and for firing a weapon. He actively participated in the ambush that took Adams' life by using his car to block hers as his co-conspirators rushed her car to shoot Adams, who was eight-months pregnant at the time. Carruth was on the phone with the gunmen throughout the incident. The baby was delivered by Caesarian section; Adams died from the gunshot wounds a month later. According to court documents, Carruth conspired to murder Adams to avoid paying child support.[166]

KURT COBAIN - drug use, suicide

Kurt Cobain was the lead singer of the multi-platinum Seattle band,

Nirvana. The band's second album, Nevermind, was a smash success selling millions of copies and bringing the band, and Cobain, to national prominence. In 1993 Cobain overdosed on heroin, and then in 1994 he was hospitalized for drug abuse and depression. A week after his release from the hospital, Cobain committed suicide with a shotgun. Controversy has surrounded the circumstances of Cobain's death; some sources and expert opinions assert the logistic impossibility of Cobain shooting himself in the head. Nevertheless, Cobain's death was ruled a suicide and is officially considered such.[167] Cobain was posthumously awarded a Grammy in 1995.

- D -
MIKE DANTON - conspiracy to commit murder
(see earlier text on sports celebrities)

ROBERT DOWNEY, JR. - drug, alcohol use
Oscar nominated actor Robert Downey Jr. has a long history of drug charges, including possession of cocaine, heroin, marijuana, and controlled substances. His drug and alcohol use reportedly started at age eight when his father gave him marijuana. It is responsible for erratic behavior, including an instance when he entered a neighbor's house and fell asleep in the neighbor's child's bed; and for losing his critically acclaimed role on the television show Ally McBeal. He spent a year in a California prison because of his perpetual run-ins with the law, including several weapons offenses, and was released in August of 2000. He has been admitted to rehab many times.[168]

-F-
HEIDI FLEISS - "Hollywood Madam"
Heidi Fleiss, the mastermind behind an elite prostitution service in Hollywood in the early 1990s, was charged and convicted in 1993 with pandering, tax evasion, conspiracy, and money laundering. She began a three-year prison sentence in 1999. She was released in 2001. Her case attracted much attention because of the status of her clients in the Hollywood community and around the world. Her roster of talent was reported to work for no less than $1,500 per night, and actor Charlie Sheen testified during the trial that he spent approximately $53,000 on Fleiss' services in 1992. Recently, Fleiss has been the subject of the trial of actor Tom Sizemore, with the accusation that he abused her throughout their two-year relationship.[169]

-G-
GANGSTA RAP - violence, gang warfare, offensive lyrics
Gangsta rap is a hard core form of hip-hop music evolving in the late

1980s and known for its controversial lyrics reflecting urban gangland themes of violence, misogyny, promiscuity, drug and alcohol use, homophobia, and attacks on authority. Los Angeles rapper Ice T is generally regarded as the first gangsta rapper for his 1987 song "Cop Killer." The L.A. group NWA (Niggaz with Attitude) made the genre popular with their 1989 album *Straight Outta Compton*, featuring the song that got the FBI's attention: "Fuck tha Police." Public Enemy did the same on the other side of the country. The music and its artists are known for their West Coast versus East Coast rivalries for dominance in the genre, represented by the competing record labels Death Row Records (L.A.) and Bad Boy Records (New York).[170] Many famous gangsta rappers have had serious troubles with the law. The following are a few examples.

Multi-platinum rapper and actor Tupac Shakur became a prominent voice for the urban angst of young Americans in the early and mid-1990s. He voiced many of the concerns and daily struggles of urban youth through his music. Although he didn't have an arrest record until after he became a recording artist, his rap sheet quickly grew. In 1992, he was arrested for a fight at a street festival in California in which an innocent bystander, a six-year-old boy, was killed by a stray bullet. He settled with the boy's family and the charges were dropped. In 1993, Shakur shot two off-duty officers who were harassing a black motorist; however, charges were dropped because the officers were drunk and were using stolen weapons. Later the same year, Shakur was convicted of sexually assaulting a woman in New York; he was sentenced for four and one-half years and was incarcerated for eight months. In 1994, Shakur was shot five times during a mugging at a recording studio in New York. He died in September 1996 at the age of twenty-five, the victim of a drive-by shooting that was never solved but was widely blamed on gang members. Shakur sported an abdominal tattoo that read "THUGLIFE" and stood for "The Hate U Give Little Infants Fucks Everybody." He is quoted as having once said, "I was raised in this society so there's no way you can expect me to be a perfect person. I am going to do whatever I like: I am not a role model."[171]

Brooklyn-born rapper Notorious B.I.G. (a.k.a. Biggie Smalls; born Christopher Wallace) was once a friend of Tupac Shakur and later a bitter rival. He was shot to death in Los Angeles in March 1997, six months after Shakur. Wallace was rumored to have been involved in Shakur's death, but neither murder has been solved and no one has been charged.[172]

Rapper Snoop Dogg (born Calvin Broadus) became an immediate celebrity in 1992 when he collaborated with Dr. Dre on the song "Ain't Nothin' But a G Thang." His early work reflected the years he was in and out of prison during his late teens. In 1993 he was arrested for the shooting death of a rival gang member who had been stalking him; Snoop Dogg and his bodyguard were both acquitted on the grounds of self-defense. In 2002 he announced he was giving up drugs and alcohol and has become a mainstream television and film actor.[173]

Rap recording artist/producer, and owner of Bad Boy Records, Puff Daddy (a.k.a. P. Diddy; born Sean Combs) was charged with the possession of a firearm stemming from a violent incident at a Manhattan club in December 1999, in which a gun was fired at another patron. Combs was also alleged to have tried to bribe his driver to accept responsibility for the shooting with $50,000 and some expensive jewelry. At the trial, Combs was acquitted of all charges against him.[174]

Eminem, born Marshall Mathers, is a successful and controversial rap recording artist and actor from Detroit, Michigan. He rose from poverty to super stardom in the late 1990s singing about contemporary social problems with lyrics that have often been criticized for being violent, misogynistic, homophobic, and profane. He was been sued by his mother for $10 million for slander and emotional distress; a claim for which she has received about $1,600 after legal fees. His volatile relationship with his ex-wife has been widely publicized. In June of 2000, Eminem was charged with possession of a concealed weapon when he struck a man with a pistol after he caught the man kissing his ex-wife in a club. He received two year's probation. A civil suit brought by the victim against Eminem resulted in a $100,000 settlement. In 2003, Eminem won an Academy Award for Best Song and a Grammy for Best Rap Album.[175]

Grammy-nominated rapper Mystikal, born Michael Tyler, was charged, along with two of his bodyguards, with aggravated rape for a videotaped attack on a woman in Louisiana in July 2002. He was sentenced to six years in prison in January 2004; the bodyguards received three- and four-year sentences. Tyler also received five years probation after pleading guilty to an extortion charge relating to the same incident: he accused the woman, his hair stylist, of stealing $80,000 worth of checks and threatened to turn her into the police if she didn't perform oral sex on the men. He gave the woman an undisclosed settlement to prevent her from filing a future civil suit.[176]

DWIGHT GOODEN - drugs

The career of former New York Mets pitcher Dwight Gooden was overshadowed by drug use and consequent problems with law enforcement officials, Major League Baseball (MLB), and the Mets baseball club. He first spent time in a rehabilitation clinic in 1987 after testing positive for cocaine. Continued testing, mandated by MLB, over the next several years led to Gooden's suspension from baseball by the MLB Commissioner in September 1994 for the remainder of 1994 season (strike-shortened) and the entire 1995 season.[177]

HUGH GRANT - lewd conduct with a prostitute

British actor Hugh Grant was arrested and charged with lewd conduct in Los Angeles in June 1995. He pleaded no contest to the charges and was subsequently fined $1,800, placed on two years probation, and ordered to attend an AIDS awareness conference. At the time of his arrest, Grant had been involved in a long-term relationship with model and actress Elizabeth Hurley. After the incident, his appearances on talk-shows, such as *The Tonight Show with Jay Leno*, were the salvation for his career according to many Hollywood industry critics.[178]

-H-

PARIS HILTON - sex video

An heiress of the Hilton hotel fortune, Paris Hilton's celebrity status peaked in late 2003 when a sex video of Hilton appeared on the Internet. Hilton was nineteen at the time the video was filmed and her then-boyfriend, Rick Salomon, was thirty. Her regular appearances in the society pages were instantly replaced by global tabloid coverage. Rather than being a cause for disgrace, the video propelled her film career: Hilton has had several cameo roles in major films and she currently appears in the reality TV series *A Simple Life*.[179] Salomon has recently indicated to the press his intention to sell a new, longer version of the original tape.

HOCKEY DADS - violent confrontation leads to murder

In July 2000, a father enraged by the way his son's hockey practice was being officiated became violent with the referee. Thomas Junta beat Michael Costin to death in front of Costin's son, who was also participating in the practice. At the trial, Junta was convicted of involuntary manslaughter and sentenced to serve six to ten years in state prison.[180]

WHITNEY HOUSTON/BOBBY BROWN - drug use, spousal abuse

Six-time Grammy Award winner Whitney Houston eclipsed her successful singing career during the late 1990s and early 2000s with highly publicized erratic behavior; most notably, her absence from a scheduled appearance at the 2000 Academy Awards show. Speculation that drug use was responsible for her behavior was confirmed after she was stopped in the Honolulu airport and charged with possession of an illegal substance. (The charges were later dropped.) Houston admitted in December 2002 to abusing alcohol, marijuana, cocaine, and prescription drugs; she was admitted to a rehabilitation center again in late March of 2005.

Houston and her husband, Bobby Brown, have also been in the media over charges of spousal abuse on the part of Brown. Brown was alleged to have slapped Houston in an airport parking lot, but the reports of this incident have been refuted by both Brown and Houston. In December 2003, Houston accused Brown of hitting her in their Atlanta home, and police noted Houston had a cut lip and a bruised cheek when they arrived on the scene. Brown turned himself in to the police a day after the incident. Brown's legal troubles started earlier: in 1996, he was convicted of drunk driving and was arrested in 2002 for speeding, marijuana possession, driving without a license, and not having proof of insurance. He was sentenced in February 2004 to sixty days in jail for misdemeanor battery for hitting his wife, as well as five probation violations.[181]

STEVE HOWE - drugs

Baseball player Steve Howe may be better known for being the first player to receive a lifetime ban from the major leagues for substance abuse, than for his baseball stats. In 1983, Howe checked himself into a drug rehabilitation clinic; a year later, he was suspended for the 1984 MLB season. Continued drug problems, specifically cocaine addiction, culminated in Steve Howe's lifetime suspension from baseball in 1992. The ban was overturned by an arbiter who decided Howe needed the cocaine to treat his Attention Deficit Disorder and Howe pitched for the New York Yankees minor league in 1994. At the end of his career, he held the record for the most drug-related suspensions in Major League Baseball: seven. In June 1996, Howe was arrested at Kennedy International Airport for carrying a loaded gun in his luggage. He received three years probation and 150 hours of community service.[182]

-I-
ALLEN IVERSON - gun possession and assault
(see main text)

-J-
MICHAEL JACKSON - accused of child molestation

Michael Jackson has managed to occupy more airtime minutes and pages of print than probably any other human being in memory. He has been making the news for more than three decades, first for his musical talents that resulted in the best selling pop albums of all time, later for his various cosmetic surgeries and more recently for his penchant for young children and his bizarre antics with his own. In November 2003, the singer's surrender to Santa Barbara authorities on child molestation charges overshadowed any other news event for several weeks. A decade earlier, a similar media circus ensued when Jackson settled a similar charge out of court, allegedly paying $23 million to a boy and his family after conceding "negligence" but not sexual abuse.[183] Since then Jackson has invited public comment several times: dangling his infant son over a balcony in Germany in front of fans and cameras; defending (in interviews) his practice of sleeping with children (not his own) in a non-sexual manner; having his children wear masks and veils in public; laughing and putting on a show before entering the California courthouse to answer multiple molestation charges in 2004.

Despite-or because of-this stream of bizarre behavior, Jackson still manages to maintain a loyal and obsessive fan base; those of us who are not fans still watch his antics in lip-curled fascination. Some Californians, however, managed to manifest their outrage in a productive way. After the 1993 case, when the boy who accused Jackson of engaging him in masturbation and oral sex refused to testify, public pressure led to a recent California law change that makes it more difficult for alleged child-abusers to offer large settlements to bypass criminal proceedings.[184] Not much is made of that fact, however, because we are more interested in the adventures at Neverland than the more serious legal issues surrounding his segue from freak to felon.

JUDAS PRIEST - accused of unintentionally aiding suicide attempt

Multi-platinum British heavy-metal band Judas Priest was accused of liability in the dual suicide of two Nevada teens in 1990. The civil suit, brought by the families of the deceased teenagers, sought damages for the band's culpability; the suit charged that the band used subliminal messages encouraging self-inflicted violence in the lyrics of the song "Better By You Better Than Me." The trial concluded with a finding for the band. While the judge ruled that subliminal messages would not be protected as free speech under the First Amendment, there was not sufficient evidence to support the assertion that the band had intentionally masked surreptitious messages (termed, "backwards masking") to its listeners persuading them to commit suicide.[185] In January 2004, former drummer for the band, David Holland, was convicted of one charge of attempting to rape a seventeen-year-old boy to whom he was giving drum lessons, as well as five counts of indecent assault.[186]

WYNONNA JUDD - DUI

In November 2003, Grammy Award winner Wynonna Judd was arrested and charged with driving under the influence in Nashville, Tennessee. Judd registered a .175 blood alcohol level, more than twice the .08 legal blood alcohol level in Tennessee. She pleaded guilty and was sentenced to two hundred hours of community service and lost her driver's license for a year. She received a twelve-month suspended sentence and parole.[187]

-K-

R. KELLY - child pornography; accused of having sex with minors

Three-time Grammy Award winner R. Kelly was indicted for twenty-one counts of child pornography in Chicago in June 2002, for allegedly video recording his sexual relations with a girl who was supposedly fourteen at the time. In January 2003, he was arrested and charged again for possession of child pornography. Kelly previously settled lawsuits brought by two women who accused him of having sex with them when they were minors. There was speculation (neither confirmed nor denied) that Kelly married his protégé Aaliyah, when she was fifteen and the marriage was later annulled. (Aaliyah died in a plane crash in the Bahamas in 2001 at the age of twenty-two.) A third lawsuit filed in Chicago alleges that Kelly impregnated another woman while she was a teenager and then forced her to have an abortion.[188] In between his court appearances, Kelly has continued his very successful recording career, winning multiple awards and releasing several chart-topping albums. In June 2004, Kelly was given court permission to go on tour for two months starting in October. He is quoted as saying, "Osama bin Laden is the only person who knows exactly what I'm going through."[189] In September, he was invited to perform for the Congressional Black Caucus, a move that was vehemently defended by South Carolina Congressman James Clyburn (D) on the Fox News program *The O'Reilly Factor*.

JASON KIDD - spousal abuse

Jason Kidd, an All-Star NBA player, was charged with assault after punching his wife in the mouth. They had been arguing about the feeding of their toddler son. The charges against him were dropped in return for his attendance at anger and domestic violence counseling and payment of a two hundred dollar fine.[190]

-L-
MARTIN LAWRENCE - drug abuse

Comedian and actor Martin Lawrence was arrested in the summer of 1996 at the Burbank Airport for carrying a loaded gun in his suitcase; he was sentenced to two years probation. A few months prior to that incident, he was hospitalized for ranting at drivers on a California boulevard; he was carrying a loaded gun in his pocket. He was ordered to perform community service a year later after punching someone at a nightclub. In 1999, Lawrence nearly died from heat exhaustion while jogging in heavy clothes and under the influence of drugs. When he awoke from a three-day coma, he decided to get clean and focus on his Hollywood career. He reportedly earned $20 million for his 2003 movie *National Security*.[191]

TOMMY LEE - corporal injury to a spouse

Former drummer for the rock band, Mötley Crüe, Tommy Lee is well-known for his wild life, both on the stage and at home. After a seven-year marriage to actress Heather Locklear ended in 1993, Lee married actress Pamela Anderson in 1995, five days after they met. The marriage was probably best known for the sex tape the two made while vacationing, which was widely distributed over the Internet. The marriage ended in

1998 after Anderson alleged Lee hit and pushed her while she was hold-ing their son. Lee was convicted and jailed for corporal injury to a spouse, child abuse, and a weapons offense. (He was brandishing a fry-ing pan.) He spent four months in prison and was ordered to complete 450 hours of community service. In 2001, a four-year-old guest attending a party for Lee's son drowned in Lee's backyard pool. Lee was cleared of any culpability.[192] He spent five more days in jail and received another three years probation for breaking the terms of his probation for the assault conviction. Lee is currently filming a prospective reality TV show in which he takes classes at the University of Nebraska and plays drums in the school's marching band.[193]

RAY LEWIS - accused of murder

Former Baltimore Ravens linebacker Ray Lewis was charged with mur-der after his involvement in a brawl at an Atlanta nightclub in the hours after the 2000 Super Bowl. Lewis and five friends were attending a post-game party to celebrate the game and ended up in a bar fight that result-ed in the stabbing deaths of two men. Lewis and his associates fled the scene in his limo. During the trial, Lewis pleaded guilty to the lesser charge of obstruction of justice in exchange for testifying against the remaining two defendants. He was sentenced to twelve months probation. Lewis, who was the highest paid linebacker in the NFL-he had a four-year $26 million contract with the Ravens-was not suspended from the league or the team, as he was found innocent of the murder charges.[194]

COURTNEY LOVE - drug abuse, violence, disorderly conduct

Rock performer and actress Courtney Love has a history of drug abuse and court battles. In July 2004, a warrant was issued for her arrest after she failed to appear at a California court hearing related to felony assault charges; the charges were for attacking a woman with a liquor bottle at her ex-boyfriend/manager's house in April. At the time of the arraignment, Love was in New York being taken to a hospital for a rumored miscarriage. She also faces charges for illegal possession of prescription painkillers.[195] Love is notorious for her outrageous public behavior, such as flashing David Letterman on his talk show and inviting a public rela-tions student to suckle her breast in front of a camera outside of a Manhattan Wendy's restaurant.[196] She recently pleaded guilty to disor-derly conduct after she was charged with striking an audience member with a microphone stand during a performance in New York in March 2004. Love was granted a conditional discharge, meaning she had to pay the victim's medical expenses, undergo drug counseling, and not commit any further crimes (doing so would net her fifteen days in jail.)[197] In October 2003, Love was arrested on drug charges after an overdose; she temporarily lost custody of her eleven-year-old daughter, Frances, who was present during the overdose. Frances had been previously taken away from Love and father Kurt Cobain, shortly after she was born in 1992, after Love admitted to using drugs during her pregnancy. The child was returned to her parents after a lengthy court battle.[198] In November 2003, Love and her band were sued by their lawyers for unpaid legal fees; they have until February 2005 to reach a settlement.[199] Love, forty, is the widow of Kurt Cobain.

-M-
MATTHEW MCCONAUGHEY - drug possession
Actor Matthew McConaughey was arrested in 1999 for possessing marijuana and resisting arrest in Austin, Texas, during a post-football game celebration at his home. Reportedly, McConaughey was playing the bongos naked in his house when the police arrived to answer a noise complaint call. It was ruled in court that the search of McConaughey's house was illegal and the charges were dropped. He pleaded guilty to violating a local noise ordinance and paid a fifty-dollar fine.[200]

MARTY MCSORLEY - violent tendencies
Marty McSorley, long-time professional hockey player, was given a one-year suspension from the NHL as the penalty for striking an opposing player in the head with his hockey stick. McSorley was playing for the Boston Bruins in 2000, when he struck Donald Brashear of the Vancouver Canucks in the head with his hockey stick. He was convicted of assault with a weapon in a Canadian court and received a suspended sentence. The NHL suspension, the most severe for on-ice violence in league history, effectively ended McSorley's professional hockey career. McSorley had ten times the number of career penalty minutes as he did career points.[201]

-N-
NICK NOLTE - drinking and driving
Oscar-winning actor Nick Nolte was arrested and charged with suspicion of driving under the influence (of the drug GHB) in Malibu, California in September 2002. He pleaded no contest to the charges and was fined five hundred dollars, sentenced to three years probation, and ordered to attend counseling for drug and alcohol abuse.[202]

-O-
OZZY OSBOURNE AND FAMILY - drug/alcohol abuse,
incessant foul language
Ozzy Osbourne, lead singer of the heavy metal band Black Sabbath in the 1970s, is famed for his long-term drug addiction and stage stunts, such as biting the head off of a live bat. He regained the attention of

American pop culture in 2001 with the MTV reality TV show about his dysfunctional family. The Osbournes is laced with profanities, which are bleeped out for the television audience. It details the lives of the teenaged siblings who indulge in frequent underage drinking and late night partying and includes such segments as brain-addled Ozzy tossing eggs over the fence into his neighbor's yard because they don't like each other. The show won Emmy Award for Outstanding Non-Fiction Reality Program in 2002. In 2003, Jack Osbourne, the seventeen-year old son, went into rehab for his addiction to alcohol and OxyContin.[203]

-P-
KIRBY PUCKETT - sexual assault
Hall of Fame baseball player Kirby Puckett was accused of sexual harassment in Minneapolis in 2002 for allegedly forcing a woman into the men's restroom and fondling her against her will. The case went to trial in Minneapolis in April 2003, and Puckett was acquitted of all charges. Other incidents have been documented, but not corroborated or prosecuted, involving Puckett and his treatment of women. His former wife alleged that Puckett held a gun to her head while she was holding their daughter and that he threatened to kill her on several occasions. His former mistress revealed that he resumed his long-time affair with her seven weeks after his marriage in 1986, and he frequently cheated on her, as well as his wife. He is reported to have committed several lewd acts in public, such as urinating in mall parking lots. His disdain for his fan base belies his title of a member in the World Sports Humanitarian Hall of Fame. One story described how, the day after he retired, Puckett dismissed a visit to a children's hospital saying, "I don't give a shit. It's just another kid who's sick."[204]

-R-
PAUL REUBENS- public lewd conduct, possession of child pornography
Paul Reubens, more widely known as Pee Wee Herman, hosted a children's television show in the late 1980s and early 1990s. In 1991 he was arrested in a Florida adult bookstore for allegedly exposing himself in public. He pleaded no contest to the charges and was ordered to pay fifty dollars in court fines and do community service. Ten years later, in November 2001, Reubens faced charges of possession of images of child pornography. In March 2003, he pleaded guilty to a misdemeanor obscenity charge for possessing 170 images of minors engaged in sexual conduct. He called the photos part of his erotica art collection and was sentenced to three years probation; during this time he is not allowed unsupervised contact with minors. He agreed to register as a sex offender, undergo counseling, and pay a one hundred dollar fine. Once his probation is completed, his record will be expunged.[205]

DENNIS RODMAN - assault

Former NBA star Dennis Rodman became a staple of the media coverage of basketball and pop culture in the 1990s. He is well-known for his romance with Madonna and one-year marriage to Carmen Electra, as well as his bizarre stunts on and off the court. Rodman has been arrested for obstruction of justice; repeatedly cited for noise violations at his California home; and charged for public drunkenness. In 1999, he pleaded guilty to a DUI charge in California. In October 2003, Rodman was charged again for drunk driving after he crashed a borrowed motorcycle outside a Las Vegas strip club. Other legal troubles include charges by four women that he fondled them at a hotel casino in 1998. He reached a settlement with the last complainant in 2003.[206]

PETE ROSE - gambling on baseball

Pete Rose, Major League Baseball's all-time leader in hits, was banned for life from baseball after a league investigation determined he had wagered on games while he was manager of the Cincinnati Reds in 1987 and 1988. Rose had denied the allegations for years. (Professional baseball players and those with a stake in the day-to-day performance of the team are barred from wagering on any baseball games.) In his autobiography published in January 2004, Rose admitted to betting on baseball four to five times a week during his tenure with the Reds. In his defense, Rose asserted that he never bet against his own team.[207]

WINONA RYDER - shoplifting

Actress Winona Ryder was convicted of grand theft and vandalism after a shoplifting spree in December 2001. Ryder was charged with having stolen more than $5,500 worth of clothing and merchandise from a Saks Fifth Avenue store in Los Angeles. Ryder was sentenced to three years probation and 480 hours of community service, as well as ordered to pay approximately $6,500 in restitution to the store, $2,700 in fines and attend drug and personal counseling. In his appeal to the judge for leniency, Ryder's attorney, Mark Geragos, said, "One day of bad should not trump what I believe to be a decade of exemplary work."[208]

-S-

O.J. SIMPSON - accused of murder

O.J. Simpson, NFL Hall of Fame running back, was tried for the murder of his ex-wife and her friend. On June 12, 1994, Nicole Brown Simpson and Ronald Goldman were murdered outside of Brown Simpson's home in Los Angeles, California. O.J. Simpson was accused, arrested, and tried for two counts of homicide. The nine-month criminal trial/media circus became an enduring television event, and it ended in an acquittal; however, the jury in the civil suit brought against Simpson found him liable for the death of Ronald Goldman and awarded $8.5 million in compensatory damages to the Goldman family. The jury also found Simpson guilty of having committed battery against his ex-wife.[209]

TOM SIZEMORE - physical abuse of girlfriend

Actor Tom Sizemore was convicted in August 2003 of six misdemeanor counts of harassing, annoying and physically abusing his ex-girlfriend, Heidi Fleiss. He was sentenced to six months in jail and three years probation and ordered to attend counseling for his drug, anger and domestic violence issues.[210] In September 2003, Sizemore was sued by a former personal assistant for harassment and sexual battery. The assistant claimed he had made unwarranted passes at her and demanded sex and sexual acts as part of her job responsibilities.[211]

JERRY SPRINGER - public forum for moral turpitude

The former mayor of Cincinnati, Jerry Springer, achieved notoriety as a "Trash TV" talk show host with a questionable reputation. The show is patterned after the Phil Donahue format where guests talk about a particular subject in front of a live studio audience. Springer's shock-and-awe style is to engage and confront guests who, more often than not, resort to foul language, nudity, and violence to emphasize their revelations and points of view on outrageous topics. Titles of Springer's past shows have included "Home Sweet Home-Wreckers," "Mistress Marathon," and "Classic Springer: My Boyfriend Is a Girl!" to name a few. The antics of Springer's shows have reached millions of households around the world. Springer is considered by many to be a cultural icon.[212] In 2002, Springer was sued by the son of a guest who was murdered by her ex-husband shortly after their appearance on a show was aired in July 2000.[213]

DARRYL STRAWBERRY - drugs, drunk driving

Baseball outfielder Darryl Strawberry's rap sheet is legendary. In 1987, his wife petitioned for separation and accused him of punching her in the nose after a game. In 1990, he was arrested for assault with a deadly weapon after hitting her and threatening her with a semi-automatic handgun; he was released on $12,000 bail and no charges were ever filed. In 1993, he was arrested for hitting his girlfriend; again no charges were filed. In April 1994, his chronic drug problems became obvious and after failing a MLB drug test, he entered the Betty Ford clinic for substance abuse treatment. It evidently didn't work; the next year he was again suspended by the league for sixty days for a positive test for cocaine. In 1995, Strawberry was convicted of tax evasion through unreported income and was sentenced to six months of house arrest. The same year, he was charged with failing to provide child support. In February 1999, he became a spokesman for the National Council on Alcoholism and Drug

Dependence; three months later he pleaded no contest to cocaine possession and solicitation of a prostitute (who was an undercover officer). He was sentenced to eighteen months probation and one hundred hours of community service. In 2000, he was suspended from baseball for a year for a third cocaine offense. He was arrested several times in the next two years for numerous probation violations and causing a traffic accident while under the influence of pain killers.[214]

-T-

LAWRENCE TAYLOR - drugs

In an interview with *60 Minutes* in November 2003, NFL Hall of Fame linebacker Lawrence Taylor talked openly about his cocaine and crack addiction during his professional football playing days. In his book *LT: Over the Edge*, he claimed to have once had a one-thousand-dollar-a-day habit for drugs and call girls. He admitted that he evaded the NFL-mandated drug testing by having teammates give him their urine. Taylor defended this practice by saying, "Well, like well, you gotta understand though. It didn't affect my play." He also admitted to paying call girls to entertain players from opposing teams the night before football games to tire them out. Taylor was given a four game suspension for a violation of the NFL drug policy in 1988. He was arrested in 1996 and 1998 for possession of crack. After the 1998 conviction, Taylor opted for treatment rather than jail time and emerged from rehab in 1999 clean and sober. Later that year, he was elected to the Pro Football Hall of Fame.[215]

MIKE TYSON - rape, violent history

Heavyweight boxing champion Mike Tyson had an early start with the legal system; he was been arrested for purse snatching at the age of twelve. He was expelled from high school in 1982. In 1987 and 1988, Tyson was involved in numerous incidents: assault of a parking attendant in 1987 (he settled out of court); a street brawl in 1988; and a purported attempted suicide the same year. He was accused of being violent by his wife Robin Givens in 1988, and she divorced him a year later. In 1991, Tyson was accused of rape by Desiree Washington at a Miss Black USA contest in Indianapolis. He was convicted of rape and two counts of criminal deviate conduct and sentenced to six years in a state prison. Tyson, commenting on his accuser, said, "Now, I really do want to rape her." He was released in 1995...after serving three years of his sentence and began his boxing comeback. In 1997, Tyson infamously bit off a portion of Evander Holyfield's ear during a match. More jail time followed in 1999, after Tyson was convicted in a road rage incident in Maryland.[216] In 2003, Tyson was involved in a brawl in a Brooklyn hotel and was divorced from his second wife.

This compendium of criminal behavior by many of the biggest celebrities in the entertainment and pro-sports industries is telling evidence that our attention and adulation is entirely misplaced. It must be granted, they're not all bad. The Talmud asks, Who is a hero? He who conquers his urges. Under that definition, some of those described in the alphabetical list would be granted the title, and others would never reach it. It would also be unfair not to acknowledge that there are a few star personalities who overcome tragedy to inspire others. Christopher Reeve was a super-hero both on- and off-screen: he was involved in the Christopher Reeve Paralysis Foundation, which has raised $47 million for spinal cord research, since his horseback riding accident in 1995. Angelina Jolie, apart from her colorful and unconventional Hollywood persona, spends a great deal of time and money traveling to war-torn countries in Africa, Asia, Latin America, the Balkans, and the Caucasus as a goodwill ambassador for the United Nations High Commission for Refugees; she raises awareness and financial support for the displaced and forgotten. Other celebrities who use their fame to leverage political and social change, such as performers Bruce Springsteen and Bonnie Raitt on the Vote for Change concert tour, may also qualify as justifiable role models. But typically, it is everyday normal folk contributing quietly to the improvement of life in the world around them-volunteers, emergency and health care workers, teachers-who are the true mentors that teach by example. These are the people upon whom we need to bestow the title of hero; we need to teach our children to properly admire them and aspire to emulate them.

We need to recognize how our values are influencing and are influenced by the way celebrities are treated in our society. There is a huge disparity between punishments meted out to famous lawbreakers and those given to the general population. Justice is not blind to wealth and privilege, and we are so blinded to it we fail to see the glaring preferential treatment given to the rich and famous. In the summer of 2004, Atlanta Braves' baseball player Rafael Furcal was arrested twice for drunk driving, but he didn't have to start serving his twenty-one-day jail sentence (for violating his probation) until after the Braves were eliminated from the playoffs. Jamal Lewis, a player for the Baltimore Ravens, pleaded guilty to taking part in a drug deal, but he didn't have to serve his four-month sentence until the 2004 NFL season was over. Synchronized swimmer Tammy Crow was allowed to compete in the Athens Olympics, despite the fact that she crashed her car and killed two people. She was given a ninety-day sentence to be served after the games.[217] It would seem that if you have some measure of fame and celebrity, the courts are willing to give you a break. If you are wealthy enough, your expensive team of attorneys will find the loopholes to let you walk.

So just how are everyday Americans supposed to have faith in a judicial system that favors the privileged of society? How are we to expect the actions and attitudes of our supposed role models to be exemplary, when it is clear to them (and to us) that they are not held accountable? Aren't we learning to exhibit (and admire) a similar lack of accountability in our own lives? It is no wonder that our measure of heroism is as limited as it is: Ralph Waldo Emerson said, "Every hero becomes a bore at last."

Boring is what most of these personalities are not; that is why they are so eagerly emulated by fans young and old. To be fair, there may be a measure of heroism in redemption: celebrities who have overcome personal (or criminal) trials and have managed to straighten themselves out, are possibly good models for youth. Ideally we would wish our children not be exposed to the drinking, drugs, sex, and violence that are part of many of their idols' lives; however, there may be a deterrent factor or a lesson in the realization that people can learn from their mistakes. No one is perfect-even our heroes-but those who make an effort to reform are more deserving of our respect and praise than those who don't.

Parents need to steer their children away from the fantasy of flash and fortune and all that stems from it: they need to expose their kids to real-life heroes; provide themselves as good examples; and emphasize real achievement within their families, their communities, and the greater world. We need to recognize, and point out to our children, the pervasive and primarily unhealthy influence that celebrity has on us and demand better.

---

[119] "Super Bowl Gets Super Ratings," Feb. 2, 2004, http://money.cnn.com/2004/02/02/news/companies/superbowl_ratings (retrieved Sept. 13, 2004).

[120] http://www.superbowl.com/features/general_info (retrieved Sept. 13, 2004).

[121] Peter Kafka. "The Celebrity 100," *Forbes*, June 18, 2004, http://www.forbes.com/2004/06/16/04land.html. (retrieved Sept. 14, 2004).

[122] John MacIntyre. "Figuratively Speaking," *Chronicle-Herald*, Halifax, NS, July 17, 2004 (quoted from investigative reporter Jeff Benedict in *Out of Bounds: Inside the NBA's Culture of Rape, Violence & Crime*).

[123] USA Today Sports Salaries Database, http://www.usatoday.com/sports/salaries/index.htm (retrieved Sept. 14, 2004).

[124] "Lakers' Bryant Settles Civil Suit," *CBC Sports Online*, March 2, 2005, http://www.cbc.ca/story/sports/national/2005/03/02/sports/kobe050302.html.

[125] "Former Jazz Center Convicted of Assault," *CNN.com*, June 25, 2002, http://archives.cnn.com/2002/LAW/06/25/ctv.penalty.box (retrieved Oct. 7, 2004).

[126] *Milwaukee Journal-Sentinel*, July 23, 2002,

http://www.jsonline.com/sports/buck/jul02/60912.asp (retrieved Oct. 7, 2004).

127 "Pacers Artest Suspended for Season," *CBC Sports Online*, Nov. 23, 2004, http://www.cbc.ca/story/sports/national/2004/11/21/sports/basketball_brawl/041121.html (retrieved Nov. 23, 2004).

128 "Latrell Sprewell Suspended by NBA," *CBC Sports Online*, Dec. 7, 2004, (retrieved Dec. 8, 2004).

129 "Phelps Gets Probation for Impaired Driving." *CBC Sports Online*, Dec. 29, 2004, http://www.cbc.ca/story/sports/national/2004/12/29/Sports/phelps041229.html (retrieved Jan. 7, 2005).

130 "Giambi Used Steroids, Growth Hormone: Report." *CBC Sports Online*, Dec. 2, 2004.

131 Tom Verducci. "Totally Juiced." *Sports Illustrated*, June 3, 2002, http://sportsillustrated.cnn.com/si_online/flashbacks/2002/year_in_review/steroids (retrieved: Oct. 7, 2004).

132 http://www.cbc.ca/story/sports/nation/2004/10/15/sports/caminiti_deadO41015.html (retrieved Oct. 18, 2004).

133 Eric Fisher. "MLB Toughens Drug Rules," *Washington Times*, Jan. 18, 2005, http://www.washingtontimes.com/national/20050114-121305-1065r.htm (retrieved Jan. 18, 2005).

134 "BALCO Founder Settles Civil Lawsuit: Report." *CBC Sports Online*, Oct. 27, 2004.

135 "Sprinter Collins Appealing Doping Ban." *CBC Sports Online*, Jan. 6, 2005.

136 "Foul Play: Sports, Doping and Teens, A Roundtable Discussion." http://www.drugstory.org/feature/foul_play.asp (retrieved Sept. 14, 2004).

137 Jerry Adler. "Toxic Strength," *Newsweek*, Dec. 20, 2004, p. 45.

138 "Muscle Madness: The Ugly Connection Between Body Image and Steroid Abuse," March 2003, http://www.drugstory.org/feature/drugs_doping.asp (retrieved Sept. 14, 2004).

139 "Russians Ask Sports Court to Strip Hamilton of Cycling Gold." *CBC Sports Online*, Oct. 20, 2004, http://www.cbc.ca/story/sports/nation-al/2004/10/20/sports/tylerhamilton041020.html (retrieved Oct. 25, 2004).

140 "U.S. Relayers Want to KEEP SYDNEY GOLDS." *CBC Sports Online*, Oct. 20, 2004, http://www.cbc.ca/story/sports/national/2004/10/20/Sports/usre-lay041020.html (retrieved Oct. 25, 2004).

141 "Sprinter Alvin Harrison Suspended Four Years." *CBC Sports Online*, Oct. 19, 2004, http://www.cbc.ca/story/sports/national/2004/10/19/sports/alvin041019.html (retrieved Oct. 25, 2004).

[142] http://www.wada-ama.org/en/tarchive.asp (retrieved Sept. 14, 2004).

[143] "The Enforcer: Q and A interview with Dick Pound," *CBC Sports Online*, Jan. 19, 2003, http://www.cbc.ca/sports/indepth/drugs/stoires/qa_dickpound.html (retrieved Jan. 7, 2005).

[144] Heather Svokos. "Naked Ambition: American Olympians Expose Themselves to the World," *Chronicle-Herald*, Halifax, NS, August 25, 2004 (reprinted from the *Fort Worth Star-Telegram*).

[145] Joe Drape. "A Winning Combination: Sex Appeal, Athleticism are not Necessarily Mutually Exclusive," *Chronicle-Herald*, Halifax, NS, August 15, 2004 (Reprinted from the *New York Times* News Service).

[146] "Numbers," *Time*, Canadian Edition, Sept. 6, 2004, p. 11.

[147] Steve Wilstein. "No Crowds, No Buzz, Not Much Fun at Athens Games," *Herald-Coaster,* Fort Bend, Aug. 17, 2004, http://www.herald-coaster.com/articles/2004/08/18/sports/sports02.txt (retrieved Oct. 19, 2004).

[148] Steve Seepersaud. "The Richest Teams in Professional Sports," http://www.askmen.com/sports/business_100/100_sports_business.html (retrieved Sept. 14, 2004).

[149] Erik Brady. "How Free Should Speech Be at Games?" *AOL News*, Feb. 7, 2004.

[150] Chris Kahn. "Virginia Tech QB Vick Gets Suspended Jail Sentence," *AOL News*, Sept. 13, 2004.

[151] Robert Weller. "New Sex Allegation Emerges at Colorado," *AOL News*, Feb. 19, 2004.

[152] "Hoffman Promises 'Sweeping' Changes in Athletics." *ESPN Sports*, May 27, 2004, http://sports.espn.go.com/cnf/news/story?id=1810657 (retrieved Oct. 13, 2004).

[153] http://www.packers.com/team/players/favre_brett/ (retrieved Oct. 27, 2004).

[154] http://www.cbsnews.com/stories/2004/05/17/earlyshow/leisure/celebspot/main617738.shtml (retrieved Sept. 14, 2004).

[155] Kafka, Peter. "Celebrity 100." June 18, 2004.

[156] Robert Lafranco. "Money Makers," *Rolling Stone.com*, Feb. 10, 2005, http://www.rollingstone.com/news/story/_/id/6959138/prince?pageid=rs.Home&pageregion=single2&rnd=1109495883956&has-player=true&version=6.0.12.1040 (retrieved March 30, 2005).

[157] Jonathan Durbin. "Star Stricken," *Maclean's*, June 21, 2004, p. 56.

[158] http://www.thesmokinggun.com/archive/janetsuit/html Feb. 5, 2004 (retrieved Sept. 13, 2004).

[159] Matthew Gilbert. "Famous Felons Next Hot Reality Concept," reprinted from the *Chronicle-Herald*, Halifax, NS, October 4, 2004, *Boston Globe*.

[160] Courtroom Television Network. "Marv Albert Sexual Assault Trial," *CourtTV Online*, October 24, 1998, http://www.courttv.com/archive/casefiles/marv/marvalbert.html (retrieved Jan. 5, 2004).

[161] "Charles Barkley Mugshot," *Absolutecelebrities.com*, http://www.absolute-celebrities.com/mugshot/charles_barkley.html (retrieved on January 6, 2004).

[162] Marcus Errico. "Halle Charged in Car Crash," *E! Online News*. March 31, 2000, http://www.eonline.com/News/Items/0,1,6259,00.html (retrieved November 14, 2003).

[163] "Judge Orders Robert Blake to Stand Trial." *CNN Law Center*, March 13, 2004, http://www.cnn.com/2003/LAW/03/13/blake.trial (retrieved Oct. 10, 2004).

[164] Associated Press, "Judge: Bryant Accuser Must Be Identified." Oct. 6, 2004, http://www.allstarz.org/kobe/kobetrial030.htm (retrieved Oct. 7, 2004).

[165] Bob Carter. "Teenage sensation became destiny's child," *ESPN.com Classic*, http://espn.go.com/classic/biography/s/Capriati_Jennifer_0808.html (retrieved November 17, 2003).

[166] Judge rejects Carruth request to vacate convictions, *Sports Illustrated*, (Jan. 23, 2001, http://sportsillustrated.cnn.com/football/nfl/news/2001/01/22/carruth_trial_ap/ (retrieved November 17, 2003).

[167] Marcus Errico. "Who Killed Kurt Cobain?" *E! Online News*, February 7, 1997, http://www.eonline.com/News/Items/0,1,656,00.html (retrieved on January 5, 2004).

[168] Robert Downey, Jr. – Biographical Information, *tvtome.com*, http://www.tvtome.com/tvtome/servlet/DetailsServlet/epid-0/showid-0/person-id-5450/moduleid-38 (retrieved on November 18, 2003).

[169] Vicky Allan. "Heidi Fleiss: Hollywood Madam," *Sunday Herald Online*. June 29, 2003, http://www.sundayherald.com/34898 (retrieved November 19, 2003).

[170] http://en.wikipedia.org/wiki/Gangsta_rap (retrieved Oct. 20, 2004).

[171] http://en.wikipedia.org/wiki/Tupac_Shakur (retrieved Oct. 20, 2004).

[172] *Wikipedia*, S.V., 'Notorious B.I.G.," http://en.wikipedia.org/wiki/Notorious_B.I.G (retrieved Oct. 20, 2004).

[173] "Snoop Dogg: Bio," *MTV.com*, http://www.mtv.com/bands/az/snoop_dogg/bio.jhtml (retrieved on January 7, 2004).

[174] Harriet Ryan. "Puffy Acquitted on All Charges," *Court TV Online*, March

16, 2001, http://www.courttv.com/trials/puffy/verdicts/verdict-acquittal.html (retrieved December 5, 2003).

175 "Facts and Figures: Everything You Need to Know About Eminem." *E! Entertainment Television*, http://www.eonline.com/On/Holly/Shows/Eminem/Facts/ (retrieved November 19, 2003).

176 Jon Wiederhorn. "Mystikal Sentenced to Six Years Behind Bars for Sexual Battery," *VH1.com*, Jan. 26, 2004, http://www.vh1.com/artists/news/1484411/01162004/mystikal.jhtml (retrieved Oct. 20, 2004).

177 Dwight Gooden – *BaseballLibrary.com*, http://www.baseballlibrary.com/baseballlibrary/ballplayers/G/Gooden_Dwight.stm (retrieved November 20, 2003).

178 "Hugh Grant Scandal," *Cable News Network*, *CNN Showbiz News:* http://www.cnn.com/SHOWBIZ/HughGrant/ (retrieved November 20, 2003).

179 "Paris Hilton seeks to halt sex video," *USAToday.com*, November 7, 2003, http://www.usatoday.com/life/2003-11-07-hilton-sex_x.htm (retrieved December 4, 2003).

180 "'Hockey Dad' Gets 6 to 10 Years for Fatal Beating," *CNN.com*, January 25, 2002, http://www.cnn.com/2002/LAW/01/25/hockey.death.verdict (retrieved Sept. 14, 2004).

181 Todd Peterson. "Bobby Brown Sentenced to Jail Time." *AOL.com*, Feb. 27, 2004.

182 http://www.baseballlibrary.com/baseballlibrary/ballplayers/H/Howe_Steve.stm (retrieved Oct. 19, 2004).

183 Stephen M. Silverman. "Jackson Paid $23 Million to Accuser," *People*, June 16, 2004, *AOL News On-line*.

184 David J. Jefferson and Andrew Murr, "From Moon Walk to Perp Walk," *Newsweek*, Dec. 1, 2003, 38-40.

185 http://heavymetal.about.com/cs/metalbandshr/p/JPbio.htm (retrieved Oct. 19, 2004).

186 Associated Press, "Former Judas Priest Drummer Convicted of Attempted Rape of Teen." Jan. 23, 2004, http://www.sfgate.com/cgi-bin/article.cgi?file=/news/archive/2004/01/23/international1004EST0532.DTL (retrieved Oct. 20, 2004).

187 Associated Press, "Wynonna Judd Gets Community Service." Dec. 17, 2003, http://launch.yahoo.com/read/news.asp?contentID=215693 (retrieved Oct. 19, 2004).

188 "R. Kelly Arrested in Child Porn Case." *CNN.com*, June 6, 2002., http://archives.cnn.com/2002/SHOWBIZ/Music/06/05/r.kelly/ (retrieved Oct.

Jeff Shiring

19, 2004).

[189] http://www.rockonthenet.com/artists-k/rkelly_main.htm (retrieved Oct. 19, 2004).

[190] "Kidd Leaving Team, For Now." *ESPN.com*, January 21, 2001, http://espn.go.com/nba/news/2001/0120/1029185.html (retrieved on November 21, 2003).

[191] Kelly Carter. "Lawrence Live, and Drug-Free." USA Today, July 23 2002.

[192] Harriet Ryan. "Sex, Drugs, and Court Appearances." *COURT TV.com*, April 11, 2003, http://www.courttv.com/trials/tommylee/041003_ctv.html (retrieved November 24, 2003).

[193] "Rock's Tommy Lee Drums Up Interest in a Reality Show." *IndyStar.com*. Oct. 18, 2004, http://www.indystar.com/articles/7/187265-6687-062.html (retrieved Oct. 20, 2004).

[194] "Lewis Murder Charges Dropped." *CNN.com*, June 6, 2000, http://sportsillustrated.cnn.com/football/nfl/news/2000/06/04/lewis_agreement (retrieved Jan. 6, 2004).

[195] "Courtney Love in Hospital After Missing Court Date." *Toronto, Globe and Mail*. July 12, 2004.

[196] Durbin. "Star-Stricken."

[197] "Rocker Courtney Love Pleads Guilty to Disorderly Conduct." *Court TV.com*, Oct. 20, 2004, http://courttv.com/trials/love/102004_ap.html (retrieved Oct. 25, 2004).

[198] Gil Kaufman. "Courtney Love Fighting for Custody of Daughter Frances Bean," *VH1.com*. Oct. 21, 2003, http://www.vh1.com/news/articles/1479849/10212003/love_courtney.jhtml (retrieved Oct. 20, 2004).

[199] *The Houston Chronicle*. "Love Tries to Stay Out of Court in Case Against Law Firm." October 18, 2004, http://www.chron.com/cs/CDA/ssistory.mpl/ae/2853360 (retrieved Oct. 20, 2004).

[200] "Matthew McConaughey, *The Free Dictionary.com*, http://encyclopedia.thefreedictionary.com/Matthew percent20McConnaughey, Oct. 20, 2004.

[201] "McSorley to Coach Coyote's Top Farm Team." *ESPN.com*, June 16, 2002, http://espn.go.com/nhl/news/2002/0616/1395556.html (retrieved Oct. 20, 2004).

[202] "Nick Nolte Cops a Plea," *CBSNews.com*, Dec. 12, 2002, http://www.cbsnews.com/stories/2002/10/24/entertainment/main526796.shtml (retrieved Nov. 24, 2003).

[203] Gideon Yago. "Jack's Addiction: Jack Osbourne Talks About His Addiction and Recovery," *MTV.com*,

http://www.mtv.com/bands/o/osbourne_jack/news_feature_070803/ (retrieved November 24, 2003).

204 "The Other Kirby," *Sports Illustrated*, March 11, 2003, http://sportsillus-trated.cnn.com/baseball/news/2003/03/11/si_puckett (retrieved Oct. 20, 2004).

205 Mark Terrill. "Pee Wee Pleads Guilty to Obscenity." *USA Today.com*, March 19, 2004, http://www.usatoday.com/life/people/2004-03-19-pee-wee-guilty_x.htm?POE=LIFISVA (retrieved Oct. 20, 2004).

206 "Rodman Charged with Driving Under the Influence," *The Battalion online*, Oct. 21, 2003, http://www.thebatt.com/news/2003/10/21/PeopleInTheNews/Rodman.Charged.With.Driving.Under.The.Influence-534045.shtml (retrieved Oct. 20, 2004).

207 "Rose: I Bet on Baseball," *CNNSI.com*. Jan. 5, 2004, http://sportsillustrat-ed.cnn.com/2004/magazine/01/05/rose_excerpts (retrieved Oct. 20, 2004).

208 Matt Bean. "Winona Ryder Gets Probation for Shoplifting," Dec. 6, 2003, http://www.courttv.com/archive/trials/ryder/sentence.html (retrieved Oct. 20, 2004).

209 "Jury: OJ is Liable," *CNN Interactive*, Feb. 4, 2997. http://edition.cnn.com/US/OJ/simpson.civil.trial (retrieved Oct. 20, 2004).

210 Associated, Press, "Tom Sizemore Sentenced to 6 Months in Jail, Three Years Probation for Abuse." Oct. 28, 2003, http://www.courttv.com/trials/news/1003/28_sizemore_ap.html (retrieved Oct. 19, 2004).

211 Associated Press, "Personal Assistant Sues Actor Sizemore for Sex Battery, Harassment." Sept. 8, 2003, http://www.courttv.com/people/2003/0908/size-more_ap.html (retrieved Oct. 19, 2004).

212 "Jerry Springer Show—Meet Jerry," *Universal Domestic Television*, http://www.uni-television.com/jerry/ (retrieved on December 15, 2003).

213 "Springer Sued Over Murdered Guest," *BBC News online*, July 11, 2002, http://news.bbc.co.uk/1/hi/entertainment/tv_and_radio/2121700.stm (retrieved Oct. 20, 2004).

214 Associated Press, "Darryl Strawberry Chronology," April 2001, http://sportsillustrated.cnn.com/baseball/mlb/news/2001/04/03/strawberry_chronology_ap/ (retrieved Oct. 19, 2004).

215 "LT: Over the Edge," *CBS.com*, Sept. 14 2004, http://www.cbsnews.com/stories/2003/11/26/60minutes/main585718.shtml (retrieved Oct. 20, 2004).

216 "The Ups and Downs of Tyson's Life," *BBC News*, May 25, 1999, http://news.bbc.co.uk/2/hi/sport/196998.stm (retrieved Oct. 19, 2004).

217 Tim Dahlberg. "For Some Athletes, Justice Doesn't Seem to be Blind," *AOL News*, Oct. 9, 2004 (retrieved Oct. 12, 2004).

Jeff Shiring

3. A Wing and a Prayer

I f you believe what you like in the gospels, and reject what you don't
like, it is not the gospel you believe, but yourself.

-Saint Augustine, Bishop of Hippo (396-430)

Religion is an intensely personal and highly controversial subject; its
effect is so profound that mere mention of the topic incites the deepest
passions and opinions in the religious and non-religious alike. No matter
what faith we subscribe to, or what house of worship we attend, or
whether we reject organized religion altogether, the influence of religion
on our society is undeniably deep and wide-reaching: 85 percent of the
world's population (5.4 billion human beings) claim to be adherents of
some denomination.[218] I am not a theologian, nor do I profess to have
anything but the most cursory understanding of the major religions of
the world; however, my knowledge of the Christian tradition in which I
was raised, coupled with my research and acquaintance with the various
religions of friends and colleagues, has prompted an insight that I think
is shared by many: that the power of religion has been corrupted from its
universal origin as an expression of love, peace, tolerance, and harmony,
to something quite different-something hypocritical that has been badly
distorted and abused for mortal rather than divine purposes.

The holy books of the major religions of the world-Christianity, Islam,
Hinduism, and Judaism-all hold the same basic tenets of faith. These
include love of God and creation, respect for humanity, acceptance of
personal responsibility, and consequences for the breaching of moral and
ethical codes. Yet adherents of all of these faiths are responsible for millennia of human suffering. Radicals and fanatics of all religious persua-
sions may be responsible for much of the persecution of other faiths, but
the actions of few greatly affect many. (The terrorist attacks of September
11, 2001, are a painfully obvious case in point.) The net result is a collective shift in faith-either a critical step away from one's faith, or a more
fundamentalist embrace of it-that cannot help but influence our social
and political structure. This influence has become overwhelming in the
United States in an intensely negative way.

The Unraveling of America

Crisis of Faith

The approach of the new millennium was a time of great anticipation, as well as troubled uncertainty, particularly for the faithful. Religious persecution is as old as religion itself, but the atrocities committed in the name of religion in Israel and Palestine, Rwanda, the former Yugoslavia, Afghanistan, Sudan, and Iraq in the last decade of the twentieth century caused many to wonder how it was possible for such violence and hatred to be manifested in the name of God (or whatever name one applies to the center of one's belief system). The horrific events around the globe were deeply disturbing to both secular and laic observers, but here in the United States perhaps none had the ground-shaking effect of the erupting scandal in the Roman Catholic Church. As it emerged that thousands of Catholic priests had sexually abused parishioners-most frequently children-over the course of decades, it also became obvious that it was widely known, denied, and concealed by Church authorities. Millions of Catholics began to question their faith, accountability of the Church, and faith in God, as they had never done before.

The sheer number of allegations of sexual abuse throughout the 1980s and 1990s, as well as the phenomenal cost of lawsuit settlements, forced the Church to examine its practices and adopt reforms, which would restore trust among parishioners and enable the Church to maintain financial viability. In February 2004, the results of two nationwide investigations into the abuse scandal were released. The U.S. Conference of Catholic Bishops commissioned a report by the John Jay College of Criminal Justice in New York, as well as an inquiry by the National Review Board for the Protection of Children and Young People, a lay panel of investigators, including Leon Panetta, the former Clinton White House Chief of Staff and Robert S. Bennett, a Washington attorney.

The John Jay survey, *The Nature and Scope of the Problem of Sexual Abuse of Minors by Catholic Priests and Deacons in the United States*, was based on the completed questionnaires of 195 of 202 dioceses across the country. Although no audits were conducted to verify the accuracy of the self-reported information, a fact which abuse victims and other critics point out very likely results in underreporting, the returned questionnaires indicated that 95 percent of the dioceses and 60 percent of the religious communities had been affected by clerical sexual abuse since 1950. Since that time, 4,392 Catholic clergy were accused of abusing 10,667 people. Of the total number of accused, only 3 percent were ever convicted by civil authorities and just 2 percent received prison sentences. The study found that the total cost to the Church in lawsuits amounted to $573 million; $219 million of this was covered by insurance companies, but that did not include settlements made after 2002, such as the $85 million paid in 2003 to abuse victims from the Boston Archdiocese.[219] [By February 2005, there were more than 1,000 new allegations of abuse-although half the priests named had already been accused-and the total cost of payouts to victims totaled $840 million.[220]] Other grand jury investigations and settlement agreements completed in 2003 included the Diocese of Rockville Center (New York); the Diocese of Manchester (New Hampshire); the Diocese of Phoenix (Arizona); and the Archdiocese of Cincinnati (Ohio).[221]

The National Review Board report, *A Report on the Crisis in the Catholic Church*, highlighted several major weaknesses in the structure of the Church that contributed to the widespread abuse. The board determined there were inadequate procedures to screen out unfit priesthood candidates; a reluctance to appropriately deal with celibacy and sexuality issues within seminaries; as well as a pervasive culture of protection and forgiveness, which resulted in the failure of Church authorities to recognize the nature and scope of the abuse and penalize those responsible. The attitude that sins can be forgiven and weaknesses can be cured within the fold of the Church contributed to many accused priests being quietly moved to new communities or therapeutic retreats, only to commit the same acts again when released into a new ministry. The report stated that the responses of many bishops to allegations of abuse were "characterized by moral laxity, excessive leniency, insensitivity, secrecy and neglect."[222] The report stated further that among Church leaders and officials, there was "a failure to hold themselves and other bishops accountable for mistakes." [223]

The extent of the abuse nationwide was manifested in the explosive scandal of the Archdiocese of Boston. After conducting extensive interviews and sifting through two decades of documentation and transcripts of reported sexual abuse, the National Review Board found "the picture that emerged was that of a diocese with a cadre of predator priests and a hierarchy that simply refused to confront and stop them."[224] Between the Archdiocese of Boston and the Diocese of Springfield, the abuse scandals within the state of Massachusetts have perhaps incurred the most publicity. The high profile case of former priest Paul Shanley, accused of raping four boys in the 1980s, was back in the news in early February of 2005. Shanley, now seventy-four, was found guilty of two counts each of child rape and indecent assault and battery on a child. Most of the original charges against him were dropped as three of the four accusers were unwilling to testify or could not be found. Although Church documents showed that his superiors knew about his predilection for boys as early as 1979-he had attended a meeting that became the organization known as NAMBLA, the North American Man Boy Love Association-he was given a recommendation by Archbishop Cardinal Law as "a priest in good standing" in 1989 when he moved to California.[225] He was arrested there in 2002 and returned to Massachusetts. Shanley was only defrocked by Pope John Paul II on May 19, 2004, a month after the Church settled four lawsuits with victims who had accused Shanley of abuse.[226] He was sentenced on February 16, 2005, to twelve to fifteen years in prison-eligible for parole after eight-and ten years probation.

In November 2004, Father Stephen Fernandes was charged with possession of child pornography after five thousand explicit images were found on his parish computer.[227]

In September 2004, former Bishop Thomas Dupre was indicted on two charges of child rape, making him the first Roman Catholic prelate indicted in a sex abuse scandal in the United States.[228]

In June, priest Robert Meffan was defrocked for having recruited girls to become nuns in the 1960s and then molesting them. Although the allegations surfaced in 1980 and Cardinal Law determined he was mentally unbalanced in 1984, Meffan was not relieved of his parish duties until 1993. It took another decade to remove him from the Church payroll.[229]

In May 2004, former priest Richard Lavigne was notified he would no longer be receiving financial support from the Springfield Diocese. Convicted of molesting two boys and suspected of (but never charged with) the death of altar boy Danny Croteau in 1972, Lavigne was removed from his priestly duties in 1992. He was not defrocked until November 2003, however, and has continued to receive $8,800 a year in health insurance benefits, as well as a stipend of $1,000 a month since his conviction.[230]

Former priest James Porter pleaded guilty in 1993 to twenty-eight counts of sexual molestation; his prison sentence officially ended in January 2004, and he was recently diagnosed with terminal cancer.[231]

Perhaps the most well-known "predator priest" from Boston was Rev. John J. Geoghan, who was sentenced in February of 2002 to serve nine to ten years in prison, convicted of indecent assault on a ten-year-old boy. According to findings of the NRB, the first complaint to the Archdiocese against Geoghan was made in 1979. Ten years later, when police made inquiries about Geoghan to the Archbishop's office, they were told the priest was undergoing treatment, but numerous prior allegations against him were not disclosed. Geoghan was finally laicized (removed from the priesthood) in 1998, nearly twenty years after Church officials were made aware of his abuse of young boys. He was named in civil lawsuits of 130 alleged victims but was strangled in his cell by an inmate in August 2003.

Cardinal Law resigned as Archbishop of Boston in December 2002 and was replaced by Archbishop Sean O'Malley, who has since overseen the closure of twenty-four parishes in the Boston area, with another fifty-four slated to close under a consolidation plan. O'Malley has said declining attendance and financial hardship because of settlements with abuse victims has required a complete restructuring of the Archdiocese, but it is an unpopular process. "Trust was a precondition, but the abuse crisis did not leave significant trust in place."[232]

Jeff Shiring

Naturally there has been a great deal of soul-searching, within the Church and in the secular and laic public at large, to try to determine what cause (or combination of causes) is responsible for the behavior that has harmed so many. In December 2002, Cardinal Joseph Ratzinger, head of the Vatican's Congregation for the Doctrine of the Faith, attempted to minimize the occurrence of abuse within the priesthood saying, "Less than 1 percent of priests are guilty of acts of this type."[233] The actual number according to individual dioceses is 4 percent, reflective of the number of sex offenders in the general population, but unacceptably high within the context of a community of trusted spiritual advisors. Some surmise that many of the men attracted to the priesthood are involved with the Church from childhood and enter seminaries before they are emotionally mature enough to fully understand their own sexual urges, much less how to practice celibacy. Others say that men with tendencies toward pedophilia may enter the priesthood believing that discipline and God's work will cure their deviance. One unidentified bishop, in an interview with a member of the NRB, said, "If you're conservative, homosexuality is the problem; if you're liberal, celibacy is the problem. So you tell me who you are, and I'll tell you what the problem is."[234]

There have been measures taken to address the crisis within the Church. In June 2002, the U.S. Conference of Catholic Bishops adopted a disciplinary policy, entitled the *Charter for the Protection of Children and Young People*. Priests guilty of a single instance of sexual abuse would be immediately removed from direct contact with parishioners, and all allegations of abuse would be reported to civil law authorities, altering the historical practice of dealing with all problems internally. In the spirit of healing and reconciliation, the Charter apologizes for the suffering caused by the "evil" of sexual abuse by clergy.

The Bishops stopped short of automatically defrocking abusers-laicization can only be performed by the Pope-and many victims and survivors have criticized the policy as being too lenient. They assert that child molesters have no place whatsoever within the priesthood, whether working at a desk or wearing a collar. For their part, bishops have taken the position that priests of advanced age, who committed acts decades ago, should not be ejected from the priesthood out onto the street, but rather are owed some comfort and protection, such as counseling and living out their days "in prayer and penance" in return for a lifetime of service to the Church. Barbara Baine, founder of the Chicago-based Survivors Network of those Abused by Priests (SNAP) met the announcement of the Charter with shock and skepticism. Baine, who was sexually abused by her parish priest for four years starting when she was twelve, holds no faith in the ability of bishops to police the policy; she believes that maintaining child molesters within the priesthood "defies understanding".[235] SNAP's membership increased to nearly five thousand members at the height of the abuse scandals in 2002.

Civil legislation has been passed in twenty-one states mandating that clergy, along with other professionals who work with children, report suspected child abuse. In many states, the confidentiality of clergy-penitent communication is protected, and information about abuse learned under such circumstances (i.e. confession) is exempt from mandatory reporting. Some states, however, that identify clergy as mandatory reporters, such as New Hampshire and West Virginia, do not recognize the privilege of pastoral communication in cases of child abuse.[236]

Despite an effort, both in civil law and canonical law, to punish the perpetrators and repair the damage done to thousands of children and adolescents by the people they trusted as much as or more than their own parents, in many eyes justice has not been served. The case of former priest David Holley is one example. Holley pleaded guilty in 1993 to molesting eight boys in New Mexico in the early 1970s. Although he was sentenced to 275 years in prison, he was granted parole in May 2004. The ruling was later rescinded, only because the victims had not been informed of the hearing or the ruling. At the time of his arrest, Holley faced similar charges of child molestation in Massachusetts, and in 1996 he settled a lawsuit over the molestation of a boy there in the 1960s.[237]

Victims who are still waiting for financial compensation from their abusers and the Church-there are more than two hundred claims outstanding in the Boston Diocese alone-may find themselves unable to reach satisfactory settlements if a recent ruling in Springfield, Massachusetts, sets a precedent. In August 2004, Hampden Superior Court Judge John Agostini ruled to uphold a "charitable immunity" law. The law states that charitable institutions, including churches, are protected from prosecution of alleged crimes that occurred before 1971 and are limited in liability to twenty thousand dollars for legal wrongdoings after that date.

No amount of money will repair the physical and psychological damage inflicted on those whose sacred trust was crushed by priests across the country (and around the world: similar scandals erupted in Canada and Europe at the same time). The Church's tenets juxtaposed with its actions makes for a hypocrisy that has been difficult for millions of Catholics to accept, but flagrant misuse and abuse of power and position does not fall solely under the purview of the Catholic Church. Many ministerial leaders of other Christian denominations, as well as self-styled "prophets" of their own churches, have been guilty of their own crimes against their trusting followers.

Tainted Televangelism
Most of us remember the televangelist scandals of the 1980s that included fraud, adultery, and a breach of trust that shook the spiritual founda-

tions of millions of believers.

Jim Bakker, minister of Assemblies of God and host of *The PTL Show* in the mid-1980s, solicited millions of dollars in donations for supposed projects to complete "God's will," including the development of a Christian holiday resort community called "Heritage USA"; instead he was using these donations to support a lavish lifestyle for himself and his wife, Tammy Faye. Bakker was disgraced when his extra-marital affair with his secretary, Jessica Hahn, became public; revelations of a long-time homosexual relationship followed. Bakker was convicted of fraud in 1987 but served less than five years of a forty-five-year sentence. In 1996, a North Carolina jury threw out a class-action lawsuit brought by 160,000 of Bakker's former followers, many of whom had contributed as much as seven thousand dollars each to PTL funds.[238] In January 2003, Bakker started broadcasting another show with his new wife, Lori Graham Bakker. His current website says, "To become a partner, donate just twenty-five dollars a month and receive *The Everyday Study Bible*." It also hawks various other wares such as medallions, crystal crosses, and books written by Bakker.

Jimmy Swaggart, host of *The Jimmy Swaggart Hour* with an estimated viewership of two million, reportedly brought in $150 million a year at the height of his televangelist ministry until his fall from grace in February 1988, when it was revealed that Swaggart regularly sought the services of a Louisiana prostitute. Two years later he was pulled over for speeding and a prostitute was sitting next to him in the car. Swaggart had been an outspoken critic of the activities of Jim Bakker.[239] Swaggart has recently put himself in the hot seat for remarks he made during a September 12, 2004, televised sermon. In his oration against same-sex marriage, Swaggart said, "I'm trying to find the correct name for it…this absolute, asinine, idiotic stupidity of men marrying men…I've never seen a man in my life I wanted to marry. And I'm gonna be blunt and plain: if one ever looks at me like that, I'm gonna kill him and tell God he died." After various broadcast stations around North America received a deluge of complaints, Swaggart tendered a back-handed apology: "If it's an insult, I certainly didn't think it was, but if they are offended, then I certainly offer an apology."[240]

Robert Tilton, former minister of the World of Faith World Outreach Center Church, which claimed ten thousand members, encountered his own scandal in 1991. ABC's *Prime Time Live* reported that Tilton was raking in $80 million a year from his direct mail campaign and his *Success-N-Life* television show that was broadcast over two hundred stations across the U.S. ABC aired evidence that thousands of letters and prayer requests sent by contributors had been tossed in a dumpster in Tulsa. A subsequent investigation by the Texas Attorney General and several lawsuits resulted in Tilton's show going off the air and the collapse of his ministry. In 2003, Tilton purchased a $1.4 million property in Miami

Beach and is currently back on the direct mail trail, sending out mass mailings containing trinkets, prayer cloths, packets of oil, and pictures of "Pastor Bob" in exchange for donations. One letter, which includes a piece of paper that looks like a $1 million bill, apparently reads: "I want you to put a checkmark on the back of the Million Dollar Bill of what you need or desire, and send it back to me, along with a Seed Faith Gift of $200…This ministry has given you spiritual food, so it's time to pay your tithes."[241] Despite the blatant fraud committed more than a decade ago, apparently there are still many people willing to hand over their earnings to someone who promises them redemption or prosperity.

How can so many people be so easily taken in and so unwilling to accept the truth about their captivating, criminal, and/or morally bankrupt religious guides? American astronomer and author Dr. Carl Sagan observed, "You can't convince a believer of anything; for their belief is not based on evidence, it's based on a deep seated need to believe." This need within us-whether explained by the existence of a human gene that drives us to believe or whether the existence of divinity simply is, and therefore humans have evolved to recognize it-might explain why we tend to follow and even worship "god-like" figures who demonstrate leadership, charisma, strength, and vision, even if it is corrupt. In our need to believe, we are brilliantly adept at rationalization: all deeds are done in the name of "God's will" or, since God is all-merciful and benevolent, then our sins will ultimately be forgiven. There is a religious irony that the weakest and basest among us are the most deserving of compassion and forgiveness. With this attitude, it stands to reason that there is little accountability for those in a position of ministerial power. Everything can be justified and redeemed, even if the sins committed break all the religious and civil codes of ethics and law. Far too many in positions of influence are adherents of the "Gospel according to me."

Even some non-indicted televangelists personify hypocrisy in their public comments. Jerry Falwell, founder of the Moral Majority and now spiritual leader of The Faith and Values Coalition, has come under fire for several of his more outrageous statements. Shortly after the terrorist attacks of September 11, 2001, Falwell said on Pat Robertson's religious program *The 700 Club*, "I really believe that the pagans, and the abortionists, and the feminists, and the gays and the lesbians who are actively trying to make that an alternative lifestyle, and the ACLU, the People for the American Way-all of them who have tried to secularize America-I point the finger in their face and say, 'You helped this happen.'"[242] In an October 24, 2004, televised debate with Baptist minister Jesse Jackson on *CNN Late Edition* with Wolf Blitzer, Falwell supported the war in Iraq and said, "…You've got to kill the terrorists before the killing stops and I am for the President-chase them all over the world, and if it takes ten years, blow them all away in the name of the Lord." His comments inspired immediate condemnation from many religious leaders and theologians, who responded with shock that a Christian minister would advocate killing in the name of God. David Currie, executive director of Texas Baptists Committed, said, "Jerry Falwell's remarks defame Christianity, my faith, and the faith of most Americans...The message of Christianity is not war, hatred or murder. It is love, unconditional love. That is the nature of God. The war on terror is not a war between Christians and Muslims. It is a war between those who want peace in the world and those who want to destroy peace. To imply God has a side, other than peace, is poor theology."[243]

Church and State

Leave the matter of religion to the family altar, the church, and the private school, supported entirely by private contributions. Keep the church and state forever separate.

-*Ulysses S. Grant, 18th U.S. President (1822-85)*

In an October 2004 cover story of the Canadian edition of *Time* magazine, Jeffrey Kluger explores the roots of faith in the context of a recent book suggesting that humans are specifically adapted to spirituality by our genetic structure. In a fascinating discussion with scientists and theologians around the world, an important point raised is that spirituality is intuitive and personal, whereas religion is institutional. Individuals are capable of worshiping their deity(ies) individually, but as social beings we tend to congregate in groups, which leads to the observation of the same set of codified rules and rituals. At that point, it is a small step to move that collection of beliefs and laws from the religious into the social realm to organize and order our behavior. Kluger used early Calvinism in Geneva as a positive example of divine law being used to reform an otherwise disordered society. One professor interviewed for the article echoed this thought with a caveat saying, "Religions represent an attempt to harness innate spirituality for organizational purposes-not always good."[244] In a modern political context, we view closed religious societies, such as Iran and Afghanistan, as fundamentalist and threatening to the freedoms we have in our secular society. Certainly the rise of extremism and the birth of terrorist groups within these countries would seem to justify that view. At the same time, many argue that American society was founded on Christian principles and the political and social climate necessarily reflects the religious bent of the majority.

Although there is a strong argument to be made that the United States was founded on Judeo-Christian traditions, historical record tells us those founding fathers were very much against the blending of church and state. Specifically, our founding fathers desired to prevent a state-sponsored church like the one they had previously rejected by separating from England. Thinkers, philosophers, and activists all, the authors of our nation were deeply in favor of protecting the freedom of religion-that each citizen should have the right to practice his own faith privately-without inflicting his beliefs on others, particularly if he held public office. Thomas Jefferson, the third President of the United States and primary writer of the Declaration of Independence, asserted, "Christianity neither is, nor ever was part of the common law." Jefferson was adamant that the affairs of the state not be intertwined with affairs of the church; he called the combination of church and state "loathsome."[245] His compatriot, James Madison, felt similarly: "The purpose of separation of church and state is to keep forever from these shores the ceaseless strife that has soaked the soil of Europe with blood for centuries." Paradoxically, the Declaration of Independence has five references to God or a Creator, most notably in the second sentence of the preamble: "We hold these truths to be self-evident, that all men are created equal, that they are endowed by their Creator with certain inalienable rights, among these are Life, Liberty and the pursuit of Happiness." Civil libertarians would argue that these references were not intended to promote the Christian God over any other. (Similarly, the "all men are created equal" was not exactly literal either: Jefferson himself was a slave-owner.)

Over the course of the past two hundred years, religion has gradually taken on a greater significance in American public life. The original motto of the U.S. was secular in meaning: E Pluribus Unum literally translated from Latin to mean "one from many" was generally interpreted to reflect the political structure of the U.S. as one federal state comprised of many smaller units. It was also representative of a respect for diversity of opinion and belief. In 1863, the motto was changed to "In God we trust" after a successful campaign by eleven Protestant denominations to insert references to God into the U.S. Constitution and other federal documents.[246] The Pledge of Allegiance states, "One nation, under God, indivisible..."; the national anthem exhorts "In God is our trust..."; all oaths taken in a court of law or public office require one to swear, one hand on the New Testament, "So help me God"; armed forces personnel pledge "serving our Nation under God"; shipping and insurance codes have exemptions for "acts of God"; and most public speeches in the United States end with the words or the song "God Bless America."

So although we live in a secular society, the separation of church and state is quite blurred. Several U.S. courts have ruled that the use of the word God in the Pledge of Allegiance and the national motto is constitutional, finding that it does not endorse a particular religious belief. The Supreme Court has declined to review most rulings of lower courts. (It also opens each session with the words "God save the United States and this Honorable Court.") It did recently dismiss a challenge to the wording of the Pledge of Allegiance. Michael Newdow, a self-professed atheist from California, sued to have the Pledge of Allegiance banned from his daughter's school, but the case was thrown out because Mr. Newdow was found to not have sufficient legal custody of his daughter to have authority to speak for her in court. In dismissing the case in June 2004, Justice William H. Rehnquist stated that the pledge does not violate the Constitution.[247]

At the same time, the Supreme Court has variously ruled that overtly religious symbols such as nativity scenes, crosses, menorahs, pentacles, and others cannot be displayed by themselves on public property unless multiple religious symbols are displayed together and given equal prominence. While various higher courts have ruled both ways on public displays of the Ten Commandments, the 2003 case involving Alabama Chief Justice Roy Moore's insistence on displaying a two and one-half ton monument of the commandments in the rotunda of the Alabama Supreme Court building garnered much attention and debate about the separation of church and state. Moore was removed from the bench after defying a federal court order to remove the monument in August 2003. In his ruling, U.S. District Court Judge Myron Thompson said when the monument is displayed in a public building, it is a government endorsement of Christianity and violates the constitutional ban on the government promoting religion. Moore countered that the Ten Commandments are the foundation of the legal system and that forcing the removal of the monument was denying his First Amendment guarantee to freely exercise his religion. Several conservative Christian groups and individuals supported Moore, including Alabama Attorney General Bill Pryor and Governor Bob Riley; however, they did not back him publicly because Thompson promised to fine the state $5,000 a day if they refused to comply with his order.[248] Moore also enjoyed support from many of his fellow citizens. A CNN-USA Today-Gallup poll, conducted in November after the monument was removed from the rotunda to a state warehouse, found that 77 percent of the 1,009 Americans who were surveyed wanted the monument to stay at the courthouse.[249]

The issue of church and state is highly contentious. The courts are inconsistent in their rulings and opinions, and legislation is similarly contradictory, leaving much of the interpretation to be made at the state level. Depending on where you live in the country, the separation of religion and politics may or may not evident, a situation which fragments and polarizes the nation and discourages us from sharing those values we do have in common. For example, while more than 80 percent of the population declares itself to be Christian and the country celebrates Christmas as a statutory holiday, it has become taboo to actually call it "Christmas" anymore, lest it offend the 20 percent of those who celebrate other holy days or who choose not to celebrate at all. Most corporate, government, and school manifestations of that time at the end of

December appear as "the holiday season"; greeting cards say "Happy Holidays" and "Season's Greetings." The city of Pittsburgh calls the holiday-formerly-known-as-Christmas "Sparkle Season," and many cities have renamed their Santa Claus parade to "The Parade of Lights." In the case of Christmas celebrations, the pendulum of religious tolerance has swung so far to the extreme that a rabid backlash has resulted. The 2004 holiday season was marked by expressions of exasperation in op-ed pages, websites and talk TV; multitudes of voices exhorted Americans to take back Christmas and throw holiday political correctness out with the used wrapping paper. The words "Merry Christmas" were suddenly adopted as a sort of manifesto, flung at people to make a point, rather than uttered with genuine good will.

More and more, religious conservatism is appearing in the public domain, which is not surprising since President George W. Bush openly declares his faith from his office, both in addresses to the nation and through legislation. At his first inauguration, Franklin Graham, the son of evangelist minister Billy Graham, delivered an invocation, and Bush's short speech was spackled with religious references. The following day, Bush held a prayer service-where Graham again delivered a sermon-at Washington's National Cathedral and declared that day, January 21, a National Day of Prayer and Thanksgiving.[250] Bush is fond of attending National Prayer Breakfasts to discuss policy issues with officials and interest groups. He has been open in his opposition to abortion and embryonic stem cell research and has pushed several legislative initiatives based on his religious inclinations. He supported a proposed constitutional amendment to ban same-sex marriage, which was not achieved in his first term of office. In the final presidential debate before the 2004 election, Bush stated that although he didn't wish to inflict his religious views on others, his faith-based principles were "manifested in public policy." (It is unclear how both parts of that admission can be justified as they are completely contradictory.)

Shortly after he came to office in 2001, Bush established, by executive order, the White House Office of Faith-based and Community Initiatives, with the mandate of encouraging religious groups to compete with secular groups for public funds in order to provide social and community programs, such as after-school care and prison reform projects. The Office is connected to ten other government departments; within each there is a separate director and staff to oversee the mandate of procuring more financial support for faith-based social services: Agriculture, Commerce, Education, Health and Human Services, Housing and Urban Development, Justice, Labor, Veteran's Affairs, Agency for International Development, and Small Business Administration. Many of the social programs are funded at state and local levels, so exact tallies of public funding to faith-based social service providers is difficult to determine;

the Department of Health and Human Services did report a 41 percent increase in availability of funding from that department to faith-based groups during the 2003 fiscal year.[251]

One program that was announced in September 2004 is a new faith-based health care plan for federal employees in Illinois that specifically excludes payment for contraceptives, abortion, sterilization and artificial insemination. The plan, which is a health care savings account with a high deductible, is sponsored by an insurer run by a Catholic group in that state. Proponents argue that it is acceptable for people to have an option to choose how their benefits are spent based on their belief system; critics worry that the government is setting a dangerous precedent by funding such ventures and is violating the doctrine of separation of church and state.[252] Bush's agenda is apparent in recent international aid pledges as well. In July 2004, the government announced that it would spend $15 billion over the next five years on the prevention and treatment of the HIV/AIDS virus in Viet Nam, Africa, and the Caribbean. The money is targeted specifically at fourteen countries who support the U.S. policy of controlling the spread of HIV through abstinence, monogamy, and condom use, in that order.[253]

Some analysts are concerned that the President is making extraordinary use of his executive powers in order to fulfill his evangelical agenda. In a recent report entitled *The Expanding Administrative Presidency: George W. Bush and the Faith-Based Initiative*, the authors wrote, "In the absence of new legislative authority, the President has aggressively advanced the Faith-Based Initiative through executive orders, rule changes, managerial realignment in federal agencies and other innovative uses of the prerogatives of his office."[254] Some of the regulatory changes of the initiative are ringing alarm bells with civil rights proponents. For example, the federal government now allows federally-funded faith-based groups to consider religion when hiring staff. Faith-based groups are also allowed to build and renovate structures to be used for both social services and religious worship with taxpayers' dollars. These measures fly in the face of anti-discrimination labor laws, as well as government policies that prohibit funneling public funds to sectarian organizations.

In late March of 2004, Bush signed legislation expanding the legal rights of the unborn, making it a crime to harm a fetus during the commission of a crime involving a pregnant woman; abortion-rights proponents say this is the first step in recognizing an embryo or fetus as a separate person and could lead to the eventual overturning of Roe vs. Wade.[255] The move was prompted by the murder of Laci Peterson, whose husband Scott has since been sentenced to death in California for the double murder of Laci and her fetus. The Bush administration has made no secret of its intention to fill the Supreme Court with conservative justices who are likely to overturn Roe vs. Wade.

He will surely fulfill that mandate, if this appointments to the Food and Drug Administration are an indication. In October 2002, the administration was keen to place Dr. W. David Hager at the head of the Reproductive Health Drugs Advisory Committee, an influential panel on women's health policies that makes recommendations to the FDA about the regulation of drugs for contraception, infertility treatments, hormone replacement therapy, medical abortions, and various other obstetric and gynecological issues. Dr. Hager is the co-author, along with his wife, of *As Jesus Cared for Women: Restoring Women Then and Now* and an editor of *The Reproductive Revolution: A Christian Appraisal of Sexuality, Reproductive Technologies and the Family.* He was selected for the chairman position by senior FDA associate commissioner Linda Arey Skladany, a former drug-industry lobbyist with ties to the Bush family, who recommended Hager for a four-year term despite concerns from other FDA staff over Hager's views; he advocates Bible readings and prayers as remedies for headaches and PMS, and in his private practice as an obstetrician-gynecologist, he refuses to prescribe contraceptives to unmarried female patients.[256] Hager has also been public about his refusal to insert IUDs in patients or to prescribe the RU-486 pill (also known as "the morning-after pill" to some or "abortion pill" to others). In one interview, Hager said, "I am pro-life. I believe sex outside of marriage is a sin. But I am not against medication. The fact that I'm a person of faith does not deter me from also being a person of science."[257] A recent (February 2005) check of the committee roster lists Dr. Hager as a member, rather than chairman, but one would assume his faith-based attitudes towards women's reproductive health are having at least a marginal impact regarding the decisions of the FDA.

The nation's public education system also seems to be affected by a disturbing religious bias. Former Education Secretary Rod Paige demonstrated his support of the President's leanings when he stated in the media that he personally finds Christian schools preferable to public institutions because of the values taught in Christian schools. "In a religious environment the value system is set. That's not the case in a public school, where there are so many different kids with different kinds of values," he told an interviewer for *Baptist Press.*[258] His public comments seem to confirm a suspicion that the Bush administration's avowed commitment to improving the public school system, through the 2002 No Child Left Behind Act, was perhaps a parochial wolf in secular sheep's clothing. Some state courts are still reluctant to endorse the governmental shift toward public funding of religious schools. The Florida Opportunity Scholarship Program is a project of Governor Jeb Bush, which was instituted in 1999; parents of children attending "failing" public schools are granted vouchers to attend private schools. It has been deemed to violate the "no-aid provision" in Florida's constitution, barring payment of tax dollars to sectarian schools. More than half of those participating in the OSP attend religious schools.[259]

The reelection of President Bush and the emerging focus of Americans toward a more moral society may be another chicken-and-egg phenomenon. Is a national shift in thinking responsible for putting an overtly religious leader in office, or is the American mood a result of that leadership? A recent Gallup poll showed that 49 percent of Americans think religion is losing its influence on society, and 61 percent believe religion is the answer to society's problems.[260] An Ipsos-Associated Press opinion poll published a few weeks before the 2004 election found that 72 percent of white evangelical respondents planned to vote for President Bush.[261] Leading up to the election, the Vatican issued doctrinal letters to the U.S. Conference of Catholic Bishops instructing them that Catholic politicians should be bound by the Church's teachings and have a duty to uphold Catholic moral laws while in public office. Many bishops, in turn, were open in their endorsements (or condemnation) of candidates based on their public positions regarding abortion, same-sex marriage and stem-cell research.[262] Both presidential candidates even managed to preach their campaign positions from the pulpits of churches across the country, an exercise that emphasized the weight of religious influence on the electorate.

Indeed, exit polls showed that Bush had secured the white, middle class, older, church-going demographic whose primary concern in the election was "moral values," but pollsters are critical of the assumption that the white evangelical right swept him to power and claim exit polls to be notoriously unreliable. Two weeks before the election, however, twenty-five thousand people congregated on Washington's National Mall to pray and fast for "God's protection of America" and a return to moral roots. The "America for Jesus" rally was telecast internationally to over 300 million households and was attended by a culturally and ethnically diverse crowd, according to organizer Bishop John Gimenez, founder of the Rock Church in Virginia Beach.[263] Jerry Falwell wrote several newsletter memos directly before the election urging his readers to vote for pro-life, pro-traditional family candidates and return the U.S. to its religious roots. He wrote, "It is the responsibility of every political conservative, every evangelical Christian, every pro-life Catholic, every traditional Jew…and everyone in between to get serious about re-electing President George Bush." Shortly after the election, Falwell launched The Faith and Values Coalition-a twenty-first century Moral Majority-and called for the recruitment of the first one million charter members. The Coalition's stated agenda is "the confirmation of pro-life, strict constructionist Supreme Court and federal court judges; the passage of a constitutional Federal Marriage Amendment; and the election of another socially, fiscally and politically conservative president in 2008, along with conservative members of Congress in 2006 and 2008." In his memo, Falwell claimed "God allowed me to give birth to the Religious Right," and then he took credit for his role in encouraging thirty million "faith and values" voters to go to the polls and swing the election in favor of President Bush.[264]

A return to moral roots is unarguably an admirable goal for Americans to reach for in addressing our society's ills. The problem is, Whose morals are we supposed to adopt? Is there not an obvious disconnect when we are supposed to adopt a moral stance against, for example, abortion-the so-called "killing of unborn children"-when some of the very same people who are against it find it justifiable to shoot and kill doctors in their homes and workplaces? Is there not a conflict when we are supposed to follow the rules of a church whose representatives and leaders have systematically abused and deceived its followers for decades, and arguably centuries (the Crusades, the Inquisition, etc.)? Is it not incongruous that we are supposed to follow the "moral" example of our President who has sent us to war under the false guise of "good versus evil"; a war that has cost the lives of more than 1,450 American soldiers, wounded 10,000 more, and killed between 15,000 and 100,000 Iraqi civilians?[265]

Reverend Jim Wallis, editor of *Sojourners* magazine and author of *The Soul of Politics: Beyond "Religious Right" and "Secular Left,"* commented in a recent *Meet the Press* debate, "Our Jesus isn't pro-rich, pro-war and only pro-American. We don't find that Jesus anywhere in the Bible." [266] Wallis has been critical of the evangelical conservatives and prior to the election wrote a column stating, "We believe claims of divine appointment for the President, uncritical affirmation of his policies and the assertion that all Christians must vote for his re-election constitute bad theology and dangerous religion." Wallis criticized the "religious" who chose "loyalty to party over loyalty to Scripture" and who have narrowed the discussion of moral values to abortion and gay marriage, effectively denying that there are common values and social concerns shared by all Americans. He pointed out that poverty and war are moral issues, and that truth-telling is also a religious issue. It should be applied to a candidate's rationales for war, tax cuts, or any other policy. Humility is also a religious issue, and the language of the "religious empire" should be avoided as it too easily confuses the roles of God, church, and nation."[267]

I submit that we are and should be deeply affected by moral values, spiritual fulfillment and/or religious norms in our personal and social lives: those are the moves that allow us to function as part of a decent, collective society. I feel, however, that we are being subject to a narrow set of moral values imposed upon us by a hypocritical minority, highly prone to abuse, who wields enormous economic, political, and social power.

Religion in society and politics is inescapable. Politicians and leaders are human beings whose decisions and actions are inevitably guided by

Jeff Shiring

their own principles and beliefs. At the same time, the actions and words of our last two presidents have belied their stated beliefs. President Bush and President Clinton both claim to be men of the Christian faith, and yet both have demonstrated highly un-Christian behavior to the American people. For Clinton's part, not only did he repeatedly break his marriage vows, he blatantly lied about it. Many of his supporters claimed his private actions had nothing to do with his ability to run the country, but this can be debated. The Office of the Presidency is a position of the highest stature: the person occupying it is supposed to offer the country firm, honest, and direct leadership through decision making and example. When someone can so casually flout his position of authority by having extra-marital sex with a junior employee of the office that represents the highest seat of power, then repeatedly deny it, it most assuredly is a public reflection of his ability to make good decisions and ably lead the country. No matter how brilliant the man or how talented a statesman, those actions dishonor the religious doctrine of being faithful in marriage, as well as the public's faith in the integrity of the presidency. The example set is poor: it is hypocrisy and abuse of power at its most obvious.

For his part, President Bush has also demonstrated words and actions inconsistent with his professed religious beliefs. By leading the United States into a war that was based on false premises, incomplete information, and misrepresentation, the blood of tens of thousands of innocent people stains our nation. Calling the war against Saddam Hussein a war against terror (which were not related until the U.S. invaded Iraq) has led the American people to believe it is a religious battle of good vs. evil. Where was that invocation of religious justice when the U.S. government backed Saddam and funded his atrocities against the Kurds? Why did we turn the other cheek as his regime tortured and killed countless numbers of his own citizens? The answer is because at the time he served a purpose that was perceived to be more important to our political and economic interests than the lives he was destroying. Right or wrong, such is the pattern of United States involvement in the global arena; to justify it under the banner of God's will for America is preposterous.

On the domestic front, the President has blatantly defied his twice-sworn oath to faithfully uphold the Constitution: civil rights infringements in the name of Homeland Security and faith-based governance are two such policies. In his single-minded determination to impose his ultra-conservative beliefs on the entire nation, his administration has broken most of the covenants of the separation of church and state; his policies have divided the country bitterly. It is our responsibility as a people to recognize and realize that as a society we have evolved beyond the "fire and brimstone" or "eye for an eye" theology of the Old Testament that President Bush espouses. To become whole again, to reclaim our displaced youth, our social institutions, and the vision of democracy upon which our country is founded, Americans need to reembrace our common, fundamental values of acceptance, charity, respect for others, and personal accountability.

The government does have a role to play in this. A democratic government governs all people through the rule of the majority. The majority of Americans profess Christian beliefs and values; therefore in governing the majority, considerations of those values are necessary. Our laws are derived from basic moral principles founded in religious doctrine, but it is the same doctrine that also values diversity and tolerance of different viewpoints. The state needs to embrace the elements of Christianity that are common to virtually all belief systems (i.e., killing is wrong; helping others is right) without forcing extreme positions down the throats of dissenters. Church and state need to be separate entities enriched by the positive actions of the other. By protecting people's enshrined right to freely practice their faiths, while ensuring that the practice does not infringe on the rights of others to worship differently (or to choose not to worship at all), we maintain the vision of the founders of this country. Martin Luther King, Jr. said, "The church must be reminded that it is not the master or the servant of the state, but rather the conscience of the state. It must be the guide and the critic of the state, and never its tool."

The state must be also reminded that it is not the church. The government can play a valuable role in demonstrating the uniqueness of people's beliefs by also promoting the similarities between those beliefs. We need to recognize Christian traditions for what they are, and at the same time educate school children and the wider public about other religions; this can be accomplished through curriculum development and public service announcements, for example. Christmas is a statutory holiday because the vast majority of the country celebrates the birth of Jesus Christ. At the same time, other religions also recognize the historical significance of the Christian Son of God; a chapter of the Qu'ran clearly tells of the miracle birth of Jesus, and Mary is the most-mentioned woman in the Islamic holy book. It is right for our youth to understand where our traditions come from and equally right for them to understand and benefit from the knowledge of other traditions. By recognizing and emphasizing the common elements of different belief systems (such as the universal significance of birth and miracle) tolerance and peace are bred into new generations. So is an expanded sense of self; young people learn they are not the center of the universe, but rather they are part of it and their actions have consequences both for themselves and others.

It is becoming increasingly difficult to worship with those who carry the sword of righteousness but kneel at the altar of expedience. It is all so much rhetoric. History repeatedly shows us the dangers in blindly following those who invoke faith when it serves an immediate purpose, particularly when that purpose is not the exercise of morality but rather the

Jeff Shiring

accumulation of wealth, sexual gratification, or the obtainment of power. The most vocal of the faithful are also the most adept at rationalization; a skill that enables human beings to distort the tenets of our belief systems and allows us to justify actions that are otherwise unjustifiable. Frank Herbert wrote, "When politics and religion are intermingled, a people is suffused with a sense of invulnerability, and gathering speed in their forward charge, they fail to see the cliff ahead of them." In the name of God, we can always find a way to get away with harming others (and ourselves), especially at the behest of those leading us. This is what we have learned from the behavior of many of our religious and political leaders; we can be unaccountable for our actions in life because we are accountable only to God to whom we can eventually repent and be forgiven. The pervasive abuse in the Catholic Church, the greed and hypocrisy of charismatic televangelists, presidential peccadilloes, and the mislabeling of a "just war" have all served to exploit and abuse religious principles and have contributed to a floundering nation searching for genuine truths to believe. Our trust has been continually broken, and so the cycle continues; those of us searching for meaningful leadership are susceptible to powerful personalities who capitalize on that collective need by portraying a strong vision and promising to guide us to a better place. Even if those personalities are deeply flawed, they offer at least a temporary alternative to or distraction from the institutions that have let us down.

I submit that the delicate and powerful influence of religion in our social lives and conscience has been badly battered by the winds of exploitation and personal gratification, much the same as heroism. As this incredible stabilizing social force erodes, where will we turn for peace, harmony, and hope?

---

[218] David B. Barrett. and Todd M. Johnson. "Table: World Adherents of All Religions, mid-2003," *Encyclopedia Brittanica Almanac 2004*, 682-84.

[219] Agostino Bono. "Four Percent of Priests Serving Over Last 50 Years Accused of Abuse," *Catholic News Service*, http://www.catholicnews.com/data/abuse/abuse09.htm (retrieved Nov. 10. 2004).

[220] "U.S. Catholic Bishops Receive 1,092 New Sex Abuse Claims," *CBC News Online*, February 18, 2005, http://www.cbc.ca/story/world/national/2005/02/18/abuse-050218.html (retrieved Feb. 19, 2005).

[221] National Review Board for the Protection of Children and Young People, *A Report on the Crisis in the Catholic Church*, 61-62, website of the United States Conference of Catholic Bishops, http://www.usccb.org.nrb/nrbstudy/nrbreport.pdf (retrieved Nov. 10, 2004).

[222] "Highlights of the National Review Board Report on Sexual Abuse," *Catholic News Service*, http://www.catholicnews.com/data/abus/abuse07.htm (retrieved Nov. 10, 2004).

[223] *A Report on the Crisis in the Catholic Church*, p. 9.

[224] Ibid., p. 40.

[225] Greg Frost. "Boston Priest, 74, Guilty of Child Rape," *Toronto National Post*, Feb. 8, 2005, sec. A, p. 12.

[226] Theo Emery. "Priest in Boston Abuse Scandal Reportedly Defrocked," *AOL News*, May 6, 2004, http://aolsvc.news.aol.com/news/article.adp?id=20040506111409990007&_ccc=4 (retrieved Nov. 11, 2004).

[227] Associated Press, "Priest Arraigned on Child Pornography Charges." Nov. 8, 2004, http://www.wggb.com/archive/religion/churchabuse/new_bedfor_priest.htm (retrieved Nov. 10, 2004).

[228] Associated Press, "Former Head of Springfield Diocese Indicted on Child Rape Chargesm," Sept, 27, 2004, http://www.wggb.com/archive/religion/dupre/indictment.htm (retrieved Nov. 11, 2004).

[229] Ralph Ranalli. "Priest Accused of Fondling is Defrocked by Vatican," *Boston Globe*, June 2, 2004, http://www.boston.com/news/local/articles/2004/06/02/priest_accused_in_fondling_is_defrocked_by_vatican/ (retrieved Nov. 12, 2004).

[230] Associated Press, "Springfield Diocese Cuts Financial Ties to Pedophile Priest," May 28, 2004, http://www.wggb.com/archive/religion/lavigne/financialties.htm (retrieved Nov. 11, 2004).

[231] Associated Press, "Lawyer Says Pedophile Priest Dying of Cancer," Oct. 22, 2004, http://www.wggb.com/archive/religion/churchabuse/porter_cancer.htm (retrieved Nov. 11, 2004).

[232] Associated Press, "O'Malley Acknowledges Abuse Problems Created 'Crisis of Confidence'". Oct. 9, 2004, http://www.wggb.com/archive/religion/churchclosings_omalley_abuse.htm (retrieved Nov. 10, 2004).

[233] Rachel Zoll. "Church Sex Abuse Study Likely to Surprise," Newsday.com, Feb. 20, 2004, http://www.newsday.com/news/nationworld/nation/wire/sns-ap-church-abuse-survey,0,7700415,print.story?coll=sns-ap-nation-headlines (retrieved Nov. 11, 2004).

[234] *A Report on the Crisis in the Catholic Church*, p. 64.

[235] "Bishops' Sexual Abuse Policy Meets with Criticism," *Weekend Edition Saturday*, National Public Radio, June 15, 2002, audiocast from website:

http://www.npr.org/news/specials/priests/ (retrieved Nov. 14, 2004).

236 "Reporting Laws: Clergy as Mandatory Reporters," *2003 Child Abuse and Neglect, State Statute Series, Ready Reference,* National Clearinghouse on Child Abuse and Neglect Information, http://www.smith-lawfirm.com/Documents/mandatoryreporting_mandclergy.pdf (retrieved Nov. 13, 2004).

237 Associated Press, "Priest to Go Before Parole Board." Sept. 15, 2004, http://www.wggb.com/archive/religion/churchabuse/priest_parole_board.htm (retrieved Nov. 12, 2004).

2328 Jim Bakker, http://www.nationmaster.com/encyclopedia/Jim-Bakker (retrieved Dec. 17, 2003).

239 "On This Day—February 21, 1988: TV Evangelist Quits Over Sex Scandal," *British Broadcasting Corporation,* http://news.bbc.co.uk/onthisday/hi/dates/stories/frebruary/21/newsid_2565000/2565197.stm (retrieved Dec. 18, 2004).

240 Associated Press, "Swaggart Apologized for Talk of Killing Gays," Associated Press, Sept. 23, 2004, http://msnbc.msn.com/id/6074380 (retrieved Nov. 29, 2004).

241 Ziva Bransetter. "Robert Tilton: From Downfall to Windfall: Living on a Prayer," *Tulsa World,* May 4, 2003, http://www.trinityfi.org/press/tulsaworld02.html (retrieved Nov. 14, 2004).

242 John F. Harris. "God Gave U.S. 'What We Deserve,' Falwell Says," *Washington Post.com,* Sept. 14, 2001, http://www.washingtonpost.com/ac2/wp-dyn?pagename=article&contentId=A28620-2001Sep14&notFound=true (retrieved Nov. 29, 2004).

243 Greg Warner. "Call to Kill Terrorists 'In the Name of the Lord' Sparks Outcry." *Associated Baptist Press,* Nov. 5, 2004, http://www.baptiststandard.com/postnuke/index.php?module=htmlpages&func=display&pid=2518 (retrieved Nov. 29, 2004).

244 Jeffrey Kluger. "Is God in our Genes?" *Time,* Canadian edition, Oct. 25, 2004, p. 51.

245 http://en.thinkexist.com/quotes/thomas_jefferson (retrieved Oct. 28, 2004).

246 B.A. Robinson. "The U.S. National Mottos: Their History and Constitutionality," *Ontario Consultants on Religious Tolerance,* Aug. 13, 2000, http://www.religioustolerance.org/nat_mott.htm (retrieved Oct. 20, 2004).

247 Associated Press, "U.S. Supreme Court Dismisses Pledge Case," June 14, 04, http://www.undergodprocon.org/pop/SupCrtDec.htm (retrieved Oct. 26, 2004).

248 "Judge Suspended Over Ten Commandments," *CNN,* Aug. 23, 2003, http://www.cnn.com/2003/LAW/08/22/ten.commandments/ (retrieved Nov. 14, 2004).

[249] "Ten Commandments Monument Moved," *CNN*, Nov. 14, 2003, http://www.cnn.com/2003/LAW/08/27/ten.commandments (retrieved Nov. 14, 2004).

[250] "Bush Inauguration Filled with Spiritual References," *Maranatha Christian Journal*, Jan. 22, 2000, http://www.mcjonline.com/news/01a/20010123b.shtml (retrieved Oct. 28, 2004).

[251] Anne Farris, Richard P. Nathan, and David J. Wright, *The Expanding Administrative Presidency: George W. Bush and the Faith-Based Initiative*, The Roundtable on Religion and Social Welfare Policy, August 2004, p. 4.

[252] http://www.opednews.com/boyne_092604.women.htm (retrieved Nov. 14, 2004).

[253] Associated Press, "U.S. Defends AIDS Policy," *CBS/New.com*, July 14, 2004, http://www.cbsnews.com/stories/2004/07/15/health/main629866.shtml (retrieved July 15, 2004).

[254] Farris, et al., *Expanding Presidency*, p. 3.

[255] Jennifer Loven. "Bush Signs Fetus Rights Legislation," *Newsday.com*, April 1, 2004, http://www.newsday.com/news/politics/wire/sns-ap-bush-fetus-rights,0,1150294.story?coll=sns-ap-politics-headlines (retrieved Nov. 14, 2004).

[256] Karen Tumulty. "Jesus and the FDA," *Time*, Oct. 5, 2002, http://www.time.com/time/nation/printout/0,8816,361521,00.html (retrieved Feb. 8, 2004).

[257] Maureen Dowd. "Tribulation Worketh Patience," *New York Times*, Oct. 9, 2002, http://www.valleyskeptic.com/bush_fda.html (retrieved Feb. 9, 2005).

[258] Editorial, *New York Times*, April 11, 2003, *AOL Online,* (retrieved April 12, 2003).

[259] "Florida School Voucher Program is Unconstitutional, Says State Appeals Court," *Americans United for Separation of Church and State*, Nov. 15, 2004, http://www.au.org (retrieved Nov. 15, 2004).

[260] Gerald L. Zelizer. "When Religion and Politics Mix," *USA Today*, Nov. 24, 2004, http://www.usatoday.com/news/opinion/2004-11-24-religion-politics_x.htm (retrieved Nov. 24, 2004).

[261] Alan Freeman. "When Voting is a Matter of Faith," *Globe and Mail*, Oct. 25, 2004, sec. A, p. 9.

[262] Shawn McCarthy. "Catholic Leaders Condemn Kerry," *Globe and Mail*, Oct. 14, 2004, sec. A, p.15.

[263] "One Nation Under Prayer," America for Jesus: One Nation Under God, press release of Washington, Oct. 22, 2004, http://apjc.unored.com (retrieved Nov. 15, 2004).

[264] Jerry Falwell. *Falwell Confidential*, Nov. 16, 2004, http://falwell.com/cgi-

bin/mailinglist/index.cgi?0::94 (retrieved Nov. 30, 2004).

265 http://www.iraqibodycount.net (retrieved Nov. 30, 2004).

266 "NBC News Meet the Press," National Broadcasting Company, transcript of Nov. 28, 2004 broadcast, http://www.msnbc.msn.com/id/6601018 (retrieved Nov. 29, 2004).

267 Jim Wallis. "God is Not a Republican. Or a Democrat," *Sojourners Magazine*, October 2004, http://www.sojo.net/index.cfm?action=magazine.article&issue=soj0410&article=041051 (retrieved Nov. 30, 2004).

4. Mad Money

Capitalism is the astounding belief that the most wickedest of men will do the most wickedest of things for the greatest good of everyone.
-John Maynard Keynes, British economist (1883-1946)

Keynes' observation may seem at first glance to be overly cynical. After all, the United States is arguably the most capitalistic nation on earth. Adam Smith's ideal of the free-market economy, which predated Keynes by more than a century, is still fundamental to our society-our education, our labor, our culture, and our politics. Smith's concept of the invisible hand is the natural force that guides the free-market system toward equilibrium between producers and consumers through competition. This theory remains central to our collective belief that unfettered supply and demand, along with self-interested motivation, results in wealth and prosperity for all.

Keynes, however, may have been prophetic, and self-interest has been taken to the worst extreme. Entrepreneurship and the cult of the corporation have gone far beyond what any reasonable person might consider a mutually beneficial relationship with the individual in society. As an example, there is a growing industry of viral marketing and advertising agencies openly recruit children to spread the consumer germ. The multi-billion dollar "tween" market mentioned earlier is a ripe target for growing firms such as the Girls' Intelligence Agency. GIA recruits popular "alpha girls" as young as eight to host sleepover parties where new products are debuted and test-marketed. (Think Tupperware parties for the prepubescent set.) The girls' preferences for certain products influence which new products (and talents) will reach the wider market, dictating new trends in clothing, accessories, and music. GIA contracts cost clients such as Disney, Fox, and Capitol Records up to a million dollars.[268] Without a doubt this type of marketing strategy is beneficial for the companies that stand to make millions from it, but the "mutual" benefit conferred upon the youngest salespeople in the country is questionable. [Free stuff? Could this be lessons in how to manipulate friends and influence record sales?]

The perpetual quest to make more money is obviously an individual pursuit, as well as a corporate one. In 2004, the combined net worth of the four hundred wealthiest citizens of our nation reached one trillion dollars, up forty-five billion dollars from the year before.[269] Our economic evolution has proven that an unfettered free-market system is unable to modulate itself. Self-interest has become a justification for greed, theft, fraud, exploitation, the corruption of power, and the contamination of a healthy democratic process. Abuse of the capital system in the name of self-interest has altered the democratic design; we have moved away from "government for the people by the people" into "government for wealthy big business and the little people be damned." That shift has become an overriding influence on the way we think and behave, not just as economic producers and consumers, but as human beings. Our age-old ethic of "If I work hard enough, I will be prosperous" has been replaced by "The end justifies the means."

That is not to say the wealthy haven't worked hard for their reward, but we have learned, by examples set by countless individuals and corporations (a few of which are highlighted in this chapter), that there are more direct ways to get what we want than effort and altruism. We have come to expect that competition is only possible if we have some kind of edge and that success is the result of knowing how to work the system. We have forgotten the humanistic belief that underscored Smith's economic philosophy: that mankind, although inherently selfish, is also decent, honest, and compassionate; and those traits would also motivate the individual's market behavior. We are left with the modern rationalization that the free-market economy is an amoral entity, which we interpret to mean that immoral behavior is acceptable. Money makes our world go 'round, but the unbridled pursuit and spending of it is threatening to bring our world crashing down.

The State of the Economy

The morning news brings daily reports of our economy, serving up numbers too large to digest with our coffee and supersized muffin: the trade deficit; the budget deficit; the unemployment rate; the national debt. Most of us don't even fully understand what all these figures represent. Taken individually, most of the statistics don't really mean anything at all, but taken together, the overall trend is alarming and was reflected in 2004 by an eroding consumer confidence index. In November, the Conference Board reported the consumer confidence index at 90.5, down for the fifth consecutive month.[270] The December index rallied somewhat because of modest job growth and economic expansion, though Americans remained cautious about the economic health of the nation and for good reason.

The U.S. trade deficit hit an all-time high in November of 2004 at $60.3 billion, a $4.3 billion increase over the previous month, and more than $20 billion higher than November 2003.[271] The budget deficit also hit an all-time record for the fiscal year ending in September 2004: $412 billion or 3.6 percent of the national output.[272] The International Monetary Fund (IMF) has predicted that uncontrolled budget deficits will threaten not only the United States, but also the global economy, reducing the world's economic growth by more than 4 percent by 2020. The increased borrowing needed to finance the U.S. deficit will eventually drive up interest rates at home and abroad as the global supply of capital is reduced.[273] Federal Reserve Chairman Alan Greenspan echoed that warning, saying that even though the deficit has not yet triggered a significant rise in interest rates (the Fed raised them by a quarter point in February 2005) or a drastic devaluation of the dollar, the long-term stability of the U.S. economy is jeopardized by a huge federal budget deficit. "The free lunch has yet to be invented," Greenspan said at a banking conference in May 2004.[274] The U.S. dollar has indeed dropped against various foreign currencies over the past year, sparking concern among international markets. The core inflation rate-which excludes food and energy prices-rose 0.3 percent in February 2005, the biggest jump since September 2004. While the Bush administration has expressed a goal of cutting the deficit in half by 2009, it is unclear how that will happen under the current policy of continually cutting taxes to boost the economy, yet increasing spending at the same time.

In December 2004, the President signed legislation raising the government's debt limit by $800 billion, increasing the borrowing ceiling to an historic high of $8.18 trillion, or 70 percent of the size of the economy. Increasing the debt limit was necessary to cover a $388 billion spending bill and to prevent the government from going into default, but it marks an increase of $2.4 trillion in debt since Bush was elected in 2001.[275] The U.S. National Debt Clock puts the outstanding public debt at $7.6 trillion as of January 12, 2005, having increased an average of $2.17 billion per day since September 30, 2004. Each U.S. citizen's share of that debt is $25,753.16. The result is that our children, our grandchildren, and possibly our great-grandchildren will inherit the burden of paying off this debt.

While the media reports overall job growth in 2004, with the economy adding approximately two million jobs, the actual unemployment rate remained virtually unchanged from July to December at 5.4 percent. That means eight million Americans are still unemployed.[276] A significantly higher number are living below the poverty line; 12.5 percent, or nearly thirty-six million people, are struggling to survive in this country, an increase of 1.3 million since 2002.[277] While housing development has increased in the last several years, home ownership rates for low- and middle-income families have dropped. Incomes have not kept up with the rising housing costs: a study by the Center for Housing Policy found that the median price of a new home in 1978 was $55,700, about four times the median income of $14,200 for a working family with children. The median price of a new home in 2001 was $175,000, five times the median income of $35,000.[278] Bankruptcy filings reached a record high in 2003 with 1,661,996 filed that fiscal year. The number was down slightly in 2004 to 1,618,987, but still at a level nearly twice what it was a decade ago.[279]

Essentially, we are spending more than we can afford. We have become a plastic society, individually and as a nation, living on credit far beyond our means. Even the traditional cushion of the fiscally responsible-savings-is getting flatter as we gradually pick away at it to finance our current lifestyle. Some finance companies are now considering allowing people to borrow from their 401K accounts using special credit cards for easy access, a potentially disastrous move for people who might find themselves unable to pay back a loan from their retirement savings. While an interest rate of 8 percent is far better than the average bank credit card, having that option of cheaper borrowing may entice those who would otherwise leave their savings alone to dip in and carry the debt. Then they face a 10 percent early withdrawal penalty, higher income tax, and a smaller nest egg for retirement.[280]

The aging labor force poses its own set of problems, prompting the Bush government to propose a controversial overhaul to the Social Security system. Social Security is predicted to be insolvent-that is, paying more benefits than it will collect in revenue-as early as 2018.[281] The administration mounted a huge campaign in early January of 2005 touting the advantages of semi-privatizing the retirement safety net at an initial cost of at least one trillion dollars. Under the proposed plan, workers would be able to invest up to 4 percent of their Social Security payroll taxes in stocks and bonds to augment their retirement savings account. In conjunction with the private accounts, guaranteed benefits for future retirees would be reduced over the long-term by basing the initial benefit on inflation. Assurances have been made that benefits to existing retirees and workers currently over fifty-five would not be affected by the restructuring, but the thirty-six-million members of the American Association of Retired Persons (AARP) are not convinced. Their position is this: putting the responsibility of preparing for retirement in the hands of the individual is too risky. Stock market investment may see higher returns than government instruments, but they are obviously prone to drastic fluctuations, potentially allowing a lower guaranteed retirement benefit that won't come close to the cost of living. Indeed, projections for workers born in this decade (2000-2010) estimate their Social Security benefit will be 21.7 percent of their income in their first year of retirement. (Under the current system, they would receive nearly 40 percent).[282] Proponents of the plan believe it reflects the reality that fewer workers are contributing to Social Security than will be collecting from it, an imbalance that will increase significantly as the aging labor force begins to retire; and that trillions of dollars will be saved in payout benefits over the next three to five decades. Little has been said about the estimated two- to three-trillion dollars it will cost to change the current system, which according to various analysts is expected to be tapped out sometime between 2042 and 2052.

USA, Inc.

Those concerned about entrusting their future financial security to the stock market-even the relatively small annual amount proposed by the new private account plan-may have good reason. The past several decades have borne witness to unprecedented corporate mismanagement and malfeasance that has evaporated the life savings, pension plans, and livelihoods of many people. The pursuit of wealth has become a cult, and corporate America is the place of worship. Takeovers, mergers, and inflated balance sheets are simply demonstrated zeal among the faithful. Charismatic oracles that they are, market analysts, traders, and CEOs have spared no effort in promising vast rewards and predicting futures (in every sense) to induct potential investors into their particular sect of the corporate church. The problem is that the prospect of success-and excess-is so intoxicating that many enter the church and walk directly into temptation, offering their ethics at the altar.

Countless high profile financial scandals have filled the business pages in recent years: insider trading; securities fraud; accounting irregularities; price-fixing; obstruction of justice; anti-trust activities; some of the country's most highly regarded companies and executives have been caught with their hands in the world's biggest till, demonstrating the adage that "absolute power corrupts absolutely." Despite a crackdown on so-called white-collar crime that has only recently resulted in serious consequences, the elite of the business community (and their disciples) continue to demonstrate "lapses in judgment" (read: fraud, theft, and unfair business practices).

One of the largest corporate failures in history, Enron Corporation has become this generation's synonym for fraud and capital abuse. After its sudden bankruptcy filing in December 2001, a deluge of major corporations and banking institutions were exposed for similar illegal activities; the fallout may continue for decades. Before Enron's fall, the giant Houston-based energy trading and communications company was lauded as "America's Most Innovative Company" for five consecutive years; it reached number seven on the Fortune 500 list, employing 21,000 people all over the world. Its collapse and virtual overnight loss of $63 billion in stock market value prompted investigations by the Securities Exchange Commission (SEC), the Federal Energy Regulatory Commission (FERC), and the Senate. In simple terms, investigators determined that between 1992 and 2001, Enron executives, with the help of Wall Street, had set up twenty-six offshore "shell" companies in the form of energy trade deals to siphon financing to the mother company. What was essentially nine and one-half billion dollars in loans from Citigroup, JP Morgan Chase, and other banks, was made to look like fluid cash flow, rather than debt, to appease investors.[283]

It was also discovered that Enron traders openly discussed manipulating California's energy market during the 2000-01 power crisis in that state: traders were caught on tape plotting to take generating units offline to boost energy prices. A class action suit for unfair business practices was filed on behalf of California consumers against Enron. Meanwhile, as management was taking home millions of dollars in salaries and bonuses, employees were contributing to their pension plans-and Enron was matching- via company shares. When the share price plunged from nearly ninety dollars to thirty cents, thousands of people lost their retirement savings along with their jobs. This number does not include the tens of thousands of Americans whose state pension funds were heavily invested in Enron. Another allegation made against the company was the bribery of foreign governments to receive contracts to build pipelines and power plants.

Founder and former Kenneth Lay was the thirtieth person indicted in the scandal; Lay turned himself in to FBI in July 2004, but pleaded not guilty to eleven criminal counts including wire and securities fraud. The SEC has charged him with insider trading, alleging Lay made $90 million from Enron stock, which they want returned.[284] Lay, a former friend of President Bush who contributed millions to his 2000 election campaign, has repeatedly said, "I have done nothing wrong." Lay stated that he trusted his senior managers when they told him everything was fine, despite a concerned memo from vice-president Sherron Watkins regarding suspicious accounting practices. Lay exercised his Fifth Amendment rights during Congressional hearings in February 2002, refusing to incriminate himself. Ten of those senior managers, including CFO Andrew Fastow, have since pleaded guilty to various charges. In January 2004, Fastow was given a ten-year prison term; he agreed to forfeit $23.8 million in cash and property and cooperate with prosecutors. Former treasurer Ben Glisan was sentenced to five years in December 2003. Two other top executives, former CEO Jeffrey Skilling and chief accounting officer Richard Causey, have pleaded not guilty to dozens of counts of insider trading, conspiracy, fraud, and lying to auditors and investors. (As of this writing, trial dates for Lay, Skilling, and Causey had not been set.)

In July 2004, the company received court approval to emerge from its bankruptcy, which according to the Texas Attorney General's office has generated more than $665 million in fees for lawyers, accountants, and examiners. Under a reorganization plan, more than twenty thousand creditors will receive $12 billion from asset sales and stock in one of three new companies.[285]

Ashes from the Enron fallout fell heavily across the U.S. business community. Arthur Andersen LLP was the largest of the Big Five international accounting firms and was charged with obstruction of justice in the Enron scandal. David Duncan, a partner and the lead auditor in the affair, was accused of shredding two tons of documents and altering electronic correspondence. The company as an entity received five years' probation, a $500,000 fine, and lost its U.S. auditing license. Duncan was fired and pleaded guilty to the obstruction of justice charge. Because Arthur Andersen had been in this kind of trouble before, having been fined millions of dollars (but never admitting to any wrongdoing) for destroying documents during investigations of Sunbeam, Waste Management, and Asia Pulp and Paper, the court opted to impose the maximum penalty in this case, which was appealed. The Supreme Court overturned the lower court's ruling, and Duncan withdrew his guilty plea. Following Enron, the firm was implicated in investigations of several other companies including Qwest Communications, Global Crossing, Peregrine Software, and WorldCom.[286]

WorldCom, the giant telecommunications company that collapsed in 2002 and is now known at MCI, vies with Enron for the dubious title of the largest corporate fraud in U.S. history. Founder Bernard Ebbers resigned as CEO two months before the company filed bankruptcy causing shareholders to lose $11 billion. Ebbers was tried and convicted in March 2005 for his role in overstating company profits in its last year of operation by $3.9 billion dollars: specifically he was found guilty of fraud, conspiracy, and making false filings to the SEC. Among other improper practices, WorldCom allegedly gave more than $400 million in off-the-books loans to Ebbers to underwrite the inflated prices he paid for company shares. Since the WorldCom collapse, Ebbers has denied any criminal intent or wrongdoing, instead blaming former CFO Scott Sullivan of rampant book-cooking. Sullivan pleaded guilty to several fraud charges and later testified against Ebbers, claiming his boss pressured him and other corporate officers to doctor the numbers. Ebbers, who faces eighty-five years in prison but is likely to receive much less, is to be sentenced in June 2005. A preliminary settlement was reached in January of 2004 in a class action lawsuit by investors; ten former WorldCom directors agreed to pay back $54 million, $18 million from their own pockets-20 percent of their combined net worth-and the rest from directors' liability insurance. The settlement sets a precedent for holding non-executive directors accountable for the failure of the boards on which they sit.[287] It also may affect the ability of large corporations to attract board members: the WorldCom directors were paid an annual salary of $36,000 plus $1,000 per meeting-remuneration considerably less than the executives who bilked the company-and personally lost $250 million in stock value when

Jeff Shiring

the company collapsed.[288]

For its involvement with both WorldCom and Enron, Citigroup has agreed to pay $9.3 billion in settlements with investors. The financial services conglomerate has set aside $2.65 billion for claims against WorldCom and $6.7 billion for potential Enron suits, although the after-tax cost to the company is roughly half of the total (or equal to Citigroup's profit in one quarter).[289] Citigroup and one of its top market analysts, Jack Grubman of Salomon Smith Barney, have been investigated for several transgressions, including conflict of interest for recommending stock in questionable companies in exchange for investment banking business from those firms. Grubman, who allegedly earned $67.5 million between 1999 and August 2000, was fined $15 million and barred for life from the U.S. securities industry in December 2002.[290]

Merrill Lynch was also slapped with a hefty fine for the similar dubious research practices of its market analysts; they advised investors to buy stock in worthless companies in expectation of trading bonuses. The investment firm settled with New York State Attorney General Eliot Spitzer in 2002, agreeing to pay one hundred million dollars and sever all links between analyst's earnings and investment banking income.

Time Warner is the another one of the latest mega-companies to settle securities fraud charges. They agreed in December of 2004 to pay $210 million to the U.S. government and a compensation fund for civil suits arising from allegations that AOL gave money to small internet companies to buy advertising space on AOL's website, thus artificially inflating that company's revenues in order to look good to investors. Time Warner, which merged with AOL in 2001, also agreed to pay a $300 million penalty to the SEC for other AOL accounting irregularities. If all the terms are reached, Time Warner will be able to reissue stock and renew its bid for the cable company, Adelphia Communications.[291]

Adelphia has had its own problems, including defaulting on $7 billion worth of loans in 2002, which sent the company into bankruptcy protection. Three members of the Rigas family, who founded the company, were charged with hiding a $2.3 billion debt from investors. John Rigas and his two sons collected an estimated $3.1 billion from the company for personal use and were sued by the company for breach of fiduciary duties. Rigas and his son Timothy were found guilty of fifteen counts of securities fraud, conspiracy, and bank fraud. Former chief of operations, Michael Rigas, was acquitted, and a mistrial was called when the jury couldn't reach a verdict in his trial in July 2004.[292]

Another mistrial was called in the proceedings against former Tyco International CEO Dennis Kozlowski and his financial chief Mark Swartz, in March 2004, after a juror received a threatening and coercive letter. The two executives were charged with dozens of counts of securities fraud, conspiracy, grand larceny, and falsifying business records; they stand accused of looting the company of $600 million. Kozlowski faces separate charges of tax evasion for not paying sales tax on $13 million worth of artwork he purchased.[293] Jury selection for a retrial began January 18. A former director of Tyco, Frank Walsh, has been sued for taking an unauthorized finder's fee of $20 million.

Still another former top executive has recently walked after a mistrial was declared in early January 2005 in the trial of Walter Forbes, former chairman of the Cendant Corporation. Forbes and his former vice chairman, Kirk Shelton, were charged with conspiracy, mail fraud, securities fraud, and wire fraud for inflating revenues of Cendant's predecessor, CUC International, artificially driving up Cendant's stock price. Revelation of the fraud in 1998 caused Cendant's value to drop by fourteen billion dollars in one day. Shelton was convicted on twelve counts. Forbes allegedly sold eleven million dollars in Cendant stocks a few weeks before the "accounting irregularities" came to light.[294] Cendant's assets include Ramada, Howard Johnson, Coldwell Banker, Avis, and Century 21; it was created by the merger of CUC International and HFS Inc. in 1997. Although Forbes resigned from the company in 1998, taking $35 million in cash and $12.5 million in stock options with him, Cendant by-laws have forced the company to pay his legal fees that were running $1 million a month. (The company could have sued to recover the money if Forbes had been convicted.)[295]

The list of major companies involved in flagrant financial scandals goes on seemingly forever. Xerox falsified results from 1997 to 2000, overstating its profits by $1.5 billion. Without admitting wrongdoing, in 2002 the company agreed to pay a $10 million fine and restate its financials for the five-year period. Qwest Communications International admitted that it incorrectly accounted for $1.6 billion in sales. Dynegy, CMS Energy, El Paso, and several other Texas energy companies have been accused of overstating revenue by falsely counting simultaneous buy-and-sell energy trades.

ImClone Systems, the biotechnology company whose CEO, Sam Waksal, was convicted of insider trading and sentenced to seven years in prison in 2003, was at the heart of several subsequent investigations, including the trading practices of Martha Stewart and Merrill Lynch. In October 2004, Stewart, who consistently denied doing anything illegal, began serving a five-month prison sentence for lying to investigators about her sale of four thousand ImClone shares in December 2001, just one day before the FDA denied approval for an ImClone drug, sending share prices into the tank. Upon her release in March 2005, Stewart served another five months of house arrest. Her former stockbroker, Peter Bocanovic, received the same punishment; both are appealing their convictions.

Computer Associates, the fourth-largest software maker in the world, agreed to pay $225 million to shareholders to defer criminal prosecution for a company-wide accounting scheme; the scheme resulted in fraud and obstruction of justice charges against former CEO Sanjay Kumar, former Head of Worldwide Sales Stephen Richards, and several other top company executives. In 2000-01, the company falsely claimed $2.2 billion in premature earnings on their financial statements. In 1998, the company's top three executives-founder Charles Wang, Russell Artz, and Kumar-allegedly divided a $1.1 billion bonus.[296]

Microsoft has been found guilty of violating U.S. and European anti-trust laws for maintaining a monopoly on various software technologies within its Windows operating system, which runs on 90 percent of personal computers worldwide. In March 2004, the European Union fined Microsoft $613 million for "abusively wielding its Windows software monopoly." Microsoft, which earned $32 billion in 2003, has appealed the ruling.[297] In April, the software giant reached a settlement with Sun Microsystems, agreeing to pay Sun $700 million for anti-trust issues and $900 million for patent disputes over a ten-year period. In November, Microsoft settled with rival company Novell for $536 million over claims involving Novell's NetWare operating system. In May 2003, the company paid $750 million to Time Warner in an agreement that included a deal to cooperate on software distribution and digital media.[298]

The Royal Dutch/Shell Group, the world's third largest oil company, was also determined by U.S. and British regulators to have knowingly overstated its oil and gas reserves for years, leading to a $150 million fine by the SEC in 2004 for misleading investors. CEO Jeroen Van der Veer claims to have known about the failures in finding reserves but not about the accounting maneuvers used to cover them up. In January 2004, the company agreed to recategorize its reserve filings and removed from its books 4.47 billion barrels of oil, or about 23 percent of the total.[299]

Conrad Black, former CEO of Hollinger International, is the latest corporate magnate to come under investigation by the SEC and U.S. federal prosecutors. Black resigned his positions as CEO and Chairman of Hollinger in early 2004, when allegations were made that he and his right-hand man, David Radler, received more than seven million dollars in unauthorized company payments. The SEC filed civil fraud lawsuits in November 2004 against Black, Radler, and Hollinger Inc.; the U.S. government announced a criminal investigation in March 2005.

Clearly the culture of business is one of unrestrained greed: countless corporations are driven by the desire to make (or at least show) unrealistically high profits to please shareholders and fatten executive bank accounts. It would seem the level of talent required to reach the highest echelons of commerce would mean all those MBAs and CAs would be smart enough to know insider trading rules and securities laws and avoid breaking them. Rather, it is that very knowledge that leads corner office occupants to believe they will not get caught; or because everyone else is doing it, then it is accepted practice. Management and board directors either willfully engage in, or turn a blind eye to, double-jointed accounting acrobatics that somehow became as standard as the generally accepted accounting principles (GAAP). When the tightrope broke and the safety net tore, the balancing act was over, and billions of dollars of investment, savings, and retirement funds plunged straight into the "gaap." The result of the colossal injury has been a deep public cynicism of Wall Street and its players.

Cleaning House

The Enron debacle and its ripple effects led Congress to take action to reform security laws and restore investor confidence in the markets. In 2002, the Sarbanes-Oxley Act was passed, establishing new and heightened standards for the corporate governance of all U.S. public company boards, management, and public accounting firms. The most recent, stiffer penalties handed out to companies and their masterminds are a direct result of the Sarbanes-Oxley Act; it has given the SEC a broader mandate and a larger budget for investigations both in the U.S. and abroad. Because the SEC has jurisdiction over any public company that lists their shares or bonds in the U.S., it has taken civil action against several foreign companies such as Parmalat SpA (charging that the Italian dairy company inflated its assets by nearly five billion dollars); Mexico's TV Azteca SA (insider trading); France's Vivendi Universal SA (misleading investors about corporate finances); and the Netherlands and Great Britain's Royal Dutch-Shell Group (overstating energy reserves). The multi-million dollar settlements, when collected, are returned to investors by the commission.

While the SEC has improved its policing of the domestic and securities markets, it has been criticized for not doing enough-i.e., not pursuing "market-timing" and late-trading practices-and for being too slow to act. In late 2003, the commission announced a new office of risk assessment designed to provide an early warning of market problems; this was only after congressional hearings into how it handled and failed to anticipate the mutual fund scandal.[300] Some observers believe that the SEC, which regulates securities, is caught up in a power struggle with the Federal Reserve, which oversees banking; and this occasional overlap of authority interferes with effective action. Others complain that the SEC relies heavily on the industry to police itself through compliance departments that are supposed to regulate their own activities (and frequently don't). Also, because the law allows companies to reach settlements and agree to structural changes without admitting guilt, investors often have difficulty trying to win redress against brokers in arbitration cases.[301]

New York State Attorney General Eliot Spitzer has bared sharper legal teeth in his single-minded crusade to clean up the corporate cesspool on Wall Street. Since his election to the top law enforcement position in the state in 1998, Spitzer has taken on the giants of commercial industry. In 2002, Spitzer's attack on the fraudulent stock research of the major investment banks forced them to overhaul their practices and shell out $1.4 billion in settlements.[302] The following year he targeted the mutual fund industry for the practice of late trading; favored clients could make lucrative trades that were not available to the average investor. Fund managers were letting hedge funds, or unregulated investment pools, buy and sell shares in mutual funds and flip them at a rate far more frequent than the average investor, allowing them to profit from out-of-date prices. Since the scandal began, dozens of class action lawsuits have been filed against mutual fund companies for improper trading activities, such as paying brokerage firms to be on a preferred list (which the brokers sell from); not disclosing excessive brokerage fees; failure to pay investors required discounts on sales commissions; and charging double loads.[303] One high profile target was Strong Financial Corporation, whose founder, Richard Strong, was handed a lifetime ban from the industry.

Spitzer has also shaken up the insurance industry, accusing large firms such as Marsh & McLennan of price-rigging, setting up artificial bids, and paying contingency commissions to brokers (who earned extra fees for sending business to particular insurance companies). Marsh & McLennan CEO Jeffrey Greenberg resigned under pressure in October 2004.

In late 2003, Spitzer filed dozens of lawsuits, along with Microsoft, against spam marketing companies for sending millions of fraudulent emails. While most of the suits are still pending, Spitzer settled with the so-called spam king Scott Richter and his Colorado-based company OptInRealBig.com in July 2004 for fifty thousand dollars, considerably less than the twenty million dollars initially sought. Spitzer imposed conditions to ensure that Richter meets industry standards, but he failed to prove that the company directly violated the federal CAN-SPAM (Controlling the Assault of Non-Solicited Pornography and Marketing) Act. Microsoft has been more successful in its litigation on the West coast; it won approximately fifty-four million dollars in settlements with various companies, including four million dollars from California-based Pointcom Inc., for using MSN and Hotmail addresses to send bogus spam mail. Microsoft has its own suit pending against Richter's organization.[304] Despite the CAN-SPAM regulations introduced in 2003 and dozens of anti-spam software programs available to consumers, it is very difficult to trace, find, and prosecute spammers, although the process may get easier after the landmark felony conviction of spammer Jeremy Jaynes in November 2004. The Virginia man faces up to nine years in prison for illegal distribution of junk e-mail.[305]

Conflicting Interests

Despite the apparent crackdown on corporate misbehavior, corporations and financial firms are still gambling with investors' dollars; investors continue to trust the markets to provide them with a comfortable retirement cushion. Government involvement is no guarantee of corporate integrity. A case in point is Fannie Mae, the nation's largest mortgage financing company, which is chartered by the federal government and, along with its rival Freddie Mac, owns or guarantees approximately half the mortgages in the U.S. (about $3.8 trillion in mortgages).[306] In October 2004, federal prosecutors, as well as the SEC, began investigating Fannie Mae after a report was issued by the Office of Federal Housing Enterprise Oversight accusing the company of violating accounting rules. This included deferring $200 million in expenses in 1998 in order to ensure earnings targets and hefty executive bonuses. When it directed Fannie Mae to reissue financial statements from 2001, the company said compliance would show a loss of $9 billion in reported profits. OFHEO was alerted to the irregular accounting practices by whistle-blower Roger Barnes, an accountant with Fannie Mae. CEO Franklin Raines and CFO Timothy Howard were both fired in December 2004, along with auditing firm KPMG. Raines is reported to have cashed in $7 million in stock over a period of eighteen months.[307] His "golden parachute" is supposed to be another $8.7 million in deferred compensation, plus $1.3 million a year for life. Howard, who owns at least $5.5 million in company shares, is supposed to receive more than $36,000 a month for life.[308] The severance packages are being looked at by investigators. A default by the corporation could mean a massive bailout by the government; consequently, regulators and shareholders are concerned about the viability of Fannie Mae. They should also be outraged that two people overseeing a $9 billion mistake are to be rewarded so extravagantly for their services.

Another quasi-public entity, the New York Stock Exchange, has been forced to see the errors of its ways after the retirement-pay scandal of former chairman Dick Grasso in September 2003. Under the terms of his contract, Grasso was able to cash in his retirement savings prior to his actual retirement; however, when it became public that the amount was roughly $140 million, the public outcry was so loud that Grasso was forced to resign. After resigning, he claimed he was owed an additional $48 million under the terms of a 2003 contract renewal. Despite the fact that the NYSE board approved Grasso's annual salary of $1.4 million, as well as perks that amounted to a combined salary of $80.7 million between 1999 and 2002 (almost the total net income of the exchange for that period), board members cried foul and asked the SEC to file suit against Grasso to return up to $100 million.[309] (Interestingly, SEC chairman, William Donaldson, is Grasso's predecessor at the exchange.) New York State Attorney General Eliot Spitzer also sued Grasso under the state's Not-for-Profit Corporation Law, which states that executive pay for nonprofit companies should be "reasonable" and "commensurate with

Jeff Shiring

services provided." Spitzer has argued that Grasso's Incentive Compensation Plan, Long-term Incentive Plan, Capital Accumulation Plan, Supplemental Executive Retirement Plan, and Supplemental Executive Savings Plan, all awarded above and beyond his salary, are totally unreasonable.

Grasso has defended himself by saying his remuneration was on par with top banking executives in the private sector, an argument that hasn't washed with many in the industry, primarily because Grasso was not only the head of a nonprofit corporation, but he was also a market regulator. (To compare, Grasso allegedly made $30,550,000 in 2001 in salary and incentives; Alan Greenspan, head of the Federal Reserve and one of the most influential people in the world, took home $171,900 that year.)[310] That position put Grasso firmly in the conflict-of-interest seat when it became clear that the board members who approved his pay were also banking officials from companies registered on the exchange. Whether or not he did so, it would appear that Grasso was able to use his influence to solve those firms' regulatory problems in exchange for compensation approval. As a result, Kenneth Langone, the former head of the committee that approved Grasso's package, has also been sued by Spitzer.

Corporate governance at the NYSE has been overhauled since Grasso's departure, most significantly by no longer selecting board members from institutions regulated by the exchange, but problems have continued. More than $35 million in legal bills have accrued over the past two years in efforts to recoup the bulk of Grasso's platinum parachute, and it has put the exchange in debt; it may cost more to recover the funds even if they win the suit.[311]

Private companies that do business with the government are not immune to impropriety either, but the ramifications for politicians are somewhat more significant. Since stepping down from his position as CEO of Halliburton Corporation to run in the 2000 election, Vice President Dick Cheney has remained firmly in the political hot seat. Halliburton and its subsidiary KBR (formerly known as Kellogg, Brown and Root) are one of the Pentagon's prime contractors and have made billions from the wars in Afghanistan and Iraq: Halliburton's prime contracts with the military increased from $483 million in 2002 to $3.9 billion in fiscal year 2003.[312] Meanwhile, Mr. Cheney continues to collect up to $1 million a year in deferred compensation from the company.[313] While that money is probably his severance package that Cheney opted to receive in installments (rather than pay income tax on the lump sum), the close relationship between Cheney and Halliburton is troubling, particularly when billions of dollars in taxpayer's money is going to a contractor mired in controversy. In December 2003, Halliburton came under fire from the Defense Contract Audit Agency for refusing to turn over internal documents showing that the company knowingly overcharged $61 million for work done in Iraq by KBR.[314] KBR allegedly charged the military for hundred of meals in Iraq and Kuwait that were never served and over-charged millions of dollars for gasoline delivered for civilian use in Iraq. Halliburton, while defending its contractual obligations, set aside $141 million to settle the meal issue after the DCAA recommended withhold-ing $159 million in payments to the company.[315] Other examples of profligate spending and outright fraud include millions spent on mono-grammed towels for the KBR health club in Kuwait, vehicles for contrac-tors leased at $7,500 a month, and $6.3 million in kickbacks to two for-mer workers in Kuwait.

Halliburton is not the only company who gorged on the $209 billion pie served to defense contractors in the 2003 fiscal year. The Pentagon's "Big Three" contractors, Lockheed Martin, Boeing, and Northrop Grumman, split $50 billion that year. Michelle Ciarrocca, a Senior Research Associate with the World Policy Institute, analyzed the rapid increase in military contracts and apparent war profiteering by U.S. com-panies. "To put this in perspective, Lockheed Martin's Pentagon awards, at $21.9 billion, are greater in value than the entire budget for the feder-al government's single largest welfare program-Temporary Assistance for Needy Families-which is meant to keep several million single parents and dependent children out of poverty."[316]

Northrop Grumman was slated to receive an even larger chunk of the $368.2 billion defense budget for the fiscal year 2004, despite its own lin-gering controversies. In a case that has been pending for years, the gov-ernment is seeking $369 million in damages from the company that allegedly overcharged for equipment sold to the Defense Department in the 1980s. In June 2003, the company paid $111.2 million to settle a suit alleging that a subsidiary, TRW, overcharged on government space projects in the 1990s. The same month, Vinnell Corporation, another subsidiary of Northrop Grumman (NG), was awarded a $48 million one-year contract to train troops in the Iraqi army. The company did such a poor job-more than half of the first battalion deserted after six months-that the Jordanian Army was called in to help with the effort.[317] Nonetheless, Northrop Grumman, together with Raytheon, received a missile defense system contract from the government in 2003 worth a potential $10 billion.

NG has been a significant political donor in recent years, contributing $3.8 million to federal campaign coffers since 1998 and spending nearly $7 million on defense contract lobbying efforts in 2000 alone.[318] At least seven former officials, shareholders, or paid consultants held positions in the Bush administration in 2003, including Secretary of the Air Force James Roche (former head of an NG department); Deputy Secretary of Defense Paul Wolfowitz (former NG consultant); and the former Administrator of NASA Sean O'Keefe (former NG Advisory Board member).

In addition to Dick Cheney and the Northrop Grumman team, there are several highly placed individuals in the Bush administration with what could (and should) be viewed as conflicting positions in the private sector. Transportation Secretary Norman Mineta, for example, was a senior vice president for Lockheed Martin from 1995-2000, and his major campaign contributors included Lockheed, Boeing, and the American Trucking Associations. Mineta continues to hold more than 18,000 stock options in Lockheed. Mineta's Deputy Secretary until January 2004, Michael P. Jackson, was a chief operating officer at Lockheed, and prior to that he was a vice president with the American Trucking Associations.[319] Jackson moved from the cabinet to sit on the President's Commission on Implementation of United States Space Exploration Policy, chaired by former Air Force Secretary Pete Aldridge, a Lockheed Martin board member. As Lockheed has received billions of dollars from the U.S. government in contracts and stands to win even more through space contracts, the contact web is rather unseemly. National Security Advisor Stephen Hadley has also been allied with Lockheed; he was a partner in the legal firm Shea and Gardner, which represents both Lockheed and Boeing, before joining the Bush administration in 2001.

Boeing rounds out the top three with its own Pentagon scandal: in 2001, Boeing won a $23.5 billion tanker-leasing deal after top air force acquisition official Darlene Druyun was promised an executive position with Boeing and a salary of $250,000 a year during the contract negotiations. Boeing CEO Philip Condit was forced to resign in December 2003 over the scandal.[320] Druyun pleaded guilty to criminal conspiracy and received a nine-month prison sentence. Former CFO Michael Sears pleaded guilty to illegally negotiating employment in November 2004. The contract has since been cancelled.

The Bush Administration itself treaded firmly on conflict-of-interest ground in early 2003, when the administration attempted to block a lawsuit investigating Dick Cheney's various meetings with energy industry executives (including Enron's Ken Lay) while forming the government's energy policy in 2001. To its credit, the U.S. Court of Appeals denied the White House any authority to intervene in the case, but the request itself raised alarming issues. For one, the National Energy Policy Development Group, which Cheney headed after taking office, was required by law to conduct public meetings and maintain publicly available records. Cheney repeatedly refused to release those records to Congress and litigants during investigations of the Enron affair, citing "executive privilege." Enron documents, however, have provided evidence that the company (and others) significantly influenced the task force's final report: seventeen policies sought by Enron, which clearly benefited the company and were included in a three-page "wish list" handed to Cheney by Ken Lay in April 2001, were included in the final report.[321]

The mutual back-scratching between the vice president and Enron was evident long before the energy fiasco. While Cheney was the head of Halliburton, its subsidiary (now KBR) built the sports stadium formerly known as Enron Field in Houston; it is well-known that Enron contributed significantly to the Bush-Cheney campaign. Halliburton's pervasive influence on Capitol Hill goes beyond Cheney: former Attorney General John Ashcroft also received campaign dollars from Enron; former Army Secretary Thomas White was an Enron executive; current Trade Representative, Ambassador Robert Zoellick, served on Enron's advisory council.[322]

Many corporate watch-dog groups have expressed concern about the revolving door policy of business and government: executives move into political positions to "serve" the public interest; politicians and bureaucrats retire from public life into high-paying industry jobs with an impressive list of contacts clutching the public purse. Complaints by industry outsiders that contract deals are based on who you know are not mere jealous whining. Billions of taxpayers' dollars have gone to sole-source contractors, such as Halliburton, without any bidding process whatsoever. The result of this cronyism is a lack of accountability and an unconscionable waste of money.

The mismanagement of resources in the war in Iraq is a devastating example of this. In the first half of 2004, nearly half of the $5 billion in reconstruction funds disbursed by the U.S.-led Coalition Provisional Authority could not be accounted for when the United Nations commissioned an audit. A large chunk of that money-$1.4 billion-was deposited in a bank in northern Iraq, but no one knows what happened to it. Another $1 billion was spent on large and small contracts (many non-bid, sole-source) for which there were no records, purchase orders, or receipts filed. Some of the money was given to Iraq's Ministry of Finance, which kept two sets of books and did not reconcile. The $5 billion came from the $20 billion Development Fund for Iraq, conceived by the United Nations in 2003, a combination of Iraqi oil revenue and international aid.[323] That money is completely separate from the $18.1 billion the U.S. government set aside in 2003 for reconstruction efforts during and after the war; only 1.3 billion had been spent as of October 2004. An independent report by the Canadian Security Intelligence Service estimates that 15-30 percent of disbursements in Iraq have been eaten up by fraud, corruption, and mismanagement, stating "no U.S. government source attempts to estimate the exact amount of money that has been lost to these causes."[324] The primary sources of the CSIS report were audits by the Office of Inspector General of the Coalition Provisional Authority and KPMG, commissioned by the United Nations to find out where the money was being mismanaged. The Pentagon was in no hurry to tally up the numbers, especially prior to the 2004 election. Inexplicably, the voting public was either unaware of the scale of fiscal ineptitude and mismanagement in Iraq, or they didn't care.

Global Consequences

Wasting another country's money while occupying it is enough to outrage the foreign community, if not the domestic population, but the U.S. government has been an international economic bully for decades. Volumes of literature have explored the subject in far greater depth than the scope of this book allows; however, some of the recent evidence is worth mentioning here, such as the November 2004 ruling against the U.S. by the World Trade Organization. The WTO, on behalf of Canada, the European Union, Brazil, Mexico, South Korea, India, Japan, and Chile was asked to impose sanctions against the U.S. for continuing to operate under the Byrd Amendment. That legislation, passed in 2000 to protect the American steel industry and ruled illegal by the WTO two years later, allows the U.S. to impose duties on imported products sold at below-market prices; a portion of these are then given to competing U.S. companies. The penalties imposed on disputed U.S. exports could amount to more than $150 million a year.[325] Although the Bush administration has promised to comply with the ruling, Congress has been unwilling to repeal the Byrd Amendment, which other countries feel is unfairly protectionist; even American interest groups consider it unpopular. The Consuming Industries Trade Action Coalition, which represents manufacturers, farmers, retailers, and other businesses, has called the legislation "the equivalent of a tax on American consumers."[326]

At the same time that Washington is crying foul about foreign exporters "dumping" onto American markets, we continue to do exactly the same thing with our agricultural commodities to other countries. A February 2004 analysis by The Institute for Agriculture and Trade Policy (IATP) found the U.S. is the worst offender for exporting food commodities at prices below their production costs: in 2002, for example, wheat was exported at 43 percent below the cost of production.[327] The artificially low prices cripple farmers abroad because they can't compete in the world market, giving rise to a cycle of poverty and insecurity in the developing world, where agriculture is often the primary industry. In a poignant editorial that appeared in the New York Times in December 2003, links between current U.S. trade policies and global poverty were addressed. "The World Bank estimates that an end to trade-distorting farm subsidies and tariffs could expand global wealth by as much as a half-trillion dollars and lift 150 million people out of poverty by 2015."[328]

For all its Republican bluster about the virtues of free trade, the government is unwilling to act on its principles. Instead of competing fairly in an open global market, and after repeatedly calling for an end to trade-distorting policies in other countries, Bush signed the Farm Security and Rural Investment Act in 2002. The legislation increased taxpayer spending on agriculture by more than 80 percent over the 1996 farm bill. The increased subsidies will likely produce even greater gluts of agricultural commodities that will be dumped on foreign markets; destroying even more farming livelihoods in developing countries for the benefit of wealthy American agribusiness. One example of how this works is in cotton production: cotton subsidies protect American producers from decreases in world market prices, but at the same time the subsidies encourage them to continue producing. The surplus is then dumped into the world market, further depressing the price and threatening foreign farmers who do not have any subsidy protection. New subsidies mean that the average U.S. cotton farmer (whose average net worth is $800,000) will get half their money from the government, although just twenty-five thousand of the nation's two million farmers grow cotton. This practice ends up costing African countries $250 million a year. [329] Clearly the interests of the few-need we be reminded that those few in the bread basket states are a significant part of President Bush's voting base-take precedence in Washington.

We are not practicing what we preach, politically or fiscally. The hypocrisy of the U.S. wielding the principles of free trade and democracy as a sword in the "fight against tyranny" around the world is stunning. Even more stunning is the announcement that the president, exercising his traditional privilege of nominating the head of the World Bank, has chosen his Deputy Secretary of Defense Paul Wolfowitz for the post, despite initial concerns from our European counterparts. While Wolfowitz is widely regarded as a brilliant man, with over twenty-four years of political experience under six presidents, he is also credited with being the architect of the war in Iraq as well as forming the present administration's policy of establishing "a new order" whereby America is supreme.[330]

The reality is we use our economic might to enforce our actions both at home and abroad. At some point, the effects of our economic policies in the world trade arena, as well as on Wall Street, are going to have disastrous repercussions. The International Monetary Fund has warned us that uncontrolled deficits threaten the entire global economy, not to mention our own, which some analysts predict is teetering on the brink of a disaster the scale of the Depression. Peter Schiff, CEO and chief global strategist of Euro Pacific Capital, has warned that ballooning consumer debt and the current real estate bubble are all about to pop. Trade and current account deficits are 6 percent of gross domestic product. The dollar has lost a third of its value against the euro in the past two years.[331] We are spending and consuming more than we are producing. We are saving less than ever and accumulating huge debt. Huge companies such as United Airlines, are failing, and average Americans are paying the price, through losses on the stock exchange as well as lost jobs and pensions (and increased tax allocations when government agencies assume responsibility for part of those pensions).

Americans are even losing their lives because of federal policies; those governing the Food and Drug Administration prevent that agency from successfully monitoring the effects of new drugs on the public. In the early fall of 2004 the discovery that the arthritis drug Vioxx doubled the risk of heart attacks in patients drew attention to the fact that the FDA has limited resources to track drug safety. In 1992 an agreement with the drug industry guaranteed that pharmaceutical companies would pay millions of dollars-$200 million in 2003-to the FDA in exchange for increasing the number of new drug reviews.[332] The result has been a drastic shift of FDA resources toward approving new drugs at the expense of tracking the safety of existing drugs on the market. This has also caused the sticky situation of requiring the FDA to reexamine the safety of drugs it had already approved.

Meanwhile, no one takes responsibility. Accountability is the new mantra, but it is still far from becoming the norm. Most of the corporate wrongdoers mentioned in this chapter have yet to serve any jail time, even for convictions up to three years ago. Sentences are frequently deferred for months (or years) in return for cooperation with prosecutors. White collar criminals who are removed from their positions either make a lateral career shift to another company or industry or invest their enormous buyouts, ensuring they never have to swing through the corporate jungle again.

So where do we go? I submit that the free-market system that underpins our society is essentially right and good. The ebb and flow of supply and demand are as dependable and continuous as the tides. Competition is absolutely necessary for the benefit of the consumer, and ultimately the producer; but I do believe the system needs significant further checks and balances to correct the current abuses and gross lack of accountability. The flagrant exploitation of the system by a minority of ethically-challenged executives and politicians has had a stunning impact on the lives of millions of people; that should not be allowed to happen. In a *Newsweek* article about the Grasso scandal, Allan Sloan wrote, "The whole drama-or farce-is a classic example of how powerful people can rationalize anything, bending or rewriting rules to fit the game they want to play."[333] That comment is absolutely true of corporate America. Those in positions of power and influence have a duty-moral and fiduciary-to engender and uphold the public trust by following the rules, particularly when they are holding someone else's purse. When they breach that trust, they should be held strictly and immediately accountable with both criminal and monetary penalties. Agencies like the SEC and Government Accountability Office have the right mandate, but they do not always have the resources or the power to enforce their directives in a meaningful way to deter similar future behavior.

Most of us-not on the Forbes 400 list-have lost a great deal since the late 1990s, not least of which has been our faith in the fabled "American Dream." But that dream had become based on false assumptions: "money for nothing"; "everybody else is doing it, so why can't we?"; and "the lights are always on in Las Vegas." Since when are we entitled to incentives above and beyond our salaries? Isn't getting paid to do a job incentive enough to perform? The reality is that the system is built on choices. Capitalism at its finest requires all participants to make informed decisions and act when it benefits them. Consumers and investors cannot make those informed decisions when insider trading is a standard market practice. The electorate cannot make informed decisions when the media is controlled by the same companies that are having lunch with lawmakers and then expensing the bill (or shredding it). There is no free lunch!

The evolution of our capitalist system most assuredly reflects Keynes' views rather than Smith's idealism. More than half a century ago, Keynes stated, "Capitalism, wisely managed, can probably be made more efficient for attaining economic ends than any alternative yet in sight, but that in itself is in many ways extremely objectionable." He also said, "The difficulty lies, not in the new ideas, but in escaping the old ones, which ramify, for those brought up as most of us have been, into every corner of our minds." As we look forward and consider the governance of our capital, political and social systems, we need to be cognizant of that social and intellectual development of which Keynes speaks. The old ideas have caused us to evolve in a way that predisposes us to rationalize twisting and bending our underlying values of integrity, industry, and fair play toward the pursuit of material accumulation, consumption, and gratification. The resulting hump has left us stooped and crooked. It is time to ask ourselves, "When is enough, enough?"

---

[268] "Tweens: A Billion Dollar Market.," *CBSNews.com*, December 15, 2004. Website: , www.http://www.cbsnews.com/stories/2004/12/14/60II/printable660978.shtml.   Retrieve(retrieved Feb. 1, 2005).

[269] David Armstrong, David and Peter Newcomb (eds.), editors,. "The 400 Richest Americans.s," *Forbes.com*, Sept. 24, 2004. Website: http://www.http://www.forbes.com/lists/forbes400/2004/09/22/rl04land.html. Retrieve(retrieved Jan. 19, 2005).

[270] www.http://www.conference-board.org/economics/consumerconfidence.cfm.   (retrieved Dec. 17, 2004).

[271] http://money.cnn.com/2005/01/12/news/economy/trade_balance/index.htm. Retrieve(retrieved Jan. 12, 2005).

[272] Glenn Somerville, Glenn. "Cutting US Budget Deficit a Top Priority.," *Reuters.com*, Nov. 17, 2004. Website: ,

www.http://www.reuters.com/financeNewsArticle.jhtml?type=bondsNews&stor yID=6837601. Retrieve(retrieved Dec. 10, 2004).

273 Martin Crutsinger, Martin. "IMF Says U.S. Deficits Threaten World Finance.," *APaol.com*, April 15, 2004., Website: http://aolsvc.news.aol.com/news/article.adp?id=20040415002609990004&_mp c=news% percent2e...

274 Martin Crutsinger, Martin. "Greenspan Says the Bill for Soaring Deficits Will Come.," *APaol.com*, May 6, 2004, . Website: http://aolsvc.news.aol.com/news/article.adp?id=20040506121309990018&_mp c=news% percent2e6

275 "Bush Signs Debt Limit Hike.," *CBS News.com*, Nov. 19, 2004. Website: , www.http://www.cbsnews.com/stories/2004/11/20/politics/printable656797.shtml. Retrieve(retrieved Dec. 9, 2004).

276 Bureau of Labor Statistics:, *The Employment Situation-—December 2004*. Website: , www.http://www.bls.gov/news.release/empsit.nr0.htm. Retrieve(retrieved Dec. 18, 2004).

277 www.http://www.census.gov/Press-Release/www/releases/archives/income_wealth/002484.html. Retrieve(retrieved Dec. 18, 2004).

278 Genaro C. Armas, Genaro C. "Fewer Low-Iincome Families are Buying Homes.," *APaol.com*, May 18, 2004. Website: , http://aolsvc.news.aol.com/business/aricle.adp?id=20040518100909990002&_ccc=5. Retrieve(retrieved May 18, 2004).

279 Administrative Office of the U.S. Courts, *"Bankruptcy Filings Down in Fiscal Year 2004.,"* Administrative Office of the U.S. Courts. Dec. 3, 2004. Website: , www.http://www.uscourts.gov/Press-Releases/fy04bk.pdf. Retrieve(retrieved Jan. 5, 2005).

280 Amey Stone, Amey. "Tapping Your 401(k) with Plastic.," *Business Week online*, Nov. 3, 2004. Website: , http://pf.channel.aol.com/bw/credit/401kcreditcard. Retrieve(retrieved Dec. 9, 2004).

281 Peter Grier, Peter. "Social Security's Battle Over Values.," *Christian Science Monitor* (on-line), , Jan. 12, 2005. Website: , www.http://www.csmonitor.com/2005/0112/p01s03-uspo.html.

282 Tami Luhby, Tami. "Bush Privatization Plan.," *Newsday.com*, Jan. 12, 2005. Website: , www.http://www.newsday.com/business/ny-bzsoc094112233jan12,0,3522643.story?coll=ny-business-headlines.

283 Edward Iwata, Edward. "Did Banks Play Role in Enron sScandal?" *USA Today*, Money Ssection, July 23, 2002.

284 "Enron's Kenneth Lay Pleads Not Guilty on 11 Counts.," *CBC News Online*, July 11, 2004.

285 Kristen Hays, Kristen. "Enron Re-emerges.," Associated Press.

Rreprinted in The *Chronicle-Herald*, Halifax, N.S., July 16, 2004, sec. C, p. 3.

286 Tom Fowler, Tom and Mary Flood,. "Arthur Andersen gGet the Maximum Sentence." *Houston Chronicle.com*, Oct. 16, 2002. Website: , www.http://www.chron.com/cs/CDA.story.hts/topstory2/1619985. Retrieve(retrieved Jan. 12, 2005).

287 "WorldCom Directors to Pay Millions.," *CBC News Online*, Jan. 6, 2005. Website: , www.http://www.cbc.ca/story/business/national/2005/01/06/world-com.050106.html. Retrieve(retrieved Jan. 6, 2005).

288 "Recent Settlements Will Likely Affect Future Outside Director Negotiations.," *Fulcrum Financial Inquiry*, January, 2005. Website: , http://www.http://www.fulcruminquiry.com/article75.htm. Retrieve(retrieved Feb. 15, 2005).

289 "Citigroup Could Pay More Than $9B US to Settle Tech Cases.," *CBC News Online*, May 10, 2004. Website: , www.http://www.cbc.ca/story/business/national/2004/05/10/citigroup040510.html. Retrieve(retrieved Jan. 6, 2005).

290 Kenneth Lambert, Kenneth. "Salomon Smith Barney: Worst Offender, Top Fine.," *AP, USA Today.com*, April 29, 2003. Website: , http://www.http://www.usatoday.com/money/industries/brokerage/2003-04-28-ssb_x.htm. Retrieve(retrieved Jan. 12, 2005).

291 David Lieberman, David and Jayne O'Donnell,. "Time Warner to pPay $510 mMillion.," *USA Today.com*, Dec. 16, 2004. Website: , http://www.http://www.usatoday.com/money/media/2004-12-15-time-warner-settlement_x.htm. Retrieve(retrieved Jan. 13, 2005).

292 "Mistrial in Case Against Adelphia's Michael Rigas.," *CBC News Online*, July 11, 2004.

293 Associated Press, "Tyco Judge Declares Mistrial." *AP, MSNBC News*, April 2, 2004. Website: , http://msnbc.msn.com/id/4638162. Retrieve(retrieved Jan. 12, 2005).

294 Associated Press, "Jury Convicts Ex-Cendant eExec of fFraud.," *AP, MSANBC News*, Jan. 5, 2005. Website: , http://www.http://www.msnbc.msn.com/id/6789153. Retrieve(retrieved Jan. 13, 2005).

295 Gretchen Morgenson, Gretchen. "Before There Was Enron, There Was Cendant.," *NY Times.com*, May 9, 2004. Website: , www.http://www.nytimes.com/2004/05/09/business/yourmoney/09watch.html?ex=1084766400&en.

296 Frank Eltman, Frank. "Former CA CEO Kumar Indicted.," *AP, Information Week*, Sept. 22, 2004. Website: , http://informationweek.com/story/showArticle.jhtml?articleID=47901105. Retrieve(retrieved Jan. 14, 2005).

297 Paul Geitner, Paul. "EU Hits Microsoft With Record Fine.," *AP, AOL Business News*, March 24, 2004.

298 Dawn Kawamoto, Dawn and Matt Hines,. "Microsoft to Pay Novell $356 Million Settlement,." *CNET News.com*, Nov. 8 2004. Website: , http://news.com.com/Microsoft+to+pay+Novell+$536+million+settlement/2100-1014_3-5442389.html. Retrieve(retrieved Jan. 12, 2005).

299 Chip Cummins, Chip and Almar Latour,. "Changing Drill: How Shell's Move to Revamp Culture Ended in Scandal.," *The Wall Street Journal*, Nov. 2, 2004. Website: , http://www.http://www.globalpolicy.org/socecon/crisis/corporate/2004/1102shell.pdf. Retrieve(retrieved Jan. 14, 2005).

300 "SEC Outlines Fund Reforms.," *CNN/Money*, Nov. 18, 2003. Website: , http://money.cnn.com/2003/11/18/funds/fundsfire_donaldson. Retrieve(retrieved Jan. 15, 2005).

301 Charles Gasparino., Charles. "The Street's Dark Side.," *Newsweek*, December 20, 2004, pp.40-42.

302 Weston Kosova, Weston. "Keeping a Close Eye on Wall Street.," *Newsweek*, Dec. 29/Jan. 3, 2004 issue. Website: , www.http://www.msnbc.msn.com/id/3770497/site/newsweek. Retrieve(retrieved Jan. 13, 2005).

303 Jane Bryant Quinn, Jane. "Fighting the Fund Cheats.," *Newsweek*, December 8, 2003, pp. 44-45.

304 *Advertising@manatt Newsletter*, Volume II, Issue 30, July 26, 2004. Website: , www.http://www.manatt.com/shownewsletter.asp?ID=1077&Type=AdvertisingLaw@manatt. Retrieve(retrieved Jan. 13, 2005).

305 Associated Press, "Convicted Spammer's Bail Set at $1 Million.," AP, Nov. 9, 2004. Website: , http://abcnews.go.com/Business/wireStory?id=237996&CMP=OTC-RSSFeeds0312. Retrieve(retrieved Jan. 14, 2005).

306 Robert J. Samuelson, Robert J. "The Trouble with Fannie.," *Newsweek*, January 10, 2005, p. 49.

307 Greg Farrell, Greg. "Fannie's fFacing a Criminal Probe.," *USA Today*, Oct. 1, 2004, sec. B, p. 1B.

308 Virginia Citrano, Virginia. "Raines: Fannie Mae Ex-CEO Could Get $1.3 Million Yearly For Life.," *Forbes.com*, Dec. 28, 2004. Website: , http://www.http://www.forbes.com/work/2004/12/28/1228autofacescan01.html?partner=rss. Retrieve(retrieved Jan. 15, 2005).

309 "The People's Lawyer Strikes Again.," *Economist.com*, May 26, 2004. Website: , www.http://www.economist.com/agenda/displayStory.cfm?story_id=2704015. Retrieve(retrieved Jan. 18, 2005).

310 "Comparing NYSE Dick Grasso's Compensation.," *About.com*, Website:

http://www.http://www.mutualfunds.about.com/cs/investmentfraud/l/blgrasso.ht
m. Retrieve(retrieved Jan. 18, 2005).

[311] Charles Gasparino, Charles. "Paying for Grasso Again.," *Newsweek*,
December 20, 2004, p. 42.

[312] "Contractors Are Cashing in on the wWar on tTerror.," *World Policy
Institute*, February 24, 2004. Website: , www.http://www.corpwatch.org/arti-
cle.php?id_10110. Retrieve(retrieved Jan. 16, 2005).

[313] Pratap Chatterjee, Pratap. "Halliburton Makes a Killing on Iraq War.,"
World Policy Institute, March 20, 2003. Website: , www.http://www.corp-
watch.org/article.php?=id=6008. Retrieve(retrieved Jan. 16, 2005).

[314] Reuters, "Report Says Halliburton is Stonewalling.," *Reuters, AOL News*,
Dec. 19, 2003. Website: ,
http://aolsvc.news.aol.com/news/article.adp?id=20031219053509990012&_mp
c=news% percent2e.

[315] Matt Kelley, Matt. "Pentagon to Withhold Millions from Halliburton.," *AP,
AOL Business News*, May 18, 2004. Website: , http://aolsvc.news.aol.com/busi-
ness/article.adp?id=20040312032709990005&_ccc=4.

[316] Ibid. www.corpwatch.org/article.php?id=10110.

[317] Dean Calbreath, Dean. "Iraqi Army, Police Fall Short on tTraining.," *The
San Diego Union Tribune*, July 4, 2004. Website: ,
http://www.http://www.signonsandiego.com/uniontrib/20040704/news_mz1b4ir
aqi.html. Retrieve(retrieved Jan. 16, 2005).

[318] Frida Berrigan, Frida. "Northrup Grumman: 'Defining the Future' or
Profiting from War?" *Economists Allied for Arms Reduction Newsletter*,
November 2003. Website: , http://ecaar.org/Newsletter/Nov03/berrigan.htm.
Retrieve(retrieved Jan. 16, 2005).

[319] Sherrie Gossett, Sherrie. "Corruption in High Places.," *Accuracy in
Media*, Nov. 24, 2004. Website: ,
www.http://www.aim.org/media_monitor/A2157_0_2_0_C. Retrieve(retrieved
Jan. 17, 2004).

[320] Charles Pope, Charles. "Guilty pPlea in Boeing Hiring Scandal.," *The
Seattle Post-Intelligencer*, Nov. 16, 2004. Website: ,
http://seattlepi.nwsource.com/business/199821_sears16.html.
Retrieve(retrieved Jan. 17, 2005).

[321] John Nichols, John. "Enron: What Dick Cheney Knew.," *The Nation*,
April 15, 2002. Website: ,
www.http://www.thenation.com/doc.mhtml?i=20020415&s=nichols.
Retrieve(retrieved Jan. 19, 2005).

[322] Ibid. (Nichols).

[323] Bryan Bender, Bryan. "Iraq Audit Can't Find Billions.," The Boston
Globe, Oct. 16, 2004. Website: ,

www.http://www.boston.com/news/nation/articles/2004/10/16/iraq_audit_can't_ find_billions?mode=PF. Retrieve(retrieved Jan. 17, 2005).

324 Canadian Security Intelligence Service, *Progress or Peril? Measuring Iraq's Reconstruction*. Canadian Security Intelligence Service, Post-Conflict Reconstruction Project Report, October 2004. Website: , www.http://www.csis.org/isp/pcr/iraq_funds.pdf. Retrieve(retrieved Jan. 17, 2005).

325 "U.S. Trade Law Draws WTO Sanctions.," *CBC News Online*, Nov. 26, 2004,. Retrieve(retrieved Nov. 28, 2004).

326 Leigh Strope, Leigh. "WTO Approve Sanctions on U.S. Imports.," *AP, AOL News*, Nov. 27, 2004.

327 The Institute for Agriculture and Trade Policy, "Widespread Ag Dumping From US Food Companies Continues, New Analysis Finds.," press release, The Institute for Agriculture and Trade Policy, Feb. 10, 2004. Website: , http://www.http://www.iatp.org/iatp/library/admin/uploadedfiles/Widespread_A g_Dumping_From_US_Food_Companies_C.pdf. Retrieve(retrieved Jan. 17, 2005).

328 "The Unkept Promise.," Editorial, *New York Times*, *editorial*, December 30, 2003. Website: , http://www.http://www.mindfully.org/WTO/2003/Harvesting-Poverty-Editorial-NYT30dec03.htm. Retrieve(retrieved Dec. 31, 2004).

329 Anuradha Mittal, Anuradha. "Giving Away the Farm: the 2002 Farm Bill.," *Food First Backgrounder*, Ssummer 2002, Vol. 8, No. 3, . Website: http://www.http://www.foodfirst.org/pubs/backgrdrs/2002/s02v8n3.html. Retrieve(retrieved Jan. 17, 2005).

330 "A sSheep in Wolf's cClothing?" The Sunday Times, rReprinted in The the Chronicle *Herald*, Halifax, NS, Canada, March 20, 2005, secp. A, p. 11.

331 Dan Ackman, Dan. "Doom for the Dollar—and Everything Else.," *Forbes.com*, Jan. 14, 2005. Website: , http://pf.channel.aol.com/forbes/invest-ing/doomdollar.adp. Retrieve(retrieved Jan. 17, 2005).

332 Gardiner Harris, Gardiner. "Critics Question FDA's Coziness with Drug Companies.," *The New York Times*, Nov. 18, 2004. Website: , http://aolsvc.news.aol.com/news/article.adp?id=20041118084309990001&_mp c=news% percent2 ...Retrieve(retrieved December 9, 2004).

333 Allan Sloan, Allan. "Here's the Real Grasso Scandal.," *Newsweek*, September 29, 2003 issue. Website: , http://msnbc.msn.com/id/3068760. (rRetrieved Jan. 18, 2005).

5. High on Democracy

Public confidence in the integrity of the Government is indispensable to faith in democracy: and when we lose faith in the system, we have lost faith in everything we fight and spend for.

-Adlai Stevenson (1990-1965)

Confidence. Integrity. Faith in the system. Mr. Stevenson adroitly captured all of the themes of this discourse in his observation about one of the most important influences on our society. America is the bastion of democracy, founded on the principle of "government of the people, by the people, for the people." Honest Abe's famous words have succinctly described our Constitution, our judicial and electoral systems, and have been the model for political reform around the world. In theory, as equal citizens we all have a voice in determining our government; we are all builders of the structure of our nation. In practical terms, however, we have managed to construct a castle in the sky. Our democratic government has become a millionaire's club: access is granted only to the well-heeled corporate and social elite. Membership requirements are a personal or corporate agenda, unstinting campaign contributions, and a sense of entitlement.

Why have we lost faith in democracy? One explanation may be that Americans are suffering from an epidemic of CFS, or campaign fatigue syndrome. CFS, like many disorders, is manifested differently in different individuals. Symptoms may include damage to illusions accompanied by political apathy and severe faith-loss. Affliction in others is characterized by vivid political pigmentation (typically red or blue), extreme mood swings, myopia, and feverish outbursts of hostility. It is triggered by a virus that invades the White House halfway through every four-year term of office and is spread via press secretaries, media outlets, campaign buses, and fundraising dinners. Carriers quickly deteriorate through exposure to public mud-slinging, false promises, misrepresented facts, and the dispersal of fortunes. The effects of national pain and suffering are chronic and debilitating; recovery is slow. Few treatments are currently available, although experimental therapies are being tested (not at the FDA). Complete elimination of hypocrisy and abuse of power, as well

Jeff Shiring

as a steady diet of responsibility, is recommended.

This facetious analogy is just an example of the cynicism surrounding our so-called democracy. While not new, it has become pervasive among many moderate Americans and has eclipsed the much discussed polarization of political camps in this country.

Two-Party System

One of the primary reasons for this state of affairs is the evolution of our two-party political system; one that allows a 3 percent margin of victory to be considered a broad mandate for the winning side. In the 2004 presidential election, 60.7 percent of eligible voters exercised their right to vote (sadly a modern day record). President Bush earned 50.8 percent of those votes, winning him a second term in office based on the support of less than a third of the voting population (31.7 percent). Seventy-eight million people opted not to participate in the process; this was more than either candidate received in votes and is indicative that the phrase "government of the people" is an ideal reserved for rhetoric rather than reality.

By its very nature, our electoral system is based on a "winner take all" format, rather than proportional representation as in many comparable democracies. Instead of a situation where a group with 25 percent of votes gets 25 percent of seats, our "first past the post" system effectively eliminates smaller parties, as well as broad debate on the issues. Alternative voices are given neither credibility nor broadcast, because third-party candidates and their supporters who challenge the status quo are considered fringe spoilers; they are criticized for taking votes from the mainstream parties. Another factor that alienates potential voters from taking part in the election process is that it has become a highly dramatized ratings war of Red vs. Blue, a clash of the tycoons pitching "radical liberals" against "dangerous conservatives." Moderate voters who find themselves outside the divide in no man's land end up voting for the lesser of two perceived evils, rather than for a government they trust will operate for the greater good. There is also the adversarial nature of "us" versus "them" within Congress; it leads to more posturing than the achieveent of real change or progressive legislation that would benefit the country as a whole. The deafening roar of partisan battles being waged in Washington eclipses the true purpose of politicians: to solve the problems of the governed majority.

Image has become more important than ideas in the political arena; personality is pitched as being more presidential than honesty, integrity, and service to the country. The two-party popularity contest lends itself to focusing on how well the leaders deliver a speech, rather than their office track records or the broader party policies they represent. Finally, in a two-party system there is always a risk the opposition will fail to garner enough power to ensure balanced decision making and maintain at least some political equilibrium. The result is a government susceptible to hegemony.

Some may consider labeling the current administration as hegemony somewhat extremist. Indeed, although the current Republican administration has a majority in the House and the Senate, the Democrats maintain respectable numbers (202 Democrat Representatives to 232 Republicans; 44 Democrat Senators to 55 Republicans; with one Independent in each house). Hegemony is the control or dominating influence of one person or group over others; by that definition, it is not much of a stretch to apply the term to our current government. While the disadvantages of the two-party system have been evolving over decades, not just since the 2000 election, our existing administration offers multiple examples of why our system of democracy does the American people a disservice.

President Bush has made no secret of his desire to spend his political capital to bring the government in line with his personal beliefs, even when that agenda conflicts not only with party policy but with the majority will of the people he is governing. In a Time magazine article about the 2004 Republican Convention, the seat of power in Washington is described as a CEO White House run with a mission to restore constitutional authority-that is, unchecked power-to the presidency. The writers point out that Bush and Cheney have felt justified in bypassing Congress to draft energy policy in secret, create military tribunals by executive order, withhold budget figures about Medicare reform costs, and misrepresent the costs of the war on terrorism.[334] While many Republicans balked at these unilateral decisions from the President's office, they were expected to toe the line or be considered an enemy (like the Democrats) or even far worse-labeled as "unpatriotic." Perhaps not quite: Senate minority leader Harry Reid might argue there is no enemy so detested as a Democrat. He, like his predecessor Tom Daschle, has been the subject of a smear campaign by the Republican National Committee. The RNC circulated a document to approximately one million people-donors, party activists, and reporters-labeling Reid an obstructionist for doing his job (that is, not automatically bowing to the will of the White House).[335] Such action not only belies the calls from President Bush for bipartisanship, but it demonstrates the bald agenda of the government to stifle democratic debate. The smear campaigns exist on both sides of the partisan divide; for every partisan attack, valid or invalid, there is usually an equally charged counterattack. Back and forth we go, until Americans do not know who or what to believe.

Another example of this "prime directive" of the GOP is the micromanagement of public events involving members of the West Wing. There have been dozens of instances of speeches and debates being controlled to the extent that they might well have been closed Hollywood sets. When

Condoleeza Rice spoke at the elite Sciences Politiques in Paris in early February of 2005, only a fraction of the student body was allowed near the auditorium and questions were vetted in advance by the State Department and the school. Prior to the 2004 election, "Ask President Bush" campaign sessions were held around the country; voters had to take written pledges of support before they were allowed in, and there were town hall debates where undecided voters were not allowed to ask questions at all.[336]

The Democratic Party is not without sin in the realm of spin either, particularly in their collusion with the tightly controlled presidential debates. Taking over the task from the nonpartisan League of Women Voters, the Commission on Presidential Debates (CPD) was formed by the Republican and Democratic parties in 1986 to legitimize their self-imposed rule that third-party candidates with less than a 15 percent average of support at five national polls could be excluded. (As such, the CPD is actually a bipartisan organization rather than a nonpartisan one.) Despite its stated mission to "provide the best possible information to viewers and listeners," the CPD virtually ensures that televised debates are open only to the two major parties. Ross Perot's appearance in 1992 is the only notable and recent exception to this shameful practice.

National Public Radio reported on the debate format in September of 2004. Before participating, the Kerry and Bush campaign teams agreed to a thirty-two-page contract itemizing every possible detail of the debates, including minutiae such as the size of dressing rooms and permitted camera angles. While supposedly a debate, the CPD format does not allow one candidate to question the other; there are no rebuttals or follow-up questions, and extended discussion of an issue cannot exceed thirty seconds. The contract makes it illegal for the candidates to debate each other anywhere else during the campaign. It also details rules for the audience, which must include 100 to 150 self-declared "soft supporters" of each candidate who must watch in immobile silence. The CPD is corporately funded by major campaign contributors who also sponsor the debates; the co-chairs are corporate lobbyists. With those vested interests, it is not surprising that in the 2000 debates between Bush and Al Gore, not a single mention was made of child poverty, homelessness, NAFTA, corporate crime, or the drug war.[337]

The lack of true debates on the issues during presidential campaigns underscores the partisan nature of our two-party system and why it makes difficult, if not impossible, for the government to come together for constructive problem solving. This country has been facing the same social problems for decades: most pressing are a lack of accessible and affordable health care and insurance for millions of Americans and the inability to provide quality public education to children across the nation. President Bush inadvertently highlighted another chronic social and economic problem when he spoke to a closed meeting of African Americans in January 2005. While pushing his Social Security privatization plan, the president said, "African-American males die sooner than other males do, which means the system is inherently unfair to a certain group of people."[338] The problem for African-Americans is not Social Security, it's the fact that they die sooner than other racial groups! Why haven't successive government administrations adequately addressed the life-expectancy gap over the last decades?

The paradox is, while Republican and Democratic lawmakers are quite often paralyzed in their decision-making tug-of-war, it is easier to yank one team across the line in times of crisis than to haul on a rope gripped by multiple political fists. After the terrorist attacks of September 11, 2001, the Bush administration managed to pass the U.S. Patriot Act with lightning speed (forty-five days) and virtually no discussion in the House. The unprecedented powers given to the FBI (to trample civil liberties) have since prompted significant debate, but at the time, it was accepted by both parties under the banner of national security. Sections of the Act remove the expectation of privacy at all levels from all Americans: the FBI can search and survey your home without a warrant; seize property; access your bank, credit, and medical records; trace your library loans, book purchases, and Internet habits; listen to your phone and coffee shop conversations; and they don't have to let you know it has happened. They have the power to violate your First Amendment rights by arresting and detaining you indefinitely without probable cause or a warrant; they can do this without telling anyone, simply by labeling you a terrorist suspect. Acts of civil disobedience can also result in the loss of U.S. citizenship (or deportation in the case of non-native-born Americans). The opposition did not oppose; they did not even blink. To block passage of the Patriot Act, or seriously debate it, would have invited the dreaded brand of anti-American. The White House capitalized on that fear and took giant steps toward their goal of expanding constitutional authority.

Invoking the term "national security" has become the preferred way for the administration to achieve its goals. When there is criticism over decisions related to the war on terrorism (and/or Iraq), the administration waves the patriotism flag. If you don't support the war, you don't support the troops, and that makes you un-American. An article that appeared in the *Houston Chronicle* a few days before the 2004 election emphasized just how much the public can be manipulated by the government's use of fear. The American Civil Liberties Union signed an agreement with the government promising not to hire and in return, to fire anyone who was on an official watch list of suspected supporters of terrorism; this could include anyone who ever gave money to a humanitarian organization alleged to support a terrorist group or anyone with the same name as someone who had donated. (Ironically, ACLU Executive Director Anthony

Romero found himself on that list, as did Senator Edward Kennedy and Georgia congressman John Lewis.)

The ACLU signed this agreement as a condition of being part of a program that would allow federal employees to make charitable donations to nonprofit organizations through payroll deductions. When the *Chronicle* exposed the story, the ACLU retracted its promise, and Romero told NPR that as many as two thousand nonprofits receiving money through the same program were expected to sign the same agreement. Essentially the government asked private employers to police individuals with "suspicious associations" by firing them because the Bill of Rights prevents the government from going after them without solid evidence. Employers are not bound by such constraints.[339] The article cited an example of an Alabama woman who was fired by her boss for sporting a Kerry-Edwards bumper sticker on her car, while her boss distributed pro-Bush fliers around the office. Fear on a national level evidently trickles down to fear in the workplace, and democratic rights get washed down the drain either way. Tom Ridge inadvertently emphasized this fact when he stepped down from his post as Secretary of Homeland Security on November 30, 2004, saying, "We don't do politics in the Department of Homeland Security."[340]

As Americans, we make much of our democratic freedoms, and no one has made more use of the word freedom than President Bush himself. In his second inaugural address, he used the words "freedom" and "liberty" more than forty times in twenty minutes; but democratic rights and freedoms are not necessarily guaranteed-they belong to some and not to others in this country. For example, former felons who have served their sentences-five million Americans-are not allowed to vote. According to the U.S. Commission on Civil Rights, 13 percent of African-American males are disenfranchised because of a felony conviction. The commission has also reported on minority voters being deterred from casting ballots because they are asked to produce a driver's license at the polling stations. They are mistakenly (either inadvertently or deliberately) turned away by poll workers, even though by law photo identification is not required for voting unless one is a first time voter who registered by mail. In a 2004 report, the commission said that in the 2000 election in Florida, where President Bush won by 537 votes, black voters were ten times more likely than non-black voters to have their ballots rejected, and many were prevented from voting because their names were "erroneously" taken off the registration lists.[341]

The recent foreign policy push to spread freedom and democracy around the world gives rise to skepticism in many quarters considering the fragility of freedoms here at home. The double-standard of decrying human rights abuses in China, Russia, and the Middle East is difficult to swallow while foreign nationals, particularly Arabs and Muslims, are subject to military tribunals, detention, and torture (and more than two dozen suspicious deaths) by American hands. Many observers decried the president's nomination of Alberto Gonzales to replace John Ashcroft in the post of Attorney General. Before eventually accepting the nomination, the Senate Confirmation Committee objected to Gonzales. While he served as White House counsel, he wrote several memos that seemingly advocated tactics labeled "torture" under the Geneva Convention as acceptable methods of interrogation for U.S. authorities to use on alleged terrorists and prisoners of war. Senator Patrick Leahy was particularly vocal in his disapproval of Gonzales' involvement in drafting numerous policies that "have tarnished our country's moral leadership in the world and put American soldiers and American citizens at risk."[342] Gonzales also wrote the Presidential Order authorizing military tribunals to try terrorist suspects, a move decried by rights advocates as completely antithetical to both the Geneva Convention and the U.S. Constitution. [Note: A recent ruling by a federal judge extended the right of detainees at the U.S. Naval Base in Guantanamo Bay to challenge their confinement in U.S. courts, overturning previous decisions. The current government tribunals to determine if prisoners are "enemy combatants" were deemed unconstitutional.[343]]

The double standard is applied whenever it is convenient to do so. President Bush welcomed "my friend Vladimir Putin" to Camp David in September 2003, publicly stating, "I respect President Putin's vision for Russia: a country at peace within its borders, with its neighbors, a country in which democracy and freedom and the rule of law thrive."[344] The fact that Russia has been cited by the U.S. Agency for International Development for shutting down independent media, rigging elections, and committing atrocities in Chechnya is apparently irrelevant so long as Putin supports Bush's war on terrorism. Also irrelevant is Russia's development of a new nuclear missile, a weapon which is not "and will not be possessed by other nuclear powers."[345] As long as the public reason for such weaponry is "defense from international terrorism," then all is forgiven. The same acquiescence is not extended to North Korea, Iran, or Syria.

Essentially, the phrase "you're either with us or you're against us" is meant not only for other sovereign nations but also for Americans here at home. The two-party system encourages this line of thinking, and it is not only alienating but destructive. If you don't agree with all the policies of the president or the methods used to put those policies in place, then you must be a left-winger. If you do, you are a right-winger. There is no room for compromise or even respect for the other side. This attitude pits neighbors and family members against each other, promotes intolerance, and chokes the life force out of democracy. It moves the rights and interests of individual citizens into the hands of entities that benefit from a two-sided, rather than a multi-sided, power struggle.

Campaign Spending

It is fair to say that those entities are almost entirely corporate, not surprisingly, since it is very difficult to get elected to national office without very deep pockets. Wealth and politics have gone hand-in-hand since the U.S. was still a colony: individuals running for public office had to pay their own way before the advent of political parties, so naturally socially prominent and well-to-do family names typically gravitated toward the seat of power. With the formation of parties, financial power for political purpose increased exponentially, drawing even more of the wealthy into the affairs of state, either to increase personal fortunes or to heighten social status. Many U.S. presidents have been millionaires (in 2004 dollars) including George Washington, Thomas Jefferson, Theodore Roosevelt, Herbert Hoover, Franklin Delano Roosevelt, John F. Kennedy, Lyndon Johnson, and both Presidents Bush.[346] The 2004 election campaign was notable for slating possibly the richest candidates in history. John Kerry is reported to hold four trusts worth between $430,000 and $2.1 million in his own right, while his wife's income on her $500 million inherited fortune was $5 million in 2003.[347] Kerry's running mate, John Edwards, has a net worth of between $12 and $60 million according to financial disclosure statements as reported by Forbes. The magazine estimated Dick Cheney's fortune at $50 million and President Bush's at $15 million, based on his sale of the Texas Rangers.[348]

The presidential campaign itself was the most expensive in history: more than $1 billion dollars was spent. As their party nominees, each candidate received $74.6 million in public funds to conduct the election, and although they were entitled to government matching funds during the primaries, both declined to avoid federal spending caps. Democrats spent $250 million on advertising alone from March 2004 until Election Day; the Republicans spent $240 million.[349]

The 2002 Bipartisan Campaign Reform Act, designed to prevent political parties from collecting money directly from corporations and unions, simply shifted the source of political contributions to interest groups that are allowed to raise unlimited amounts of "soft" money to support candidates (i.e., through issue advocacy, voter mobilization, etc.). While corporations and unions are not allowed to directly contribute to the candidates' campaigns, they are allowed to donate to the 527 groups and political action committees (PACs). As long as the PAC is registered with the Federal Elections Commission, it can solicit contributions by individual company owners, employees, or union members to advocate the election or defeat of a candidate. Contributions can then be made directly to candidates or parties in the name of the PAC. (Consequently, there is a Microsoft PAC, a Teamsters PAC, a National Rifle Association PAC, and so on.) In total, 527 groups raised more than $400 million for the 2004 election.[350] They spent almost half ($192.4 million) on advertising for or against one of the candidates.[351] The 2004 Democratic National Convention alone cost $150 million; one-third of that money went toward security. The Republicans paid an estimated $166 million for their convention. Another $40 million was shelled out for the 2005 inauguration festivities; $20 million came from private donations and the other $20 million covered security for President Bush. While there was significant public disapproval over the extravagance of the event-in light of the ongoing insurgency in Iraq and the tsunami devastation that occurred less than three weeks earlier-one writer pointed out that the 1997 inauguration of Bill Clinton cost $42 million at the time (which is roughly $49.5 million in 2004 dollars when adjusted for inflation.)[352] Then again, President Clinton was not fighting a war.

Al Gore, during his campaign for the presidency in 2000, blamed the structure of the two-party system and campaign funding rules for his own questionable conduct in the days leading up to the 1996 election. He came under fire after the 1996 campaign for making fundraising calls from the White House (a forbidden practice) even though he said he paid for the calls with a private credit card. Gore also attended a 1996 fundraising luncheon at a Buddhist temple in California that was later determined to be an illegal campaign donation scheme. Democratic fundraiser, Maria Hsia, was convicted in 2000 of illegally diverting more than $100,000 in contributions, including donations through the temple, to the Clinton-Gore '96 Democratic National Committee. The FBI investigated Gore's involvement in 1997 and asked then-Attorney General Janet Reno to appoint independent counsel. Reno found no grounds for pursuing the case and closed it. In September 2002, the FEC imposed $719,000 in fines against the DNC, the Clinton-Gore campaign, the Buddhist temple, and several individuals and corporations for having made illegal contributions. When repeatedly asked about his actions by PBS news anchor Jim Lehrer in a March 2000 interview, Gore replied, "Well, I've acknowledged my mistakes and the...the '96 campaign saw both political parties pressing the limits and I think that it demonstrated the pressures that all campaigns in the current system and the need for change."[353] Gore famously claimed in a press conference that there was "no controlling legal authority" that had found him guilty of breaking any laws.

Regardless of campaign finance reform, it still costs millions to run for higher public office, and many hopefuls end up sinking their own money into the endeavor. Twenty-one House and Senate candidates in the 2004 election spent more than one million dollars of their personal funds and lost at the polls.[354] Just 2 percent of American households make more than $200,000 a year, effectively eliminating the possibility of ever running for president for all but the smallest sliver of the populace. This fact is acceptable to the voting public. We trust that the more privileged among our citizenry will assume their civic duty and work for the betterment of the "have nots." Perhaps this is an honest motivation in the hearts of some politicians, but it would be naïve to think that the primary interests of Washington extend far beyond the boardrooms of the nation.

Consider this: one-third of President Bush's top fundraisers for the 2000 election (or their spouses) were given political appointments in the first administration, including three who became cabinet secretaries: Don Evans at Commerce, Elaine Chao at Labor and Tom Ridge at Homeland Security.[355] Whether or not the appointments reflected the stellar qualifications of the recipients is beside the point in the eyes of the public: clearly their fundraising finesse earned them the President's eye and ear. Apparently it is standard practice in Washington to reward the "$100K Club": Bill Clinton gave ambassadorships to five of his top contributors in his first year in office. Bush topped that with more than two dozen diplomatic appointments. In 2002, the White House approved $1.44 million in cash bonuses to 470 political appointees, reversing an eight-year ban on the practice introduced by the Clinton government. Many union workers were unimpressed, as the Bush administration initially fought the 4.1 percent pay increase approved by Congress for two million ordinary civilian federal employees.[356] Clearly, corporations, special interest entities, and individuals that contribute heavily to their preferred candidates and parties have a vested interest in policy-making: they paid for a seat at the table. This makes sense from one perspective: if I am buying the groceries, then I will decide the dinner menu. The problem is that these vested interests do not generally represent the public, which is the mandate for elected government. The voters cast their ballots for a candidate or a party, not truly knowing what game is being played or even what the rules of the game are.

There are those who throw out the rules altogether. In January 2005, it came to light through unsealed federal court documents that Hilary Clinton's finance director for her 2000 campaign filed false reports with the FEC. David Rosen has been indicted for allegedly understating contributions from and the costs for a fundraising gala for the Senator in order to have more money for her campaign. The Associated Press article that carried the story also reported that during President Clinton's administration, more than two dozen individuals and two corporations were charged by the Justice Department for fund-raising irregularities and abuses from the 1996 election.[357] A Center for Public Integrity analysis of FEC documents prior to the 2000 election showed that the FEC was backlogged by cases of campaign fraud and abuse by presidential candidates after the 1996 election, but that only one-quarter had been looked into. Al Gore was named in seventeen "Matters Under Review".[358] Prior to the passage of the Bipartisan Campaign Reform Act in 2002, the vague and contradictory campaign finance rules and loopholes made it commonplace for candidates in previous elections to break the rules by exceeding contribution limits and receiving contributions from illegal sources. The sheer volume of complaints-numbering in the thousands-and the limited resources of the FEC prevented most of them from ever being reviewed.

Government Transparency and Accountability
The lack of investigation into questionable behavior by politicians and government officials is preferred in Washington. According to various consumer and media groups, there has been a shift toward heightened secrecy and smokescreens in the federal government. One month after taking office in 2001, President Bush signed an executive order repealing the 1978 Presidential Records Act that allows all presidential papers to become historical public documents after twelve years. The order effectively blocked the release of 68,000 documents relating to his father's tenure as vice president under Ronald Reagan, as well as several members of his current administration. After a lawsuit was filed to by a watchdog group called Public Citizen to block implementation of the order, the administration released the documents in question. By invoking executive privilege, however, a former president, vice-president, or a member of their family can still indefinitely prohibit the release of information related to their term in office.[359] According to a report by Public Citizen who studied the trend toward secrecy, fourteen million new documents were stamped "secret" in 2003, a 60 percent increase from 2001, at a cost of $6.5 billion dollars.[360]

Many of our past and present elected officials have good reason to support keeping information about them under wraps, although ethical lapses and downright criminal behavior can apparently be overlooked by our forgetful electorate. Carol Moseley Braun ran for the 2004 Democratic presidential nomination despite a scandal involving her campaign manager (later her fiancé) during her 1992 bid for the Senate. Kgosie Matthews was variously accused of misappropriating campaign funds, violating immigration law, and sexually harassing members of Moseley Braun's staff. The Senator apparently did nothing to address any of the situations and reportedly took pains to cover them up. Matthews was paid a salary of $15,000 a month as campaign manager, and then an annual salary of $120,000 to develop strategies for reducing the campaign fund debt. (Moseley Braun's fundraising efforts totaled $7 million, but the fund was in debt $94,000 when Matthews resigned, nine months after he took over the debt management.) The couple was also widely criticized for an unauthorized trip to Nigeria in 1996, where they visited with the dictator Sani Abacha. Abacha was widely condemned for corruption and human rights abuses, including the execution of playwright Ken Saro-Wiwa and eight other activists who objected to the exploitation and destruction of the

Niger Delta by multinational oil companies. Moseley Braun herself was investigated by the Federal Elections Committee in 1993 after being unable to account for nearly $250,000 of campaign funds. The FEC found that she had failed to properly itemize and disclose thousands of dollars of expenditures, but formal charges were never filed. She was accused of failing to report $28,000 of income for her mother, who was a Medicaid nursing home patient at the time; she was forced to return $15,000 she had accepted as a gift; but despite all the controversy, President Clinton appointed her to the post of Ambassador to New Zealand and Samoa, where she served from 1999-2001.[361]

Former U.S. Representative Gary Condit is another high profile politician who managed to maintain his position in the House, despite serious questions regarding his involvement in the 2001 disappearance and homicide of twenty-four-year-old intern Chandra Levy. The Democratic Congressman from California served in Washington from 1989 until the end of his term in 2003, maintaining his seat throughout the Levy investigation. Despite his early denials, it was eventually discovered (and admitted) that Condit, a married father of two, had had a long-term affair with the intern. Although Condit was never an official suspect in Levy's death and passed a polygraph test, it was widely perceived that he withheld information regarding her disappearance.[362]

The Reverend Jesse Jackson, a Baptist minister, founder of the Rainbow/PUSH (People United to Serve Humanity) Coalition, and two-time presidential candidate, is another highly controversial political figure who continues to stand in the public eye. President Clinton's spiritual advisor throughout the Monica Lewinsky scandal, Jackson himself publicly admitted in 2001 to an extramarital relationship, which resulted in the birth of a child in 1999. Karin Stanford, the former head of the Washington, D.C. office for Rainbow/PUSH Coalition was paid $35,000 from the organization's funds as severance pay to move to Los Angeles with her daughter; she receives $3,000 a month in child support from Jackson personally.[363] Jackson's wife of more than forty years, Jacqueline, is the mother of their five children.

Jesse Jackson has also been accused of effectively blackmailing Anheuser Busch by organizing a boycott against the company in the early 1980s due to a dearth of distributorships owned by African-Americans. After an equal opportunity discrimination suit was filed on behalf of employees in 1997, Anheuser Busch contributed $500,000 dollars to the Rainbow/PUSH Coalition and set up a $10 million fund to help nonwhites buy distributorships. A year later, Jackson's sons, Yusef and Jonathan, purchased Budweiser's River North Distributorship for an undisclosed sum, and Jackson himself dropped his support of the boycott campaign.[364] Despite his transgressions and suspected ethical breaches, Jackson maintains relatively popular support.

In one of the more bizarre examples of politicians who can't seem to let go (and voters who inexplicably enable them), there is the story of James Traficant. The former U.S. Representative (D-Ohio) was expelled from the House by the ethics committee after being found guilty in 2002 of ten charges of bribery, racketeering and tax evasion. He is only the second member to be kicked out of Congress since the Civil War. (Gary Condit was the only member who voted to let Traficant keep his seat.) In a rare instance of reasonable punishment, Traficant was sentenced to eight years in prison and fined $150,000. That didn't seem to be an obstacle to campaigning for office again. Traficant ran as an independent for another term in the House from prison in 2002 and received 15 percent of the votes in Ohio.[365] In 2003, a group of individuals formed "Draft Traficant for President 2004" and received permission to campaign on his behalf. They filed a Statement of Candidacy with the FEC and set up a website, but they were unable to meet their funding goal and the effort was abandoned.[366]

Newt Gingrich is another politician who appears to have Teflon™ skin. During his tenure as Speaker of the House from 1995-1998, Gingrich was particularly vocal about and hostile to President Clinton over the Lewinsky affair, calling for his impeachment. Yet in 1997, he was reprimanded by the House and fined $300,000 for using tax-exempt foundations for political purposes and lying to the House ethics committee. His private life was no more moral or upstanding than the president's: the Republican congressman was found to have been having an extramarital affair with a staff clerk twenty-three years his junior during the Lewinsky scandal. He is also known for divorcing two wives while they suffered significant health problems.[367] There have been rumors in Washington that Gingrich is considering running in the 2008 presidential election.

Keeping information hidden from public view is not unique to the current administration; leaders and governments have lied to their citizenry since the formation of political systems. Some government cover-ups have such a lasting effect on the country that they need only be mentioned by a word: Watergate and Iran-Contra. Some are more minor, such as the recent federal charges against Clinton administration national security advisor Sandy Berger for removing and keeping classified defense documents from the National Archives. He has denied any criminal wrongdoing and claimed his action was "an honest mistake"; however, anyone who has done research knows that removing archives is a no-no, particularly classified ones relating to government efforts to fight terrorism. The maximum sentence that Berger is (un)likely to receive is one year in prison or a $100,000 fine, but it is probable is that he will suffer the minimum consequences allowable under the law.

Thomas Paine wrote, "A long habit of not thinking a thing wrong gives it a superficial appearance of being right." In our modern information age,

Jeff Shiring

one would think that our government would be forced to become more transparent rather than less. Ironically, perhaps because of our mass media and technology, it is actually easier to obfuscate the truth than to expose it. Public relations campaigns, which should inform the public about government policy, have become propaganda blitzes, to the tune of $88 million in the 2004 fiscal year alone (compared to $37 million in 2001). The buzz surrounding columnist Armstrong Williams' paid promotion of the No Child Left Behind Act was mentioned in an earlier chapter. Another example of government abuse of the "free" press comes from the Department of Health and Human Services. *The Washington Post* discovered in January 2005 that syndicated columnist and family affairs writer Maggie Gallagher received $41,500 in two contracts to write brochures, a magazine article, and a briefing report supporting President Bush's marriage initiative; it called for redirecting welfare funds to pay for premarital counseling and abstinence programs. Gallagher also wrote several columns supporting the plan.[368] After echoing Williams' justification that the work reflected her personal beliefs, Gallagher did admit that not disclosing the contracts was a mistake. In neither case did these journalists, or the people who hired them, accept responsibility for breaking the rules.

It is a common theme in this discourse: everyone breaks the rules and no one is held appropriately accountable. This is especially egregious at the highest levels of our democratic government: there are many who repeatedly demonstrate that if they don't like the rules, they will either ignore them or change them. After Senate Democrats blocked ten conservative judicial nominees last year, the Republicans threatened to change the rules to disallow filibusters. Even though the filibuster has been overused as a partisan tactic in recent years (by both sides of the Senate) to block policies as well as nominees, it remains a valuable mechanism to counter potential legislative railroading by the majority power. It is unacceptable that the current majority power wants to eliminate that protection because it is inconveniently doing what it was designed to do.

Another inconvenience for the government comes from rules at the state legislature level. Despite a Congressional district rule that allows for redrawing electoral district lines once a decade (after the census), the Republican Party attempted to rearrange electoral districts in Texas in early 2003 in order to give them more seats heading into the 2004 election. The move prompted an out-of-state defection by several Democratic legislators to prevent a vote. Meanwhile in Colorado, Republicans similarly tried to reapportion the district lines that had been set in 2000. Both attempts resulted in court challenges by the Democrats: in December 2003 the Colorado Supreme Court ruled that mid-cycle redistricting was an infringement of the state constitution. In doing so, it blocked a precedent for state legislators to be able to create safe seats for partisans and move opposing parties out of their seats. An editorial in the *Washington Post* put it this way, "Gerrymandering districts ensures those in power the ability to remain in power, and to augment that power. It makes them less accountable to voters because it allows them to choose the voters who will then elect them."[369] The Texas case was shuffled by that state's supreme court back to a three-judge panel of a lower court for reconsideration in late October 2004.

House majority leader Tom DeLay, who oversaw the Texas power grab, has fueled the fire of accusations that the GOP operates by its own legislative rulebook. DeLay is currently involved in a Texas grand jury investigation of alleged campaign finance violations in the 2002 state legislative races. While he has not been indicted, three of his associates and eight companies have been. The situation has prompted Republicans to reconsider a House rule that GOP leaders must step down if indicted on charges that could lead to a two-year prison term. They proposed a Republican Steering Committee that would have thirty days to determine whether an indictment was serious enough to merit removal of the representative; their recommendation would then go to all House Republicans to decide if the member in question should relinquish his or her post. DeLay has called the investigation "a partisan attack," despite the fact that he has been repeatedly reprimanded by the House Ethics Committee for "appearing to link political donations to a legislative favor and improperly persuading U.S. aviation authorities to intervene in the Texas redistricting dispute."[370] DeLay famously summed up his regard for the law when a government employee tried to stop him from lighting up a cigar on federal property, responding, "I am the federal government."

The GOP preference for party loyalty over integrity was apparent again in early February 2005 when three members of the ethics committee were replaced by members more sympathetic to DeLay's actions. Speaker of the House Dennis Hastert removed Chairman Joel Hefley, Steven LaTourette, and Kenny Hulshof, head of the sub-committee investigating DeLay's alleged campaign irregularities. They were replaced by Doc Hastings, a long-time friend of Hastert, and Texas representatives Lamar Smith and Tom Cole, both of whom contributed to DeLay's legal defense fund.[371] The move was widely perceived as a purge of those who put their personal and professional ethics before loyalty to the club.

Like a long-running play, the action, the setting, and the universal themes of questionable principles and conflicts of interest remain the same: only the cast of players changes occasionally. Vice President Dick Cheney has more or less successfully hidden behind immunity from federal court orders on constitutional, separation-of-powers grounds. He went duck hunting with a Supreme Court Justice hearing the case, possibly helping his position; although that was flatly denied by Justice Antonin Scalia, who defended the propriety of the January 2004 hunting trip they took together. The trip occurred three weeks after the Supreme Court agreed to hear the Bush administration's appeal of the requests by environmental groups to release details of the energy meetings. Scalia refused to recuse himself from the case and said that since Cheney was not being sued as a private individual, it was acceptable to socialize with him.[372]

It is interesting that the separation-of-powers argument did not apply when Mr. Cheney took the helm of the federal energy policy task force one year after serving as CEO of Halliburton Corporation (an energy company). It is also interesting that he has done a flip-flop over U.S. trade sanctions against Iran. In 1996, he told an energy industry conference that sanctions punished American companies: "The problem is that the good Lord didn't see fit to always put oil and gas resources where there are democratic governments."[373] Although Cheney maintained his opposition to the sanctions early in his first term, they were renewed by the administration in March 2001. Yet, Halliburton Products and Services Ltd., a foreign subsidiary of Halliburton Corporation which opened an office in Tehran in February 2000 while Cheney was still CEO of the parent company, does a reported $30 to 40 million business with Iran every year. (Under the law, as long as no Americans directly participate in the activities, American companies can do business with Iran through foreign subsidiaries.)

In the spring of 2003, the Pentagon gave Halliburton a contract worth more than seven billion dollars over two years to fight oil well fires in Iraq. California Representative Henry Waxman, ranking minority leader of the House Committee on Government Reform, asked the General Accounting Office how multi-billion dollar contracts were being award for work in Iraq without competition. The Pentagon defended the deal by saying that inviting other vendors to bid on highly classified work would waste money and delay war planning when KBR, the primary Halliburton subsidiary, was already in place from an existing 2001 contract; had the necessary security clearances; and could fulfill the requirements on short notice. They further said the deal was structured to control costs.[374] Meanwhile, KBR has come under fire (and fines) since 1997 for overcharging the government millions of dollars for materials and services. In 2002, the company paid a $2 million settlement to avoid criminal charges for price gouging. As of December 2004, disclosed Halliburton contracts for work in Iraq were valued at $10.8 billion.[375] Like Representative Waxman, it is incumbent upon Americans to wonder about the logic, wisdom, and legality of awarding no-bid contracts to one company as part of the war on terror when the company does business in Iran and Libya-countries that openly support terrorists-especially when there have been such blatant abuses of spending and fraud.

The White House has continually denied any involvement in selecting contractors. Perhaps this is the case, but it is difficult to believe when even a few of the dizzying array of dots are connected. One of those dots is the Bechtel Group, the largest contractor in the U.S., another major recipient of defense contracts in Iraq. Jack Sheehan is a senior vice president at Bechtel and also serves on the Defense Policy Board that confidentially advises the Pentagon on defense issues.

Bechtel's board of directors includes former Secretary of State George Shultz, who was also chairman of the advisory board of another dot, the Committee for the Liberation of Iraq. The CLI was a non-governmental organization closely aligned with the White House, created to build support for the administration's war campaign and dedicated to the removal of Saddam Hussein. The president of the committee, Randy Scheunemann worked for Donald Rumsfeld as a consultant on Iraq. The founder of the CLI was Bruce Jackson, a former vice president of Lockheed Martin (another big-time defense contractor) who also chaired the Republican Party's Platform subcommittee for National Security and Foreign Policy during Bush's 2000 presidential campaign.

The Center for Public Integrity discovered that at least nine of the thirty board members are connected to companies who were granted more than $76 million in defense contracts in 2001 and 2002.[376] Richard Perle, chairman of the Defense Policy Board, stepped down in March 2003 after Seymour Hersh of *The New Yorker* broke a story alleging that Perle was using his influence with the Defense department to drum up business with Middle Eastern investors. Perle, who stayed on as a board member, was a managing partner in Trireme Partners L.P., a venture capital company that stood to potentially profit from the war in Iraq through its investments in intelligence technologies, such as those owned by Adnan Khashoggi.[377] In a separate dealing, Perle reportedly accepted a $725,000 consulting fee from the bankrupt telecommunications firm Global Crossing to seek Pentagon approval for a proposed sale to a Hong Kong buyer, $600,000 of which was contingent upon a government go-ahead.[378]

The Heights of Hypocrisy

While the intrigue and machinations of Washington are open secrets, the Bush administration's handling of the war in Iraq, both at home and on Iraqi soil, has been much more obvious to the American public. Manipulation of the complicit mass media has already been discussed; even with the propaganda and the posturing, few could have escaped the carpet bombing of information that accompanied the U.S. invasion and occupation of Iraq. A detailed discussion of the war, which is warranted and necessary, is simply beyond the scope of this book. For our humble purposes, the war serves to underscore the hypocrisy for which our country has become known. The Duelfer Report blew the lid off the government's arguments for going to war: there were no chemical, biological, or nuclear weapons; Iraq was not an imminent threat to U.S. security; and Saddam Hussein had nothing to do with the 9/11 terrorist attacks. The Abu Ghraib scandal shot down the holier-than-thou attitude about the moral superiority of the American military and its treatment of prisoners. The deaths of 1530 (as of April 1, 2005) U.S. soldiers, the wounding of 11,600 more and the ongoing presence of nearly 150,000 troops two years after the invasion have annihilated Richard Perle's and Ken Adelman's arrogant predictions that the war would be a "cake walk."

Prior to the September eleventh terrorist strike on the World Trade Center towers, according to The Washington Post, the President spent 42 percent of his first eight months in office on vacation, including fifty days at home on his ranch in Crawford, Texas.[379] The attacks seemed to kick start our President, and he quickly found his stride as a wartime president. A full term and one war later, he now calls himself a "peace president." Somewhere in the middle of that timeline, the administration embraced a mission to spread freedom far and wide, by force if necessary.

They said, "Let there be democracy." And there was…sort of. On January 30, 2005, Iraqis were free to ignore death threats and risk their lives to vote for secret-until-the-last-minute candidates at secret-until-the-last minute polling stations in some neighborhoods in Iraq. Clearly no one expected the process to be a smooth one and under the circumstances, election officials and security forces achieved a monumental feat. People died, but there were no large scale disasters as anticipated. The initial stunning voter turnout reports of eight million Iraqis (57 percent) have yet to be verified (as of April 1, 2005) and the numbers are likely to be much lower than the cheerleading press would have us believe. Certainly large pockets of the population, particularly the Sunnis, were not represented in the election, whether by choice, intimidation, or the absence of open polling stations in their region. There was, predictably, widespread ballot tampering that hindered the tallying process. The uncertainty that continues to characterize all things political in Iraq is heavy enough to cloud Washington's crystal ball of Middle Eastern destiny for a very long time, despite the popping champagne corks of the coalition.

Those in favor of the war and those against the war can both claim righteousness. Pro-war supporters can claim victory in Iraq by virtue of the miraculous execution of a popular election. The anti-war camp can claim that "Operation Iraqi Freedom" has been a failure: the elections were hardly democratic given that a sizeable number of Iraqis were unable or unwilling to vote for a new government. Both sides are right, but that is small comfort for the men, women, and children who are still trying to survive in a decimated country with little infrastructure and no security.

The Bush administration's zeal to spread democracy around the world is, like any government's foreign policy, not to be taken at face value. Many analysts-from all sides of the political divide-have accused the U.S. of invading Iraq in order to protect its interests in and dependence upon oil. After all, the U.S. backed Saddam Hussein and the Baath Party during the Iran-Iraq war, even when it was well-known that Iraq was using chemical weapons against Iran. [Iran's Ayatollah Khomeini was the sworn enemy of the U.S., and Iraq had lots of oil.] Both the Reagan and Bush Sr. administrations authorized the sale of chemical and biological agents (including anthrax) to Iraq. Even after the 1987 gassing of the Kurds, a horror to which the current president frequently referred to as an indicator of the threat of Saddam Hussein, the U.S. extended another $1.2 billion in credits and loans to the Iraqi government.[380] As late as December 1988, Dow Chemical sold $1.5 million worth of highly toxic pesticides to Iraq, even though the government was concerned the material would be used for chemical warfare.[381] As soon as Iraq invaded Kuwait, another rich source of oil, off came the gloves. [A curious and ironic aside: Saddam Hussein was presented the key to the city of Detroit by an American delegation visiting Baghdad in 1980, courtesy of then-mayor Coleman Young.]

An important point to remember is while we have managed to remove Saddam Hussein from power, we have failed to find, detain, and prosecute the mastermind of the September eleventh attacks against the United States: Osama bin Laden. President Bush has made it clear: even if he knew then what he knows now, he would still have led our country into war with Iraq. Yes, Saddam Hussein was a brutal tyrant who flagrantly defied international sanctions and the human rights of his own people, and he should have been removed from power; but following that logic, the U.S. should be invading dozens of countries led by despotic regimes-pick a dictator. The fact remains that our government ignored public opinion and went to war in Iraq, expending thousands of lives and hundreds of billions of dollars. Saddam is gone, but the costs of the war in Iraq continue to soar, and we are no closer than we were three years ago to finding the world's most wanted terrorist, who remains a threat to the United States. This display of flawed government decision making and action, taken against the will of the American people, shows just how far we have distanced ourselves from the ideal of a democratic government.

Two years after the fall of Baghdad, we have the benefit of hindsight to some degree. But many historians and political observers point out that governments are notoriously short-sighted and senile: they forget the lessons of the past and are unable or unwilling to see the effects of their actions on the future. Our blind insistence on setting up free markets and democratic structures in developing nations to ensure our own security is a strategy that has failed time and again. As some scholars have pointed out, that model ignores essential factors such as religion, gender, history, and deeply-rooted ethnic divisions that often run along economic lines. Imposing a western-style free market-system and/or a rapid shift of political power in countries with wealthy ethnic minorities and poor

Jeff Shiring

majorities has been disastrous in many countries, such as Indonesia, Sierra Leone, Venezuela, the Balkans, Rwanda, and Iraq.[382] Too much democracy too fast can be a bad thing for countries without the conditions necessary to sustain it, but the American fervor for freedom often obscures our judgment.

That fervor also blinds us to the failures of our democratic system at home, for which we are ultimately to blame. Two months before the U.S. invaded Iraq, polls showed almost a third of the public (31 percent) were in favor of immediate action and 63 percent favored a diplomatic solution.[383] Despite the unprecedented opposition to the invasion, the President considered 31 percent to be a mandate (much like his re-election). Millions of people marched in protest here in the U.S. and around the world, to which the president's response was, "Democracy is a beautiful thing, and that people are allowed to express their opinion." Democratic governments are supposed to respond to the will of the people, not obstinately ignore it and further, accuse protesters and dissenters of being unpatriotic and anti-American. It is telling that the president began his second term with the lowest approval rating (49 percent) of any reelected U.S. president in a half century, but it is more telling of American apathy that he stood to take a second oath of office at all.

Thomas Jefferson said that dissent is the highest form of patriotism. It is up to the citizens of a democratic country to hold governments accountable for their actions. It is up to us to exercise what we take for granted to be our democratic rights. Jane Jacobs wrote, "When a culture is working wholesomely, beneficent pendulum swings-effective feedback-do occur. Corrective stabilization is one of the great services of democracy, with its feedback to rulers from the protesting and voting public."[384] If we don't use the instruments available to us to us-the media, the courts, the polls-to make our voices heard and heeded, then we have no right to traffick democracy and freedom around the world, high on principles that leave track marks but no lasting effect.

The fundamental design of democracy reads loudly and clearly "government of the people, by the people, for the people." Those brilliant words and the ideals they encompass have been lost to the shallow principles of rule by minority interests, favoritism, corruption, partisanship, money, power, and greed. The challenge at hand is to restore integrity and honor in the system with the intent of bringing back the brilliance of Lincoln's vision.

---

334 Nancy Gibbs and John F. Dickerson, "Inside the Mind of George W. Bush," *Time*, September 6, 2004, p. 21.

335 Thomas Ferraro. "Senator Reid Calls on Bush to Repudiate Attack Mailing," *Reuters*, February 8, 2005,

http://aolsvc.news.aol.com/news/article.adp?id=20050207203509990004 (retrieved February 8, 2005).

336 Maureen Dowd. "Condi Follows the Script," column from the *New York Times*, reprinted in the *Nova Scotian*, Sunday publication in the *Chronicle-Herald*, Halifax, NS, Canada, February 13, 2005, p. 7.

337 "Connie Rice: The Top 10 Secrets They Don't Want You to Know About the Debates," commentary on *The Tavis Smiley Show*, National Public Radio, September 29, 2004, http://www.npr.org/templates/story/story.php?storyId=4052162 (retrieved February 22, 2005).

338 Paul Krugman. "Little Black Lies," *New York Times*, January 28, 2005, http://www.truthout.org/docs_05/012905E.shtml (retrieved January 28, 2005).

339 Corey Robin. "Scary How Fear is Being Used to Keep Us in Line," *Houston Chronicle*, October 31, 2004, sec. E, p.1.

340 "U.S. Security Czar to Step Down," *CBC News Online*, November 30, 2004, http://www.cbc.ca/story/world/national/2004/11/30/ridge041130.html (retrieved November 30, 2004).

341 Alan Elsner. "Millions Blocked From Voting in U.S. Election," September 22, 2004, http://www.commondreams.org/headlines04/0922-03.htm (retrieved February 22, 2005).

342 Jesse Holland. "Democrats Rule Out Filibuster of Gonzales Nomination," February 1, 2005, http://aolsvc.news.aol.com/news/article.adp?id=20050201150509990009 (retrieved Feb. 1, 2005).

343 Associated Press, "U.S. Judge Allows Guantanamo Detainees to Challenge Confinement," *Chronicle Herald*, Halifax, NS, Canada, February 1, 2005, sec. A, p. 4.

344 Fred Hiatt. "Democracy on Hold," *Washington Post*, October 6, 2003, sec. A, p. 23.

345 "Putin Says Russia Developing New Nuclear Missile," *CTV.ca*, November 17, 2004, http://www.ctv.ca/servlet/ArticleNews/story/CTVNews/1100695433357_6?s_na me=&no_ads= (retrieved February 22, 2005).

346 "A Classification of American Wealth," *D.C. Shouter and RAKEN Services website*. Updated October 18, 2004, http://www.raken.com/american_wealth/encyclopedia/comment_politics_pub-lic_office.asp (retrieved February 22, 2005).

347 Genaro C. Armas. "Presidential Race Shapes Up as Millionaires v. Millionaires," Associated Press, July 7, 2004, http://www.miami.com/mld/miamiherald/news/politics/9099735.htm?1c (retrieved July 7, 2004).

Jeff Shiring

348 "History's Highest Priced Ticket," *Forbes.com*, July 7, 2004, http://money-central.msn.com/content/invest/forbes/P88669.asp (retrieved February 22, 2005).

349 "U.S. Presidential Spending Campaign Triples," *CBC News Online*, Nov. 1, 2004, http://www.cbc.ca/story/world/national/2004/11/01/us_campaign-cost041101.html (retrieved November 1, 2004).

350 The Center for Responsive Politics, "Advocacy Group Spending in the 2004 Elections," *Open Secrets.org*, Feb. 22, 2005, http://www.opensecrets.org/527s/527new.asp?cycle=2004 (retrieved Feb. 23, 2005).

351 Federal Election Commission, 2004 Presidential Campaign Financial Activity Summarized," press release, Feb. 3, 2005, http://www.fec.gov/press/press2005/20050203pressum/20050203pressum.html (retrieved Feb. 22, 2005).

352 Joseph Curl. "Inaugural Price Tag in Line With History," *Washington Times*, January 19, 2005, http://washingtontimes.com/national/20050119-103531-1062r.htm (retrieved February 25, 2005).

353 "Online Special: An Interview with Al Gore," transcript from *The NewsHour with Jim Lehrer*, March 14, 2000, http://www.pbs.org/newshour/election2000/candidates/gore_3-14a.html (retrieved April 1, 2005).

354 Steven Weiss. "2004 Election Outcome: Money Wins," press release, The Center for Responsive Politics, November 3, 2004, http://www.opensecrets.org/pressreleases/2004/04results.asp (retrieved Feb. 23, 2005).

355 Sharon Theimer. "Raising Cash for Bush Had its Rewards," reprinted in the *Chronicle Herald*, Halifax, NS, Canada, November 19, 2004, sec. A, p. 11.

356 Christopher Lee. "Report on Bonuses Raises Ire," *Washingtonpost.com*, July 11, 2003, http://wwwwashingtonpost.com/ac2/wp-dyn/A40613-2003Jul10?language=printer (retrieved Feb. 2, 2005).

537 Larry Margasak. "Sen. Clinton's Finance Director Indicted," *AOL.com*, January 8, 2005, http://aolsvc.news.aol.com/news/article.adp?id=20050107170709990004&_mpc=news percent2e (retrieved January 8, 2005).

358 Marianne Holt. "Federal Elections Panel Too Swamped to Check Campaign Finance Abuses," The Center for Public Integrity, December 1, 1999, http://wwwpublic-i.org/report.aspx?aid=584&sid=200 (retrieved February 23, 2005).

359 Public Citizen, "Limiting Access to President Records," *BushSecrecy.org*, http://www.bushsecrecy.org/page.cfm?PagesID=17&ParentID=1&CategoryID=1 (retrieved February 24, 2005).

360 Rick Blum. "Secrecy Report Card: Quantitative Indicators of Secrecy in the Federal Government," a report by *OpentheGovernment.org*, August 26, 2004, http://www.openthegovernment.org/otg/secrecy_reportcard.pdf (retrieved February 24, 2005).

361 The Center for Public Integrity, "The Buying of a President 2004: Carol Moseley-Braun," http://www.public-i.org/bop2004/candidate.aspx?cid=11 (retrieved March 31, 2005).

362 "Levy Case Opens Door on Secret Life." People in the News: Gary Condit, *CNN.com*, http://www.cnn.com/CNN/Programs/people/shows/condit/profile.html (retrieved March 31, 2005).

363 "At Church, Jesse Jackson Supporters Offer Encouragement," *CNN.com*, January 21, 2001, http://archives.cnn.com/2001/US/01/21/jackson.02/index.html (retrieved March 31, 2005).

364 *Wikipedia*. s.v. "Jesse Jackson," http://en.wikipedia.org/wiki/Jesse_Jackson (retrieved March 31, 2005).

365 *Wikipedia*. s.v. "James Traficant," http://en.wikipedia.org/wiki/James_Traficant (retrieved: April 1, 2005).

366 Malia Rulon. "Prison No Bar to Traficant Bid for President," *Cincinnati.com*, July 25, 2003, http://www.enquirer.com/editions/2003/07/25/loc_oh-traficant25.htm (retrieved April 1, 2005).

367 *Wikipedia*. s.v. "Newt Gingrich," http://en.wikipedia.org/wiki/Newt_Gingrich (retrieved April 1, 2005).

368 Jim Drinkard. "Report: PR Spending Doubled Under Bush," *USA Today*, January 26, 2005, http://www.usatoday.com/news/washington/2005-01-26-williams-usat_x.htm (retrieved February 24, 2005).

369 "Once is Enough," Editorial, *Washington Post*, December 3, 2003, http://www.washingtonpost.com/ac2/wp-dyn?pagename=article&contentId=A30081-2003Dec2&notFound=true (retrieved February 24, 2005).

370 Larry Margasak. "GOP Approves New Party Rules in Light of DeLay," *AOL News*, November 17, 2004, http://wwwfreerepublic.com/focus/f-news/1282242/posts (retrieved January 31, 2005).

371 Ari Berman. "Hastert's Heavy Hand," *The Nation*, February 8, 2005, http://www.cbsnews.com/stories/2005/02/08/opinion/main672463.shtml (retrieved February 8, 2005).

372 Gina Holland. "Scalia Defends His Hunting Trip With Cheney," *AOL.com*, February 11, 2004, http://aolsvc.news.aol.com/news/article.adp?id=20040211112309990003

Jeff Shiring

(retrieved February 11, 2004).

373 Matt Kelley. "Cheney Once Pushed to Lift Iran Sanctions," *customwire.ap.org*, October 8, 2004, http://www.billingsgazette.com/index.php?id=1&display=red-news/2004/10/09/build/nation/65-cheney.inc (retrieved December 12, 2004).

374 Associated Press, "Rep. Waxman Questions Iraq Work Given to Halliburton Subsidiary Without Competition," *customwire.ap.org*, April 11, 2003.

375 Elizabeth Becker. "Details Given on How Halliburton Contract Was Awarded," *New York Times*, April 10, 2003, http://www.informationclearing-house.info/article2854.htm (retrieved February 24, 2005).

376 Bob Herbert. "Spoils of War," *New York Times*, April 10, 2003, http://www.mindfully.org/Reform/2003/Spoils-Of-War-Herbert10apr03.htm (retrieved February 24, 2005).

377 Seymour Hersh. "Lunch with the Chairman," *New Yorker*, March 10, 2003, http://www.newyorker.com/printable/?fact/030317fa_fact (retrieved February 24, 2005).

378 Maureen Dowd. "Perle's Plunder Blunder," *New York Times*, March 23, 2003, http://www.commondreams.org/views03/0322-07.htm (retrieved April 1, 2003).

379 Derrick Z. Jackson. "While Bush Talks to Cows, Workers Get Milked," *Boston Globe*, August 29, 2001, http://wwwcommondreams.org/cgi-bin/print.cgi?file=/views01/0829-03.htm (retrieved January 2, 2005).

380 Robert Scheer. "The Wraps Come Off Bush's Colonialist Agenda," *Los Angeles Times*, March 26, 2003, http://www.thenation.com/doc.mhtml per-cent3Fi=20030407&s=scheer20030235 (retrieved February 25, 2005).

381 Michael Dobbs. "U.S. Had Key Role in Iraq Build-up," *Washington Post*, December 30, 2002, http://www.washingtonpost.com/ac2/wp-dyn/A52241-2002Dec29?language=printer (retrieved February 25, 2005).

382 Emily Eakin. "On the Dark Side of Democracy," *New York Times*, January 31, 2004, http://www.globalpolicy.org/empire/economy/2004/0131darkside.htm (retrieved February 25, 2004).

383 CBS News Polls, "Poll: Talk First, Fight Later," *CBS News.com*, January 24, 2003, http://www.cbsnews.com/stories/2003/01/23/opinion/polls/main537739.shtml (retrieved February 25, 2005).

384 Jacobs, *Dark Age Ahead*, p. 21.

III. TRAJECTORIES

Let us not seek the Republican answer or the Democratic answer, but the right answer. Let us not seek to fix the blame for the past. Let us accept our own responsibility for the future.

-John Fitzgerald Kennedy (1917-1963)

The twentieth century was without doubt "The American Century." By 1900, the United States was the wealthiest nation in the world; by the end of World War II, it was the most powerful in military and economic strength. Subsequent decades were marked by the leadership of American governments: the U.S. led the way in solving global problems through international diplomacy, foreign aid, and multilateral treaties and alliances. The United States was looked at as a model of freedom, democracy and economic success. It was the destination of choice for millions of immigrants and refugees who dreamt of peace and prosperity in America. As we forge ahead into the twenty-first century, it is clear that things have changed. The world's perception of America is not what it once was, and although Americans still hold ourselves in higher regard than the rest of the world, we are becoming increasingly uncomfortable with what we see in the collective mirror also.

On the Home Front

In an international poll of over 22,000 people in twenty-one countries, conducted by the University of Maryland's Program on International Policy Attitudes together with GlobeScan and released in January 2005, 71 percent of Americans surveyed said they see the U.S. as a source of good in the world (compared to 47 percent of the rest of the world who view U.S. global influence as negative).[385] A CBS poll released on the same day, however, found that 56 percent of Americans believe our country is headed in the wrong direction.[386] Domestic issues ranked higher in importance than the war in Iraq, indicating a growing concern about jobs and the economy. Increasingly, we are beginning to realize that we are operating in an "upside-down economy," where corporate profits reached record levels despite the first job loss recovery since the Depression.[387] Those profits have not found their way to employee

Jeff Shiring

wages and benefits, so faced with the rising costs of housing, health care, and education, middle-income earners are borrowing more than ever just to stay afloat. Many are sinking, as evidenced by the rising levels of personal bankruptcies. The result is a debt-driven economy that is unsustainable; many are beginning to worry that if we continue on this path, the U.S. will find itself squarely in the midst of a modern Depression. Indeed, job growth has been lower than expected, and in March 2005, a third of Americans ranked this problem as the most important issue facing the country, above health care, Social Security, the budget deficit, and prescription drugs.[388] The same poll found that 63 percent of Americans feel the Bush administration doesn't share their priorities on domestic issues. Nine out of ten characterize the federal budget situation as serious, and 42 percent expect the proposed budget for next year will result in a larger deficit than the current one.

With the budget deficit at 4.5 percent of the Gross Domestic Product (GDP), we have reason to be concerned. Less drastic, but still significant, is the U.S. trade deficit reaching nearly 6 percent of GDP in 2004. While many analysts, including Alan Greenspan, have downplayed the trade deficit as fairly easily correctible by market influences, others point out that our best hope for a globally competitive edge-advanced technology products (ATP)- is losing ground. Our information and communication technologies, life science products, and other high-tech manufacturing sectors ran a $37 billion trade deficit in 2004; other countries such as Japan, China, Malaysia, Ireland, and Mexico surged ahead in those areas. According to U.S. Census Bureau trade statistics, the U.S. had been in the black for ATP exports until 2000, but those surpluses disappeared in 2002.[389]

Some of the blame is being laid on funding cuts to scientific research and development. At the national meeting of the American Association for Advancement of Science in March 2005, many scientists and educators expressed concern that the 2005 federal budget reduced spending for basic research and investment in scientific education programs, and that the current administration had removed scientists from major policy-making processes, particularly if their research conflicted with government policy objectives. Kurt Gottfried of Cornell University and the Union of Concerned Scientists claimed that scientists in the Environmental Protection Agency and the U.S. Fish and Wildlife Service have been pressured to change their research to match the administration's stand on environmental issues.[390] Gottfried said the situation is critical because it is becoming increasingly difficult for federal agencies to attract and keep top talent; with 35 percent of the EPA scientists expected to retire soon, there are fears that they will be replaced with staff less inclined to challenge the status quo (a problem echoed in the FDA).

So where exactly are we headed? With a teetering economy and a dissatisfied majority, the United States is poised for significant change.

Respected author Jeremy Rifkin, president of the Foundation on Economic Trends based in Washington, D.C., and also an adviser to the European Commission, sees the country becoming so divided along partisan lines that physical borders could be redrawn creating a new North American Union. Rifkin argues that American "blue states" (the Northeast, upper Midwest, and West coast states that are traditionally Democratic) have more in common with Canada than with the rest of the continental U.S. ("red states" or those that are traditionally Republican) and that regional cross-border economic networks are already firmly established.[391] The Conference of New England Governors and Eastern Canadian Premiers, made up of six blue states and five provinces, meet annually to discuss issues that have an impact on the region and to formulate policy. Established in 1973, the NEG/ECP is currently working to establish tighter border security and a world-class information technology commercial zone to create a knowledge-based economy and regional identity. Similarly, the Pacific Northwest Economic Region (PNWER) involves five blue states and two provinces and claims to have an annual "gross regional product" of nearly $700 billion. PNWER participants are working on regional energy strategies, border security, and ways to streamline all the economic sectors that affect the region: forestry, agriculture, tourism, trade, telecommunications, and transportation. The Council of Great Lakes Governors, consisting of eight states and Ontario and Quebec, is working toward sustainable use and regulation of the Great Lakes water resource.

Rifkin makes a persuasive argument that the United States has become so divided, politically and culturally, that the logical conclusion is a blue-state alignment with Canada, a country that better reflects the values and policies of the moderate majority and liberal left than Washington and its core base of support. He also notes that the American Dream has lost its allure for millions of Americans, who are becoming less enthralled with the aggressive pursuit of self-interest and being drawn to a more global vision.

Farther Afield

In the January 2005 GlobeScan poll, 47 percent of people around the world saw U.S. global influence as negative. An average of 58 percent thought President Bush's reelection was a threat to global security, a perception shared by all western European countries polled, as well as Canada, Mexico, and Australia. (Only the Philippines, India, and Poland were positive toward President Bush.) Not surprisingly, predominantly Muslim countries were overwhelmingly negative about a second term of the Bush administration (76 percent) and said they feel worse toward the American people as a result. Not a single country had a majority in favor of sending troops to Iraq.

These numbers reflect a deepening mistrust of the United States and its mission to spread freedom and democracy around the world, a product of what is becoming known as President Bush's "liberation theology."[392] This is the belief that America's security, and that of the world, rests on the democratization of the planet. Elections in Afghanistan, Palestine, the Ukraine, and Iraq, even if marred by violence, ballot tampering, court challenges, and less than universal participation, have fuelled the engine of U.S. resolve to foment freedom. The zeal with which the U.S. has pursued the war on terror and the war in Iraq, and the self-righteousness demonstrated in both ("you're with us or you're against us"; "the coalition of the willing"), have put the rest of world literally on the defensive. After September eleventh, the U.S. launched a juggernaut in response to a threat to its security simply because it could. In 2003-2004, the U.S. spent $466 billion on defense, nearly equivalent to the $500 billion spent by all of the other 190 world nations combined, and that was less than 4 percent of our GDP.[393] Congress passed the 2006 defense bill in August 2005 allocating another $417 billion for the coming year. Most countries simply cannot afford to subscribe to the U.S. government's credo of "the need to use force to defend the peace," and frankly, despite our massive economy, neither can we. When President Bush addressed the leaders of the world and told them that the United States "expected" that they would support an invasion of Iraq, it is no surprise the majority objected to his intimidating language. The attempted (and failed) coercion of Turkey into allowing the establishment of American military bases there-with the promise of billions of dollars in aid and debt-forgiveness-was greeted with cynicism by the world and by the people of Turkey, whose opposition to the war was overwhelming (between 80 and 90 percent). The U.S. government double-speak was naturally perceived as insincere when we agreed to allow UN weapons inspectors to take one more look in Iraq, while at the same time U.S. soldiers were lining up around the borders. Now that we are embroiled in a continuing bloody insurgency and faced with the enormous costs of restructuring a destroyed (but democratic!) Iraq-a situation that was predicted by many opponents of the war-the U.S. is reaching out to the UN once more. This time the message is: "We rejected the United Nations when you didn't do what we wanted, but we can't afford this problem anymore so we need your help." The gall of such an attitude is astounding and further reinforces a negative attitude toward our country.

An instant shift of foreign policy characterized by the sudden mantra of democratization, freedom, and collective security rings false for many diplomatic ears; the Bush administration reneged on or refused to ratify five international treaties in its first year. The United States walked away from the Kyoto Protocol and failed to implement a unilateral environmental conservation alternative. According to the World Wildlife

Federation's measurement of land use, pollution, energy consumption, and carbon dioxide emissions, Americans leave the second largest "ecological footprint" on the planet. We have an obligation to participate in a global strategy to minimize that impact, which is seven times greater than the average Asian or African country.[394] We also refused to participate in or be held accountable to the International Criminal Court in The Hague, withdrew from the Anti-Ballistic Missile Treaty and the Comprehensive Test Ban Treaty, and changed the rules of the Geneva Convention to suit our own purposes. After the abuses of Abu Ghraib and Guantanamo Bay came to light, President Bush voiced his regrets but refused to apologize. Not only has no one in the Pentagon or White House been held accountable, the legal mind who encouraged the climate of abuse through his loose interpretation of the Geneva Convention was rewarded with the job of Attorney General. All these actions have dealt a huge blow to our credibility as a defender of human rights, freedoms, and the rule of law.

We have expected the United Nations to rubber-stamp our actions, and when they have objected, we've taken our baseball and bat and gone home. Some might argue that the U.S. might expect to exert considerable influence since we are the single largest contributor to the UN: we subsidize 22 percent of the regular budget-$341 million in 2004-and assume 27 percent of the cost of peacekeeping operations.[395] Nevertheless, as contribution assessments are based on a nation's share of the global economy, we actually pay less than our due: the U.S. portion of the world economy is about 34 percent. Total U.S. payments to the entire United Nations system add up to less than one-quarter of 1 percent of our federal budget, and our peacekeeping forces in 2004 totaled 1 percent of approximately 56,000 military personnel. The U.S. has also been the single largest debtor to the United Nations in history. In 2001, the U.S. owed the global body $582 million in unpaid dues, thanks to decisions made by the Reagan administration in the mid-1980s, which included resigning from UNESCO. (We rejoined in September 2003.) The U.S. House of Representatives voted unanimously to repay the debt just two weeks after the September eleventh terrorist attacks.

At the Millennium summit in 2000, the U.S. committed to helping eradicate world poverty, hunger, and AIDS but has rejected the most viable plan for achieving those goals to date. At a February 2005 meeting of the G-7, the British finance minister put forward the proposed International Finance Facility (IFF), which would double international aid to the world's poorest countries by raising another $50 billion a year on world capital markets. The response from John Taylor, U.S. Treasury Under Secretary, was, "Not only does the IFF not work for the United States, we don't need the IFF."[396] Aside from the slap in the face to the U.K., America's most loyal supporter in the Iraq war, this kind of reaction to multilateral problem-solving isolates us and erodes our global leadership. Our pledge to commit $15 billion over five years for the treatment and prevention of AIDS in fifteen target countries is overshadowed by the conditions we place on that assistance, as well as the fact that HIV/AIDS among African Americans is at record levels. In 2003, African Americans accounted for 12.8 percent of the population, but 49.3 percent of estimated AIDS cases in the United States.[397] The U.S. reluctance to promote generic anti-retroviral drugs in the AIDS fight, preferring FDA-approved (and costlier) brand name drugs manufactured by American pharmaceutical companies, has drawn loud criticism from the World Health Organization, UN Secretary-General Kofi Annan, and other world leaders including former South African President Nelson Mandela, whose son died of AIDS in January 2005.

In a March 2003 special feature, Newsweek writer Fareed Zakaria commented, "Most of the problems the world faces today-from terrorism to AIDS to nuclear proliferation-will not be solved with less U.S. engagement, but with more...The real question is how America should wield its power."[398] There is a new world order taking shape, and undoubtedly the United States can take much of the credit, as well as the blame. The U.S. goal of changing the landscape in the Middle East has certainly been met: Israel and Palestine are actively participating in achieving peace (although it may be argued that Yasser Arafat's death precipitated the new efforts); Syria has agreed to pull out of Lebanon; elections took place in Iraq on schedule. It is too soon, however, to gauge whether these shifts are temporary or a lasting testament to the power of democracy. In either case, the United States cannot blithely tell the rest of the world, "We told you so" if we hope to succeed in our goals. We are still facing enormous financial and human costs in Iraq and still bearing the wrath of extremists and terrorists. Osama Bin Laden, still at large, has partially realized his own goal of "bleeding America to the point of bankruptcy," as he stated in a videotape released a day before Bush's re-election. The mujahadeen succeeded with this strategy against the Soviet Union in the 1980s in Afghanistan; while the United States is vastly superior in economic power, our current deficit-bloated by the war in Iraq-is chipping away at our economic legs.

The U.S. government habit of responding to international situations and events in terms of how well it serves us has to change. After the fall of Baghdad, Donald Rumsfeld heralded "the era of the pre-emptive strike" aand sent a shiver of foreboding throughout the world: it appeared as though the U.S. now believes it has a prerogative of invading countries if it is in their interests to do so. Condoleeza Rice's characterization of the December 2004 tsunami disaster in Asia as "a wonderful opportunity to show not just the U.S. government, but the heart of the American people, and I think it has paid great dividends for us"[399] was an insensitive misstep in the administration's march toward a new era of diplomacy. The relationship with France and Germany, frosty since those governments refused to endorse the war in Iraq and were dismissed as "Old Europe," may be slowly warming again, but popular opinion of the U.S. remains bitter there, as it does in Britain, despite Prime Minister Tony Blair's steadfast support for the war in Iraq. (More than 100,000 protesters greeted President Bush during his November 2003 state visit to the U.K.)

Shifts in foreign policy and the response of the U.S. government to global events in recent years have rewarded us with the descriptors "arrogant" and "bullying." We are heading on a trajectory toward the loss of our status as a great power with a diminishing ability to influence world affairs. In order to change the negative world attitude about America, we might start by stifling the rhetoric about the supremacy of the American Way and acknowledging there are other models of democracy and foreign policy that are serving other nations well. In an article that appeared in *Newsweek International,* Andrew Moravcsik suggests that the world is looking to other, particularly European, examples in setting up new governments, social systems, and economies. Five of the top ten top-ranked competitive economies in the world are northern European social democracies (the U.S. ranked second behind Finland in 2004, according to the World Economic Forum). Universal health care, child care, and heavily subsidized education systems seem to be markers of success for some countries. European-style constitutions were adopted by both Kosovo and South Africa; South Africa is now becoming the model for other new democracies in Africa. Despite our president's assertions that Americans have the best medical care in the world, other countries recognize that the U.S. is the only developed democracy without universal health care. The WHO ranks our health system thirty-seventh in the world, on a par with Cuba.

The world holds its nose when the U.S. rebukes other countries for their human and civil rights records while the death penalty is enforced in thirty-eight states (executions of juveniles under age eighteen were only just banned by the Supreme Court on March 1, 2005); firearms are as common in U.S. households as camera phones; and privacy laws have been virtually tossed out the window. The world also recognizes that the yardstick of domestic and global security is not measured in increments of military power, but rather trade agreements, international law, foreign aid, and peacekeeping activities. Moravcsik writes, "Not only do others not share America's self-regard, they no longer aspire to emulate the country's social and economic achievements. The loss of the American Dream goes beyond this swaggering administration and its war in Iraq. A President Kerry would have had to confront a similar disaffection."[400]

Indeed, the current administration is not entirely to blame. The George W. Bush White House is simply the one at the helm at the

Jeff Shiring

moment. Grave mistakes have been made by previous administrations, both Republican and Democrat. Much of our recent history has been defined by expansionist governments, trade protectionism, corporate corruption, and a general attitude of entitlement that has alienated foreign governments and their citizens. This book is more about calling on Americans to recognize what is wrong with our institutions, accepting responsibility for those weaknesses, and taking action to change them, than it is about laying blame. The trajectory that we are on-that is, a unilateral course of forced democracy, retaliation, and control-is one that imminently threatens our domestic and international security. By instilling suspicion, fear, and resentment in other nations, we will continue to be a target of international terrorists. By spending billions of dollars on questionable wars that balloon our debt, we will hold our future generations hostage to an economic ransom. By continuing to blithely consume more of the earth's resources than we are entitled to (or can replenish), the American Dream will become the American Nightmare. It is time to look ahead and adjust the coordinates of our direction. "We must clearly articulate a vision of what America could be in a world in balance, a world at peace, and a world where the planet's vital natural resources are protected and renewed. This is the ultimate family value, the highest patriotism, and the most desperately needed story to guide the next generation of Americans."[401]

[385] U.S. Information Agency Alumni Association. "World Opinion Grows More Negative After Bush Re-election," Jan. 23, 2005, http://www.publicdemocracy.org/41.htm (retrieved March 1, 2005).

[386] "Poll: Low 2nd Term Expectations," *CBS.com*, January 19, 2005, http://www.cbsnews.com/stories/2005/1/19/opinion/polls/main667937.shtml (retrieved April 3, 2005).

[387] Christian E. Weller and Radha Chaurushiya, "Upside-down Economy Takes a Bite Out of Middle Class Wallets," Center for American Progress, May 28, 2004, http://www.americanprogress.org/site/pp.asp?c=biJRJ8OVF&b=84397 (retrieved April 3, 2005).

[388] "Poll: Bush Out of Step With Public," *CBS.com*, March 2, 2005, http://www.cbsnews.com/stories/2005/03/02/opinion/polls/main677661.shtml (retrieved April 3, 2005).

[389] Christian E. Weller and Tyler Tepfer, "U.S. Loses Global Competitive Edge in Hi-Tech," Center for American Progress, March 9, 2005, http://www.americanprogress.org/site/pp.asp?c=biJRJ80V&b=426201 (retrieved March 10, 2005).

[390] Associated Press, "Scientists Feel Stifled by Bush administration," *CNN.com*, February 21, 2005, http://www.cnn.com/2005/TECH/sci-

ence/02/21/bush.science.ap/ (retrieved March 10, 2005).

391 Jeremy Rifkin. "Continentalism of a Different Stripe," *The Walrus*, Toronto, Canada, March 2005, Vol. 2, Issue 2, 37-41.

392 Bogdan Kipling. "Reaction to 'Liberation Theology' No Surprise," *Chronicle Herald*, Halifax, NS, Canada, January 27, 2005, sec. A, p. 9.

393 "World Wide Military Expenditures: 2004," http://www.globalsecurity.org/military/world/spending.htm. Updated February 5, 2005, retrieved March 2, 2005).

394 Jonathan Fowler. "Group Warns Consumption is Outstripping Resources," Associated Press, October 21, 2004, http://www.commondreams.org/headlines04/1021-02.htm (retrieved October 26, 2004).

395 United States Mission to the United Nations, "The United Nations: Myth and Reality American Support," fact sheet, July 2004, http://www.un.int/usa/fact2.htm (retrieved March 1, 2005).

396 Paul Carrel and Gavin Jones, "U.S. Stalls British 67 Plan for Africa," *AOL.com*, February 4, 2005, http://aolsvc.news.aol.com/news/article.adp?id=20050204134309990025 (retrieved February 7, 2005).

397 U.S. Department of Health and Human Services, "African Americans and HIV/AIDS in the United States," fact sheet of January 2005, http://hab.hrsa.gov/history/fact2005/african_americans_and_hivaids.htm (retrieved March 6, 2005).

398 Fareed Zakaria. "The Arrogant Empire," *Newsweek*, March 24, 2003, p. 30.

399 "Condi Rice: Tsunami Provided "Wonderful Opportunity" for US," *Agence France Presse*, January 18, 2005, http://www.commondreams.org/cgi-bin/print.cgi?file=/headlines05/0118-08.htm (retrieved February 1, 2005).

400 Andrew Moravcsik. "Dream on America," *Newsweek International*, January 31, 2005, http://msnbc.msn.com/id/6857387/site/newsweek (retrieved January 28, 2005).

401 Thom Hartmann. "The Empire Needs New Clothes," *Common Dreams*, March 11, 2003, http://www.commondreams.org/views03/0311-07.htm (retrieved March 25, 2003).

IV. CHANGING COURSE

But what is liberty without wisdom, and without virtue? It is the greatest of all possible evils; for it is folly, vice and madness, without tuition or restraint.

-Edmund Burke, British statesman and philosopher (1729-1797)

The purpose of this discourse is to chronicle for the American people, particularly moderate America (more than two-thirds of the population), events that illustrate the current state of our society and the dominant forces that are causing a radical decline in the ability of this country to live up to the principles of its founders: a government of, for, and by the people with a system of free trade that allows for natural competitive market pressures to influence service and pricing. These forces, and the polarized positions that drive them, are heavily influencing the politics, the economics, the churches, the media, and the entertainment sectors of our society and ultimately the lives of each and every American. These mechanisms and the people that control them are not benefiting our society as a whole, but are causing its disintegration in the name of greed, profit, ego, and minority political interest. This book was written with an end in mind, but the current facts in this book could easily be replaced with facts from thirty years ago and the events from that era. My hope is that a book such as this will not need to be written in the future, as we will have evolved socially, politically, and economically to the point that we will have grown and matured beyond these struggles.

The radical liberal and conservative political positions are the most sensational and the loudest in the media, yet only account for a combined 15 to 35 percent of the voting population. All too often, the remaining 65 to 85 percent is left unheard, unrepresented, or far worse, stuck in the middle with a legislative solution or compromise that benefits very few, other than special interests.

That majority includes those with moderate opinions, as well as people who have been marginalized from society in some way-those who have wrestled with their own accountability, have become disillusioned with the system, or believe their voice does not or cannot count.

This book is meant as a warning sign for all of us. For those in positions of authority and control, and for the rest of us who feel we have lost any input into the status of our country's present and future, the message is clear: Danger…proceed with caution. There are significant flaws within the primary institutions of the United States that Americans not only must recognize but must radically change. Soon our systems will become so riddled in corruption and ineffectiveness that the American Dream will vanish and the American people will lose the gifts our forefathers so aptly designed for us. Profits, greed, and ego talk too much in all the American social and political systems to the detriment of the majority. These failing institutions and influences, consciously or not, are driving us away from social accountability, trust, integrity, and hard work; they are weakening us as a whole. We, the American people, have abrogated our responsibility and allowed these powers to control our destiny.

When citizens cannot rely on their government and social and economic institutions for honesty and responsibility, where can they possibly turn for inspiration, guidance, hope, and faith? Especially in light of the religious and spiritual decay and corruption around us, where can we turn? The institutions in which we are losing faith and trust were designed to work for us, protect us, and ultimately preserve a way of life predicated on the principles of liberty, democracy, and a free market. The government, our free market, and our social influences should encourage us to place our faith in them and motivate us to greater achievement and integrity. When they continually fail us, leaving us empty and searching elsewhere for integrity and trustworthy leadership, we will eventually turn away from our larger society, becoming self-absorbed, finding fulfillment whatever way we can in our own individual worlds. We become separate, scattered, polarized, and discouraged from participating in the process; we become influenced away from social accountability and become complacent by powerful and entrenched social, economic, and political attitudes including our own apathy. In the absence of our ability and will to solicit necessary change, we should be able to rely on the institution of government to lead the way. Our government, though, is a reflection of the electorate; the former will necessarily reflect (or take advantage of) the apathy of the latter, perpetuating the downward spiral toward ineffectiveness.

The American people cannot defer responsibility for the failures and corruption of our values and systems. We need to be accountable for our actions and to trust in our indomitable creative spirit and compassion, while holding all our social influences to the highest of standards. In solving the critical weaknesses in our systems, however, we need to carefully consider our current society in terms of our human development and nature. We need to thoughtfully consider and implement solutions that provide strength where our human nature is weak; solutions that provide assurances for our future and for the future of our children's children, where justice, integrity, ethics, and common sense prevail.

Although we have become a fragmented and scattered people, polarized by partisan politics and prejudices, we must learn to come together under the multi-colored umbrella of our commonality as Americans, the basis of which is freedom, faith, liberty, and the governing concept of democratic majority rule. We need to embrace our similarities, while recognizing, sharing, and appreciating our great diversity and individuality. We share common values regardless of culture or religion: love of family and community; faith in a higher power; desire for education and health care; and a need for physical and financial security. Through these values we will find the strength to acknowledge and rectify the errors of our past. Through these values we can begin a modern-day revolution to return to what we can be: a true democracy with an uncorrupted, balanced free market operated by accountable members of society. We must do this to preserve our future and our way of life.

We need to be reminded that the joint and ethical participation of all the elements-the government, the American people, the free market, and our social influences-is fundamental to the success of our country. We can benefit immensely from the liberty and opportunity afforded to us by our Constitution, but to do so requires effort, integrity, strength, and participation.

It is time for the American people to honor and uphold, through committed participation in the democratic, economic, and social processes, our responsibility as citizens of the United States.

It is time for our government, free market, and social influences to honor and uphold their responsibility to the American people.

It is time to recognize that we as a people, in part through our weakened social influences, are losing faith in critical institutions-democracy, free market, and religion-and to realize the destructive social values, including apathy, that are replacing that faith.

It is time to reflect on the greatness in design of our fundamental economic, political, and social structures and recognize how far our current practices diverge from that design. We must be conscious of the need for change before it is too late; we must realize the potential crises we face: social demise; economic collapse; elevated threats of terrorism, from within the borders of the U.S. and from without; and ultimately a collapse of the American Dream.

This discourse began with a reflection of our times and our people. Now is the time, and we are the people. This is where the revolution begins....

The People's Responsibility

In the long run, we shape our lives and we shape ourselves. The process never ends until we die. And the choices we make are ultimately our own responsibility.

-Eleanor Roosevelt (1884-1962)

The people of America are this country's richest resource. The strength of our diversity lies in embracing the common principles and values of this great country-liberty, democracy, free enterprise, integrity, and old-fashioned hard work-and accepting the necessity and responsibility of participating in these systems. The earlier pages of this book describe countless examples of the unraveling of our nation. The purpose of capturing all those frayed edges of our society's fabric was not to prophesy our inevitable doom, but rather to highlight the need to mend the seams, or the American Dream and the American model of democracy will be passed over. There are many reasons for the problems we have discussed, but there is absolutely no reason why we can't solve them as a strong and united country. We have the good fortune of living in what has been, and what could be again, the greatest nation on earth. With that good fortune, however, comes a duty to try to make the very best lives we can for ourselves and for others. We enjoy a constitutional democracy, but inherent in that democracy is a dual responsibility on the part of both the governing and the governed. It is our privilege and our right to elect our officials, but it is also our deserved loss if we fail to exercise our power. If we do not demand better of ourselves, our social constructs, and our government, then we get exactly what we deserve. [Clearly this is the state of our current social and political life!] Individually and collectively, we have control over our lives, and it is up to us to use this incredible societal power and influence.

Opportunities for success and prosperity abound in the United States; but it is important to remember that this country was built on the foundations of freedom, liberty, responsibility, and participation. It was not built on a fast buck and political favors as it seems to be today. We have internalized from our social influences an understanding that begging, borrowing, and stealing are viable paths, not only to survival but to success and wealth. These negative values ultimately conflict with the healthy design of our systems and our societal progress. We must relearn the meanings of honesty, integrity, accountability, and effort and apply these values to our own lives. In doing so, we will inevitably project them upon the society as a whole and upon future generations.

In the opening paragraphs of this book, I alluded to having "deferred accountability" in my own life. Perhaps it is time I shared some of that history to clarify my purpose for this book and my profound belief in the power of personal responsibility and its effect on my life. My parents divorced when I was twelve, and like many marital breakdowns, it was a confusing and heartbreaking period of turmoil for everyone in the family. My parents did not handle the situation well, nor did I. There was much anger, sadness, and far too many lies in the divorce process. Without any tools to cope with crisis, and without any positive influence and direction in my life, I became the personification of *The Unraveling of America*. I became detached, reserved, and leery of trusting anybody. During this period of my life, I was arrested and charged with several misdemeanors. At the age of nineteen, my girlfriend at the time became pregnant and we gave our baby boy up for adoption-a decision I regret every day of my life. I went to college but lived recklessly on credit cards so that at the age of twenty-two, my bad decision making led me into a dire financial situation, from which it ultimately took me years to rebound. In my early twenties I lived a shallow and complacent life and went through a string of disastrous relationships. I did not participate in the society around me except to survive the day and to take what I could get from it. The turning point for me came when I was twenty-seven and involved with a woman who was the loveliest person I'd ever known. I ended the relationship by having an affair and hurting her badly. By having no ability and strength of character to say "no," I destroyed an ultimate love for lust.

As I had repeatedly done throughout my youth, I took the quick and easy way to instant gratification and escape without measuring the consequences; but when I saw the suffering I had caused, the penny finally dropped. I became discouraged with my conscious and unconscious treatment of other people; I was constantly running from problems and denying my personal accountability in life. I made a deliberate decision to take control and make amends.

A decade later, I have accomplished this and am actively taking part in the lives of my family, friends, and community. I am a devoted father to my young son and strive to always be a positive role model for him. I am a successful professional, working ethically and honorably. I am, in many ways, living the American Dream in a very healthy and productive way.

This book is a reflection of my desire to participate in the broader social picture and contribute something of value to my fellow Americans who are, I believe, poised for change.

My first recommendation to begin the process of change is a call to every American to demand more of him or herself at an individual level. A critical observation of my own life and that of many Americans demonstrates that we have grown used to deferring responsibility for our lives and behaviors. The blame game has become a national pastime politically and socially. Capable Americans need to be held accountable for their decisions, and actions need to have consequences.

The first step of becoming accountable involves taking total responsibility for our individual actions and everyday choices. These actions and choices need to be founded on the virtues of honor, integrity, ethics, value for life, and respect for the law of our land.

This sounds like a very simple solution, yet can you recall the last time you or a family member or friend held themselves accountable for a flawed or failed decision? How frequently have you heard individuals taking responsibility and apologizing or remedying the consequences of their actions? Also, can you recall a time when you candidly and compassionately spoke to that same family member or friend about their decision and its consequences? Did you perhaps share knowledge and skills to help them consider other alternatives for their future decision making?

Now take that same thought and apply it to our social constructs. It has been my observation that we very rarely-usually only under direct threat-see responsibility for unlawful or erroneous decision making.

It is a shame we have not learned the grace, humility, and the strength of character gained by taking full, complete, and timely accountability for our actions. It has also been my experience that when people offer their heartfelt, sincere apology, we generally see the great compassion of our citizens surface. Our ability to forgive is truly one of our great gifts.

My second recommendation is to spend formal time-at school and at home-learning about human nature, human sexuality, who we are, and who we want to be. A wise teacher once shared with me that by the time I was eighteen, if I had not asked myself penetrating questions about how I wanted to live life and how I wanted to be recognized and remembered in life, I may never be certain if I had achieved my life's dreams and aspirations. I believe this challenging task begins with learning and developing the skill and ability to communicate honestly and openly, and includes learning the strength and grace of the word no.

We are constantly tested and challenged in life and sometimes the pressure of the moment makes it quicker and easier to bend our values; but it is at such a cost to our character. Only when it is too late do we realize how simple it would have been to choose a different path by having said "no." If we are centered in life with the knowledge of who we are and how we will lead our lives, we will not be easily moved to compromise our values and ethics. No, I will not betray the trust of my friends. No, I will not join my friends in stealing. No, I will not lie to ease the pain. No, I will not steal and lie to the employees or shareholders of this company to enrich myself and friends. No, I will not commit adultery on my spouse for quick gratification and pleasure. No, I will not legislate an action that will cost human life and waste billions of dollars without irrefutable evidence to justify the action. Simple and very profound.

As we begin to expect and demand more of ourselves, we can naturally expect to demand more and achieve more from our political, economic and social influences.

The incredible power of united Americans is the single largest force capable of bringing about healthy change in our failing systems and corrupted institutions. Corrupt politicians, unethical capitalists, hypocritical religious leaders, and irresponsible media and celebrity figures continue to dilute the powerful voice of a unified America. They carefully and often deliberately manipulate us with streams of disinformation, advertising, and double talk. They prey on our compassion, our short-term attention spans, and they profoundly affect our belief in our social institutions; and we have let them do this. A friend of mine once distributed a politically biased mass e-mail, the accuracy of which I challenged. Upon admitting there were misleading "facts" in the e-mail, she said, "All is fair in love, war, and politics." Essentially, she was condoning the distribution of misinformation as long as it benefited her own political position and interests. The attitude that it is acceptable to misrepresent facts and disseminate incomplete information is terribly damaging to the democratic process and only serves to lower the ethical bar in politics and information sharing. Nevertheless, it is a prevailing attitude in our lives, our government, our media, our free-market economy, our celebrity, and our faith. This belief needs to be reversed entirely.

My third recommendation is to demand that all persons in a position of public trust-without exception-be held to the highest standard of law. We must demand absolute legal and ethical compliance to all our political, social, and economic institutions and the power brokers who control them.

Unprosecuted violations of public trust have a tremendously negative influence on our social psyche; we have become accustomed to the attitude that any action is acceptable as long as you don't get caught. The caveat is this: even if you do get caught, favors and friendships can get you out of trouble. This belief, and the cause of it, is one of the true root diseases in human nature, and in particular with the citizens of the United States, that needs to be addressed and cured.

Every day we see authority figures and role models getting away with murder (literally and figuratively) so why should the rest of us be held accountable for similar transgressions? Fair and consistent application of the law will not only reestablish a respect for the judicial system but will serve as a necessary deterrent for everyone, including our most valuable resource-our youth.

Punishments for breaking the law and violating public trust should be significant: criminal prosecution, automatic loss of public office, loss of licenses, loss of patents, repayment of inappropriate gain, repayment of lost retirement/pension funds, punitive damages payable to the society, etc. The penalties need to be enforced by our legal system swiftly and publicly. We need to realize our actions have consequences that are measured against law...and that law is truly, universally just and blind. We must demand that our dominant institutions become accountable to the majority and are subject to appropriate enforcement of laws that reflect social integrity and justice. We have taken only small steps to reverse this trend with the Sarbanes-Oxley Act, which directly affects public company CEOs and CFOs. We need to go beyond this initial positive step and address similar legislation as it pertains to broader social influences and constructs.

We can accomplish the goal of reinstituting integrity, ethics, and legal compliance by voting individuals into office who demonstrate these values and by holding them accountable if they forget them. We can exercise our considerable power as consumers to let corporations, marketing moguls, and celebrities know we disagree with their behavior or tactics simply by refusing to buy in to their products. We need to go to the polls more and to the check-out counters less.

Our daily media diet demonstrates that American society is suffering from a slow and steady decay in family values, in our physical and spiritual health, in our financial health, and we are losing faith-in faith, ourselves, our democratic principles, our free-market design, and our social constructs. These trends will continue unless we, the American people, individually and collectively, change course and employ the recommendations above. We need to first adopt them individually and then apply them purposefully to all our social influences. As we learn to demand more of ourselves, we will naturally learn to apply that standard to our social constructs, by demanding the same of those who are in a position of public trust. Individually we can absolutely and positively change ourselves. Collectively we can absolutely and positively change our great American society. We can achieve this goal just as we have met countless other challenges; and I can think of no greater goal than to preserve our country's values-liberty, freedom, and government of, for and by the people.

Democracy: Government by the People, for the People

People often say that, in a democracy, decisions are made by a majority of the people. Of course that is not true. Decisions are made by a majority of those who make themselves heard and who vote-a very different thing.

-*Walter H. Judd, American physician, missionary, member of Congress from 1943-1962 and Presidential Medal of Freedom recipient (1898-1994)*

The United States suffers from one of the lowest electoral participation rates among industrialized democracies (Austria and Sweden, for example, often have a 90 percent eligible voter turnout during elections.) Voter apathy and complacency permeates our culture for a number of reasons: we think our vote will not count; or regardless of who is elected, current policy will not significantly change or affect our lives; or there are just not any qualified (or honest) candidates to vote into office. Some people don't know they are required to register to vote; others can't be bothered because it is inconvenient. For still others, polling station hours conflict with their work hours. Whatever the reason, the result is that 40 percent to 60 percent of us choose to not exercise our responsibility to vote. This absence of enthusiasm for democratic participation results in a government that is out of touch with the needs and priorities of that 40 percent to 60 percent and, naturally, the "winning" leadership concerns itself with the priorities of the group that put it into power; as we have seen that generally represents special interests.

In many cases, representatives to Congress are elected by winning fewer than 25 percent of the eligible vote at state polls. Fewer than 50 percent of eligible voters cast their ballots in the 1996 presidential election, the lowest turnout since 1924. Even in the hotly debated 2004 election, a mere 61 percent of the voting population turned out to offer their vote. Of course, politicians know this trend and bank on a lack of public interest and poor voter turnout when they run for office. Consequently, a slate of leadership candidates who may be unqualified to govern find themselves elected to political office; they are now able to influence policy in ways that do not reflect the needs of the majority, but rather reflects their personal agendas or the agendas of their political or corporate allegiances, who funded them on their way to victory. Special interests governing the majority is contrary to the very intent of our democratic design: government of, for, and by the majority of people. [In the 2004 presidential election, selecting John Kerry or George Bush struck many Americans as a choice between the lesser of two evils, because neither candidate reflected the needs and wishes of the majority. The electorate should never be in the position of having to settle for "the least worst".] Greater interest and participation from the voting population is necessary to offer and elect qualified leaders who can truly stand for and represent majority concerns, while balancing the priorities and realities of the state (security, finance, trade, etc.) they represent.

One of the most fundamental ways we can accomplish a significant directional shift in this country is by more actively participating in the democratic process. [This may seem an obvious point, but millions seem not to recognize it, or far worse, they simply do not care.] In the absence of a motivated populace, it is necessary for the government to support the ideology of democracy by not just requesting, but by requiring the electorate to meet a minimum standard of participation. This can only be accomplished through law.

I propose several options for reintroducing accountability, integrity, and trust back into our democratic process. My first recommendation revolves around voter turnout. For congressional and executive office elections to be considered valid, voter turnout must meet or exceed 67 percent (two-thirds) of the total eligible voter population. Anything less than that is simply insufficient to achieve the concept of democracy; government of, for, and by the people should reflect a true majority. To achieve this benchmark, we must allow longer and more flexible voting time frames. A five-day or multi-day voting period, which includes at least one weekend day and later evening hours, will allow all eligible

Americans to vote and result in a much higher turnout.

A major reason for voter apathy is that the electorate cannot easily gather and analyze factual information about relevant socio-economic issues or about the candidates themselves. Facts and issues are often so distorted by media and corporate interests and national committees that the American people do not know who or what to believe. Feeling both overwhelmed and uninformed as a result, millions simply wash their hands of the whole process. To address this problem, my second recommendation is to institute a "Truth-in-Running" policy for federal and state political candidates; an independent body, similar to the existing Government Accountability Office (GAO), would conduct investigations that include criminal background checks and disclosure statements from candidates. Similar in intent to the "Truth-in-Lending Act" that governs banking, a "Truth-in-Running" regulation would provide a public record of clear and complete information about each candidate's current and historical positions on social, economic, and political issues, their education, careers, etc. Such scrutiny, made fully and freely available to voters, would allow us access to more reliable information and a better understanding of the priorities and qualifications of the candidates. This would allow us to better choose a candidate that supports our needs in government. It would also reduce the ugly and uncontrolled public relations, media, lobbyist, and corporate spin doctoring we are subjected to today by providing an independent forum to evaluate potential candidates.

My third recommendation is to limit campaigning to six months before an election. A shorter campaign-rather than the current half-term of office-would allow incumbents to continue doing their jobs for an appropriate period of time and would reduce the consuming and negative political maneuvering that takes place during extended campaigning.

My fourth recommendation involves the funding of qualified candidates. Our government cannot deny or ignore the control leveled over them by corporate America. National committees, powerful lobby groups, and party allegiances have significantly diminished the essence of majority rule. The lack of public participation in the election process, coupled with corporate influence on the parties and candidates, brings us much closer to a one-party system: the Capitalist Party, the emblem of which is a gold dollar sign with two bold vertical stripes, one red and the other blue. I believe the most effective way to reintroduce integrity to the democratic process is an elimination of all "soft money" corporate and personal contributions, fundraisers, political action committees (PACs), and national committees for congressional and presidential elections. Even legitimate contributions create the appearance of impropriety, favoritism, or outright fraud, creating a public perception that the system is unfair and dishonest and that money buys favors or freedom. The current practice (by both parties) of rewarding successful fundraisers with plum jobs and political appointments reflects and reinforces the attitude "If you scratch my back, I'll scratch yours," whether the outcome is good for society or not. State and federal governments should allocate appropriate, limited funds to a number of approved candidates to campaign on their publicly-stated platforms. The candidates would be subject to a full public accounting of their spending and any mismanagement would result in penalties, including repayment of funds, disqualification from office, and criminal prosecution. Quite simply, the cost of electing congressional leaders should be borne by the American people via their tax contributions only. These taxpayer funds need to be the only monies made available to congressional and presidential candidates.

In order to make these proposals financially and practically viable, my fifth recommendation is for House, Senate and Presidential terms to be extended to six years, with two-year intervals between elections for each branch. [For example, in a six-year cycle, House elections would be held on year two, Senate elections on year four and Presidential elections on year six.] At the same time, term limitations should be removed. Good leaders should be allowed to govern for longer periods and a participating American populace would ensure the earlier removal of bad ones, particularly with the introduction of an election platform accountability standard. The cost to taxpayers would be minimized by strictly limited campaign funds. There is no reason why a successful campaign could not be run with limited equal funds for all parties with free and equal participation from television and media outlets. As part of their mission to inform the public, media outlets would be required to allot specific amounts of air time and print space to each candidate for the duration of the campaign, at no cost.

These are not new concerns, but they are critical issues that have not been resolved successfully or progressively, largely as a result of our failing two-party system. What has been accomplished over the past twenty-four to thirty-two years regarding education, health care, social security, judicial application, and a cumulative balanced budget? Millions of Americans still do not have sufficient health care or access to a meaningful education. Our social security fund and Medicaid are in dire jeopardy. Our judicial system is ineffective and favors the powerful and wealthy. Our cumulative deficit and overall debt is so great that it burdens generations beyond our measure. The Democratic and Republican parties continue to cater to wealthy and powerful interest groups, while using hot buttons issues and doubletalk to court the population. The cynicism and distrust are only perpetuated under a two-party system.

The ineffectuality of the two-party dichotomy is further demonstrated by the recent "nuclear option" debate. In April 2005, the Republican Senate majority wanted to change Senate rules to eliminate filibustering of judicial nominees and to allow a simple majority to carry nominations, the up or down vote, rather than the supermajority historically required to break a filibuster. The Democrats screamed foul and complained that the Republicans were trying to circumvent constitutional law. But both parties continually want to change the rules when it suits their purpose. Not so long ago it was the Democrats who wanted to eliminate filibustering. Every time I turn on the political news I am peppered with two-party partisan hate messages. This hatred forces moderate representatives into extreme positions or to turn away from politics totally. The process of partisan politics favors and severely limits choices available to the governed, and it needs to end.

My sixth recommendation is to completely and immediately eliminate the existing two-party system in favor of a five-party system comprised of (theoretically) the following positions: Liberal, Conservative, Moderate, Independent, and Environmental. A five-party system would quickly provide us the structure of a healthy government of, for, and by the people. It would also greatly reduce the opportunity for collusion and corruption from special interests (i.e., corporate power brokers, national committees, and PACs). Americans would have a much louder voice in government if they were afforded a choice of candidates that truly represented the actual range of political viewpoints and concerns that exist across the country. The multi-party system would ensure that the majority voice is heard and represented by appropriate legislation.

Another significant problem with our democratic system is the prevalence of loopholes in our legal and tax systems. My seventh recommendation is to completely overhaul our legal and tax systems to eliminate loopholes entirely. Our legal system should be restored from a money-making enterprise back to an institution of integrity that oversees order and justice in society. People have become cynical about the judicial system, as it clearly does not apply to all equally. Lawyers belong to one of the least respected professions today. The system needs to be improved to demonstrate swifter, enforceable, blind justice applied equally to everyone, including those who have a lot of money or hold positions of public trust and authority. Punishments need to be meaningful enough to deter future behavior and to encourage people to be accountable for their actions, regardless of their social status. At the same time, the trend toward over-litigating is growing out of control. Frivolous lawsuits should never see a courtroom and compensatory damages should have reasonable limits rather than record-breaking awards. Compensation for defense lawyers and prosecutors should be balanced so talent does not just shift to the defense side of the legal system and ambulance chasers have nothing left to chase but their tails.

Loopholes are often designed to bypass meaningful tax responsibilities and tend to benefit the select minority of wealthy individuals or corporations. They contribute to the separation of Americans into classes with unequal responsibilities to pay taxes. I propose to close those loopholes by changing our current tax structure and introducing a fair progressive tax on all income earned (wages, capital gains, interest, etc.) with deductions and loopholes eliminated altogether. Everyone pays tax based on what they earn-period. Earned income under a certain dollar amount would be exempt from federal income tax; higher incomes would be scaled in brackets, for example $35K to $50K would be taxed at 15 percent; $51K to $75K taxed at 16 percent, etc. As income increases, so would the appropriate tax rate, reflecting our current tax system, but without all the existing loopholes and deductions that enable high wage earners to avoid paying appropriate taxes by minimizing their income.

A similar revenue tax would be applied to corporations as well. Companies would pay a flat fee on all generated revenues, much like the requirement of a franchisee revenue contribution to a franchisor. It would simply be the cost of doing business in the United States and having access to the largest economy in the world. This tax strategy would have a profound secondary impact: it would force corporations to operate much more efficiently, as bottom line expense and cash flow management would be required for growth and viability. It would also lend great support to the prosecution of corporations fraudulently manipulating and overstating revenue figures. Corporate accountability has long been missing in the free market, and significant changes are needed to alter its current direction.

It is the social responsibility of every American to contribute to the governance of this country and the services provided for its citizens. If I am earning that much more in income, I would gladly contribute to a reasonable progressive tax for the benefit of the country to which I belong. I believe this is the feeling of most honest Americans, including the very wealthy. The threat that wealthy citizens and corporations will withhold investment in America if their tax brackets increase is baseless. This threat is regularly made by those who seek to grow their wealth without playing by the rules of the free market. They seek to influence and alter tax laws, to introduce trade barriers, and to solicit government subsidies all in the name of enhancing their profits, often at the expense of the American taxpayer. Instead, they should be relying on their ability to deliver the best quality product and service to capture the market and to maximize their profits appropriately. I make the "baseless" point predicated on the inherent nature of those who accumulate wealth: they want to make it grow. Most people I know would tell you that if they had to pay a higher tax on their $20 million dollar capital gain or golden parachute, it would not prevent them from reinvesting their net distribution in America, albeit a slightly lower one, in an effort to gain more wealth. Higher tax contributions do not restrict or deter the ability to grow wealth, but they do allow for fair tax contributions for the government to fund its activities on behalf of the people fairly and equitably.

The government pays out more than it takes in, amd as such it is constantly operating in a position of deficit; but this pattern cannot continue indefinitely. My eighth recommendation is a legal requirement for the government to operate in a position of a cumulative surplus or moderate deficit, not just for a one-year period, but for the overall cumulative financial position of the government. Realistically there will be unavoidable periods of deficit spending, but the overall balance sheet of the country needs to equate to a surplus on a regular basis. This would require the exercise of unprecedented discipline toward grants and subsidies and general government spending. Wasteful pork barrel spending of public dollars reaches into the billions each year. On our current course, our future generations will have to pay for the failures of our various leaders who have contributed to our deficits. We need to rectify this situation now by balancing the budget and bringing the cumulative deficit to zero. It is nothing short of disgraceful and embarrassing to hear the current administration suggest that the annual budget deficit will be cut in half by 2009, while passing war, highway, and energy bills that are laced with pork barrel spending and subsidies to the big contributors of the campaign coffers. It is exactly this type of thinking that will continue to bring our society to the financial brink, and it is exactly this type of thinking that American citizens need to alter.

My observations tell me that the Executive Office and the Congress of the United States under right or left control are rewriting the definition of democracy in a profoundly negative way. They are teaching us that democracy does not stand for freedom, liberty, or government of, for, and by the people. They are replacing these concepts with less than altruistic themes; namely that money, power, and relationships can buy you favors and greater wealth. The United States has the foundations in place for a great and powerful democracy, but we need to make it stronger; clear fractures in the foundation exist. We need to make it real, rather than just an ideal that is being ignored with more and more frequency.

In a true democratic environment, the citizens have the ability to elect the most qualified candidates, who in turn represent the voice of their constituents in government. The candidates should have a defined period of time to market their positions, qualifications, and differences to the American people. To make informed and educated decisions, the people need to be able to easily find unbiased factual information about potential candidates and leaders. The media should provide free and regular forums for the candidates to openly debate their differences in front of the electorate. Upon election, leaders have an absolute responsibility to execute their campaign platforms without bias, influence, or prejudice. They need to be free of corporate or minority influence so they may honor the principle of government of, for, and by the people without interference. We should be able to accomplish this within a tax base that is reasonable and provides appropriate funds to operate our government in a financially prudent and balanced manner. These changes will lift us from the "nuclear options" we face today. These changes are simple in design yet powerful in effect. Only with significant changes such as those detailed above, can we restore integrity and honor into the brilliant concept of government of, for, and by the people.

Free-Market Balance

We have the best government that money can buy.

-Mark Twain (1835-1910)

Corporations and capitalists are out of control in their influence on the election of congressmen and presidents who favor their needs. Minority free-market influence is directing American policy in a profoundly negative way. The influence takes place completely behind closed doors where favoritism and nepotism abound. This type of influence destroys the inherent design of the natural, competitive free market and compromises it completely. No longer do corporations need to creatively and constantly provide the highest quality product or service at an appropriate price level. Instead they can position themselves to purchase profits through influence or manipulation. The boundaries between our democratic system and free-market system have become so transparent it is difficult to tell the difference between the two. One subsidizes the other and all too often at the expense of the American people.

Corporations, although legally granted the rights of "persons," do not live and breathe; however, the human beings who operate them do. People are ultimately accountable for their actions and for those of the businesses and markets they operate. To have the majority will of the American people superseded by corporate influence is simply unacceptable.

There is brilliance in the conceptual framework of our free-market system; however, we need to more broadly consider our human evolution and the susceptibilities of our nature in the equation. In the free market, more than in any other of our American institutions, we need to enforce a very strong system of checks and balances-preventive measures and deterrents-to control the weaker side of our human nature and promote a higher level of social consciousness, honesty, and integrity. Our susceptibility to greed and power leaves us vulnerable to fiascos such as the failures of Enron, WorldCom, Tyco, Iraq, and dozens of others previously mentioned in these pages. These economic and political disasters have negatively influenced millions, yet they were perpetuated by only a handful of individuals.

This susceptibility, of course, does not just affect our economic status but our political reality as well. The influence of money can leave us vulnerable to major political decision making, including such debacles as the second war in Iraq, which we have subsequently learned was built on lies and deceit. This war has cost untold American and Iraqi lives and money, yet it provides substantial returns to only a handful of favored corporations.

Let us reflect on the intended design of the free-market system for a moment. The free-market capital system is designed to allow for the unfettered creation and provision of goods and services. The inherent competitive forces of the market drive quality up and prices down, which naturally benefits the end consumer and keeps the market efficient and self-regulating.

Negative human nature, exhibited by those who have the driving need to accumulate and possess power and wealth, frequently gets in the way of the otherwise healthy free-market design. A few individual capitalists, entrepreneurs, and politicians have corrupted the system with their less than altruistic motives, rationalizing the growth of their personal wealth at any cost. What these individuals have failed to recognize is that wealth is more readily generated through healthy reinvestment in the market-place rather than through control and manipulation of otherwise self-regulating market and political forces. This negative control has resulted in the suppression of creativity and progress, and has forced the middle and lower classes to bear the burdens of lost jobs, lost pensions, increased energy and health care costs, etc. Simply consider how the top ten energy and pharmaceutical companies have registered staggering cumulative profits in the past few years while receiving billions of taxpayer dollars from government provided subsidies; yet equally staggering are the number of Americans who cannot afford energy to heat their homes or drugs to survive their health issues. This equation is upside down.

Let's consider the energy industry in particular, because it is a classic example of how profit and control demands have so negatively influenced public policy and so blunted the creative spirit of the American work force. Oil, natural gas, and their by-products produce and wield phenomenal wealth and power, because oil-based energy is, today, essential for our survival. Our entire infrastructure and way of life has been built around it. As such, oil production, distribution, and consumption are among the greatest sources of corruption, conflict, and wealth in the world.

The American energy industry, in turn, is one of the most powerful lobby groups, wielding tremendous influence and control of energy policy at home and around the world. These energy conglomerates have enormous revenue, profits, and assets in the billions of dollars, and yet they continue to be subsidized by American tax dollars. In recent months they have recorded enormous profits at the expense of the American people. They have done so under false pretenses, suggesting that natural dis-

Jeff Shiring

asters and war are the primary cause of such profits. Our political leadership is deeply influenced by those enormous energy conglomerate coffers, which can and do buy a stake at any decision making table. [As one of his first acts in office, Ronald Reagan quietly removed the solar panels installed on the White House roof. It is no secret that the energy industry was one of his largest soft money contributors. Reagan's decision to steer away from the reality of the energy crisis of the1970s has proven to be one of his greatest blunders, as it has been for every president since who has failed to consider viable energy alternatives.]

Unfortunately for the industry, oil-based energy has a very limited remaining lifespan. Domestic oil production peaked in the mid-1970s sparking the oil crisis of that decade and the emergence of OPEC. Many experts believe that between 2010 and 2030, we will have depleted more than half of all the available sources of oil. We know that oil has a limited life, and it no longer be considered as a means of providing sustainable energy. Continued reliance on it is detrimental to the planet, but the fact remains that as long as there is oil, companies will find a way to collect it, and consumers will use it until it becomes unaffordable. It is clear that global demand for oil is increasing (typically by 2 percent a year) and production is dwindling (roughly 5 percent a year).[402] This results in inevitable increases in the price of a barrel (to a record-breaking $70 in August 2005). The oil that is left is harder to get at and more expensive to refine, and higher oil prices keep the cycle going until the oil runs out or people just stop paying the prices.

The fact remains that we are already incredibly late in introducing, promoting, and implementing meaningful energy alternatives into our daily lives. Meanwhile the consumer is burdened with the ever increasing cost of fuel for our vehicles and homes, as well as providing billions of dollars in subsidies to the energy industry through our tax dollars, most of which are ear-marked for technologies to discover or drill for new oil sources, rather than alternative energy research and development. This is all done while the energy industry is posting record financial profits.

Under the Reagan administration, some twenty-five years ago, the government should have established commissions and incentives to promote alternative and sustainable energy research and practices. They should have begun phasing in energy alternatives (i.e., tax incentives for development, mandatory tidal turbines in coastal regions, energy-efficiency requirements for new homes, and tax credits for retro-fitting older homes and office buildings with solar, tidal, and wind power); this would have enabled our entire societal infrastructure to evolve away from the combustion engine and fossil fuels long before we would be forced to take emergency measures. The American workforce, with the right focus and incentives, would have created viable alternative energy sources and technologies long before now. A much earlier investment in the development of alternative energy solutions could have, by now, yielded phenomenal profit returns with significant positive impact on our environment and ultimately the cessation of our dependency on oil from the Middle East. Instead we are fighting a war thousands of miles away from home, directly or indirectly to control access to a vast supply of oil, spending hundreds of billions of dollars and losing countless lives in the process.

In the very near future, we will be faced with the huge challenge of completely redesigning the entire foundation of our society to accommodate new energy sources and technologies at a projected cost of hundreds of billions more dollars. Interestingly, a handful of conglomerates will get these contracts-the major oil companies who have quietly bought up many of the patents and technologies produced over the past several decades. Oil companies such as Chevron have formed "strategic alliances" with smaller cutting edge alternative energy firms, such as Energy Conversion Devices, Inc., which are designing applications for hydrogen fuel cells and solar energy. When the oil industry crashes, "Big Oil" will have ownership of the solutions to switch over, save the day, and rob the American people a third time with the enormous costs of conversion away from fossil fuel consumption. (Some are more open about their plans than others: in their new advertising BP now stands for Beyond Petroleum, rather than British Petroleum.)

Political and industry leaders have had countless opportunities to alter the course of history, to protect the public and the environment, but they have failed to do so simply because of profit demands and wealth accumulation. Our refusal to ratify the Kyoto Protocol is largely owing to the threats of energy industry leaders who have made it abundantly clear they will eliminate jobs, if they are required to divert their own capital dollars into environmental solutions. Polls show that 71 percent of the American people (and 73 percent of policymakers) support our participation in the Kyoto treaty,[403] yet our government continues to buckle under corporate control and influence.

This is a primary example of how free-market demands can conflict with fundamental social responsibility and majority opinion, as the American public pays multiple times for the profits and subsidies of energy companies. The backward formula of minority influence, in this case a free-market industry, setting public policy while enriching itself to the detriment of the American public needs to be reversed in its entirety. Corporations have to be accountable to the society in which they participate.

I am a true believer in the phenomenal benefits of a balanced free-market system. The free market we operate, however, is not a truly free or an independent entity; it is connected to the government and the consumers/voters who underpin the whole economic system. The theoretical checks and balances are insufficient to protect consumers from being vic-

Jeff Shiring

tims of the highly evolved corporate culture of greed and mismanagement. We need to reevaluate the effectiveness of our controls over a corrupted system by implementing meaningful solutions that use inherent market forces and are more closely controlled and guided by the American people.

One way to achieve this balance is my first recommendation: institute government competition and control in the free market. Certain industries that are providing products and services essential to the survival of society should be removed from the corrupted profit demands of the free market and placed in the hands of a public trust or in public/private cooperatives with limitations on profit margins. I am not suggesting a government monopoly, but a deeper level of participation and regulation whereby the consumer is not unfairly gouged for the necessities of life. Government enterprise funds or businesses, such as the U.S. Postal Service and public water utilities, are examples of how the government can and should enter the market. These government entities are known as enterprise funds. Specifically, I propose a government enterprise fund for critical industries such as health care, including drug research and development and manufacturing; energy production and distribution including oil, natural gas, hydroelectricity, nuclear fuels, and alternative energy technologies; food production; and transportation by air, rail, and road. If these industries were controlled by nonprofit or limited profit enterprises, the benefits to the consumer and market would be incredible. The government's share of income on provision of these goods and services would go directly into providing managed costs to the people, while excess funds would be utilized toward balancing the books. The U.S. Postal Service pays for itself and provides excellent service at a price that is extremely reasonable for the consumer. This example needs to be copied in industries that provide essential products and services.

While bureaucratic inefficiency and governmental lack of integrity are obstacles, to this proposal today, they should not prevent us from thinking through viable long-term solutions to current and future free-market issues plaguing us. In trying to solve the giant problems, we need to be able to think out of the box and see past the obvious obstacles and inefficiencies that exist.

In keeping with earlier proposals for democratic reform, I reiterate a prior recommendation for free-market balance: hold any and all violators of public trust by any free-market leader, investor, CEO, or other market participant to the highest standard of law. These violators must be met with swift and severe judicial repercussions, including the loss of patents, licenses, and permits, repayment of capital gain or income, loss of privilege to operate and compete in similar businesses, and jail terms. The Sarbanes-Oxley Act is only a good first step; so much more is needed to bring a level of fair play back into the market.

My third recommendation also comes from an earlier section: completely eliminate corporate contributions and lobbying to the political process. The responsibility of influencing governing leaders and policy belongs squarely in the relationship between elected officials and the people. Instead we have lobbyists and corporate contributors pushing their agendas on congressional representatives, who then vote on policy decisions; the proper process should be elected officials acting on the behalf of the majority of their constituents. When trial lawyers and tobacco industry representatives and energy lobbyists can contribute millions of dollars to election campaigns and candidates, and yank the purse strings of domestic and foreign policy, there is a definite disconnect from democracy and a clear, unwritten rule that money does buy favors and influence policy.

We need to reestablish public trust in the free market. We need to bring back fair play, ethics, and integrity into our economic system; one that allows for economic growth while ensuring consumer protection by removing inappropriate corporate influence on our government. In doing so, we will immediately inject healthy competition and efficiency back into the system, improving the quality of products and services and restoring accountability. To counter the negative side of human nature, a strong system of checks, balances, and deterrents needs to be implemented and enforced in our economy. Strong government intervention is needed on the free market and not vice versa. Co-operatives and government-owned industry need to be implemented for industries providing life necessities. These recommendations will benefit society by providing low-cost essentials to consumers, creating jobs and providing significant revenue to benefit our federal government balance sheet. They will also force corporations and businesses to operate without the ability to buy profits: to achieve growth and wealth they will be required to produce and market products that are of the highest quality at a price the market will bear. These solutions will bring back honor, integrity, and accountability, not just to the free-market system, but to society as a whole.

The Loss of Faith

When religion and politics travel in the same cart, the riders believe nothing can stand in their way.

-Frank Herbert (1920-1986)

In my mind, nothing can so negatively affect a people or a society as a continual breach of religious faith and trust. When faith and trust are abused and wielded with incredible hypocrisy, there is a profound impact on people's ability to believe in their individual God, their religious institutions, and in the human spirit as well.

From a religious perspective I tend to lean toward Christianity, although it is a constant challenge with what I observe from those in leadership positions in the political and Christian fields. I am truly baffled with the state of Christian leadership and Christians believers who have blindly followed those who profess to be Christian leaders or leaders who profess to be Christians. I listen to the Bushs, Clintons, DeLays, and Falwells of the world declare their faith so passionately and then watch them act so passionately against the constructs of that very faith. It boils down to incredible hypocrisy. They hypocritically manage their faith with lies, deceit, and corruption; I would struggle to call them Christians. One cannot be a Christian by declaration alone, but by both our declarations and by our actions. This type of hypocrisy is peppered throughout the religious world today. It is very destructive and sad, as so many people of faith (Christian, Muslim, Hindu) are blindly following along and losing the message of hope and compassion that can be found in almost all the dominant religions. These healthy values are being replaced with values of intolerance, hate, and deception. It is truly time for members of each faith to step up and hold our professed leaders to the true constructs of our respective faiths. These constructs include accountability, compassion, honesty, tolerance, and hope. We can achieve this by openly talking about these critical and very healthy values. We can follow this up by distancing ourselves from the leaders of our faith whose actions do not support their professions of faith: individuals such as Falwell, bin Laden, Bush, and others whose actions are inconsistent with their faith. We can vote out people who profess Christians beliefs yet lie, cheat, and steal their way into office by preying on our valued Christian beliefs: people like Bush, Clinton, and DeLay, who only use Christian faith to solicit votes or to fulfill commitments to extreme positions.

Our religious and political leaders profess their faiths but demonstrate their hypocrisy daily. The Catholic Church's cover-up of horrific child abuse at the hands of hundreds of priests who were also preaching Church doctrine shattered the trust of millions. Christian Evangelists, preaching salvation to millions of other believers while preying on the weak and elderly to finance their extravagant lifestyles, have similarly breached their sacred trust. Presidents and political leaders avowing faith in God and Christian principles while flagrantly breaking them, publicly unaccountable but "forgiven by God," have further stretched the thin thread of our collective conviction and trust. When this trust is completely broken-may God save our souls.

These are the primary examples of hypocrisy in the name of God (in whatever manifestation that may be for people) that have badly damaged our spirituality and caused a breach in faith that is critical to American society and fabric. Far too many authority figures publicly profess their faith in God and yet live their lives in ways that contradict basic, shared religious principles and doctrine. By preaching one thing and practicing another, they set an incredibly profound negative example that teaches us we do not have to be accountable for our daily actions. Our own collective and individual intolerance of other people-whether it is hatred toward Muslims in the Middle East or Pentecostal Christians down the street-is a glaring manifestation of the loss of our connection to true spiritual awareness and practice to the Christian principles of acceptance and compassion.

This breach in faith and trust is causing us to lose our faith in faith itself. We are learning not to trust in any institutions, in society, or more broadly, the human spirit. We are losing our collective ability as Americans to believe that anything is possible. Instead, we are learning to believe it is possible to get away with anything. The power of belief in humanity, the one that saw us put a man on the moon, is fading to a cynical memory. I believe that once this ability to believe and to have faith is lost, all that is great and good in our spirit will be lost as well.

Our religious institutions should be restored to a level of integrity that inspires us to conduct ourselves as decent, compassionate, and moral people. Without attacking any particular belief system, I believe that we must begin to assume much more accountability in life, as opposed to relying on absolution and forgiveness in death. It's not enough to break the tenets of our faith, or misuse our positions of authority, and say, "I've made peace with God." We must first make peace with those whose trust we have betrayed and accept the consequences of our actions.

My first recommendation is to introduce an independent religious oversight body-comprised of officials from various religious affiliations, lay members, and government officials-that would investigate improprieties and apply meaningful laws that would govern all religious institutions. These laws, one of which would remove the current tax-exempt status enjoyed by religious organizations, would require strict accounting of all of collections and spending to ensure that funds are being allocated appropriately (i.e., to the benefit of their parishioners and not on luxury homes, shoe collections, or prostitutes) by the representatives of those affiliations. Religious leaders need to be accountable in the criminal justice system (not just in Canon law) so that instances of fraud and sexual abuse are dealt with publicly, swiftly, and under the common law that governs all of us. Those found guilty of breaking these laws should be permanently barred from publicly or privately representing a religious organization or affiliation in future, and of course, they should be punished to the fullest extent of the law.

Our country was founded on a desire for political and religious freedom; however, our nation has evolved with predominantly Christian values. The majority of Americans (76.5 percent) believe in Christianity and the tenets that have become an integral part of our culture and legal system and are represented in our oaths, our currency, and our anthems. My second recommendation revolves around the continued dilution of this common ground we share. I propose we embrace the faith of the majority while walking the line of separation of church and state. For example, Christmas is a sacred Christian holiday for the majority of Americans. Let us rejoice in Christmas as a Christian holiday and reject diluted holiday themes ("Sparkle Season") that were created to keep from alienating or ignoring those who are not Christians. We should celebrate our religious history and the common tenets of faith we share, but we should do so in an environment where our government continues to recognize the holidays of many other religions. The double-edged sword of a democracy is the necessity of accepting majority opinion and beliefs even when they differ from our own. At the same time, we have to preserve and respect the freedom we have to practice whatever faith we believe and to speak freely about those beliefs. We should be able to celebrate the Christian tradition for what it is and how it brings us together, while simultaneously recognizing and embracing the unique and special traditions of other faiths and religions throughout the year. We must not lose sight of what defines us as a nation. Tolerance and inclusion should be the common thread that binds us together as Americans.

This great country needs to rebuild itself from the inside out. The loss of trust and faith from all social influences has greatly affected us, but none so much as a breach of trust in the religious community. Because of the depth of this impact, we need to provide a much stronger system of oversight to ensure the activities of religious leaders can be reviewed and managed. We need to bring back hope and belief to the religious realm. We must renew our faith in those who lead and influence us. We must learn to be accountable in life. May God bless Humanity.

The Celebrity Charade

Hero-worship is mostly idol gossip.

-Anonymous

The influence of fame and celebrity on our society and culture is profound, but it is unfortunately also profoundly negative. We have all witnessed, most often through the media, the abuse of celebrity and the impact it has had on our youth. I have become so disenchanted with celebrity and the cult of personality that I very rarely watch sports or Hollywood movies. I prefer to spend time with my son and avoid television so he does not have to see basketball stars fighting on the court and in the stands, or Hollywood stars arrested for shoplifting or DUI, or Olympic athletes doping up to win gold. Steroid use and drug abuse and the books that tell about it are virtually a badge of honor among pro athletes. Sports figures and Hollywood icons, by virtue of the privileges they enjoy (fame, wealth, public adoration) hold a position of public trust. In that position, they have a responsibility to conduct themselves appropriately and act as models of behavior without deterring the ability to be unique and a creative individual. It can't be easy to be in the spotlight all the time, but the alternative is to give it up. Millions of people spend the money that supports the lavish lifestyles of their favorite athletes, actors, and musicians through ticket sales and merchandise. In return, they are entitled to expect a high standard of behavior from those celebrities. When those celebrities violate the public trust they need be held accountable: the law needs to be applied swiftly, as it would be to the average law breaker. All too often, the rich and famous seem to be given special treatment in the courts, if they get to court at all. The example set for young fans is appalling.

For their part, fans have an equal responsibility to respect the privacy of their idols and conduct themselves in a civil and orderly fashion. Stalking, game fights, parental abuse of referees, and other abhorrent behavior cannot be tolerated and needs to be dealt with in the same strict manner as any violation of public trust. Our culture needs to turn off the reality TV, heave itself off the couch, and take a giant step toward improving the quality of our individual lives. Our definition of hero needs to include an incredible parent or teacher or inventor, not a good-looking actor or athlete who nets $20 million per film or sports contract and is convicted of rape.

Athletes in particular have an obligation to their fans to perform to the best of their natural abilities. Sporting events and those who excel in them inspire near reverence in our culture. True ability and dedication in any sport is admirable and inspiring, but false excellence is ideal shattering. The use of any drug or substance that accelerates, enhances, or alters the bodies or performances of athletes in all sports at all levels should be prohibited. Frequent random drug testing needs to be implemented with strict penalties for violations including, but not limited to, immediate suspension, loss of pay, and possible banishment from the sport. Test results should be made public as a deterrent for other athletes and the fans who emulate them.

Olympic athletes are already subject to strict monitoring and severe penalties for drug use. They are also subject to the heavy pressures of sponsorship requirements and competing against professional athletes for medals. My first recommendation revolves around the Olympics. I propose we restore the Olympics to its original purpose: to be the ultimate competition between the best amateur athletes in the world. Obviously these athletes need to be able to live while they are training to win medals for their country; to that cause, they should receive enough government funding that they do not have to rely on corporate endorsements for their well-being. With big business sponsorship, we are destroying the essence of amateur sports and removing the affiliation and loyalty of teams to their community and their country.

Even at the high school level, student athletes are faced with enormous sponsorship pressure: perks, preferential treatment, and the promise of the big leagues weigh so heavily on these teens, they are frequently pressured into making decisions that could ruin their lives. My second recommendation is to allow our young people to enjoy their youth in sports by removing all corporate sponsorship and steroid use from the realm of high school athletics. This is not to say that corporations cannot contribute to a school sports program, but they should do so without strings-a high school field should not be called the "corporate" sports area, and kids should not be required to wear a corporate logo.

By allowing high school athletes to develop without the pressure of drug use or corporate sponsorship, we can provide them the opportunity to grow naturally and free of added adolescent pressures. By allowing the Olympics to be free of all drug-enhanced performances and to be held with true amateur athletes, we can bring back the incredible spirit of the games as they were intended.

The third recommendation revolves around celebrity and the application of law. It cannot be repeated too many times-those who are in a position of public trust should be held to the highest standard of law. Our youth need to learn that actions have consequences, especially for those who are in positions of trust. Violating that trust has measured consequences. This truly begins the cycle of teaching and reeducating our youth on the values of law; and what an incredible tool this can be for our youth and for our society.

Finally, in the spirit of avoiding the dreaded "cancelled season" of any sport, I recommend that team owners force league parity by eliminating free-agency and by strictly penalizing athletes who fail to play for their drafting team. Players' unions were created to enhance compensation for pro athletes, and they have fulfilled their purpose. Between unions and agents, team owners and fans are held hostage by player contracts and sky high salaries. Considering that the typical professional athlete has a career that lasts between four and ten years, team owners assume a great deal of risk. They often invest their own money into the team, betting on future success. Players argue they should have an equal share in that success, but the reality is they don't have the same liability or assume the same risk in potential failure of the team, which is a business like any other. (They also often don't want to participate in being a role model. How often do you hear of team owners humiliating themselves by throwing punches and getting arrested?) Players, through agents, should be able to negotiate fair contracts and pay, but they should not be allowed to strike or derail the sport for a season or longer.

It is important for us to remember that, individually and collectively, we can influence change. One of the most powerful tools we can use is our economic voice. If we don't like how our celebrities are behaving, then we can take away their status simply by refusing to support them. We stop going to their movies; we stop going to their games; we stop buying their music; we stop reading magazines that promote them. If there is no audience, there is no icon. We must also recognize bad behavior for what it is, not who it comes from; cheating on your girlfriend is not cool just because Usher sings about it. Throwing a phone at a concierge is not any less of an assault because Russell Crowe did it, and he's a good guy. Attacking fellow fans in the bleachers because they heckled your favorite player, or someone got fouled, is unacceptable. It's a game! It's all entertainment, not a blueprint for how we should live our lives. Here is the ability for us to learn just how powerful our economic voice can be. When we boycott a particular celebrity or athlete because of poor behavior, there is pressure on them from sponsors and owners to mend their ways (which gets translated directly into their bank accounts). We also need to ensure an equal application of existing law. To have a baseball player serve his penalty after the playoffs or to have an track star serve her time after the Olympics is destructive to the collective sense of accountability and fair play. The practice of favoring celebrity needs to be reversed in its entirety: justice, after all, is blind.

Celebrity will always play a critical role in our society. The enjoyment of a wonderful movie, the thrill of seeing our home town team win the Superbowl, the excitement of seeing a movie star will never change. What we can do is ensure the trust of the American people is more broadly defined and acted upon through celebrity.

Media Matters

All media exist to invest our lives with artificial perceptions and arbitrary values.

-Marshall McLuhan (1911-1980)

The media-everything we use to gather and disseminate information-is a collection of communication tools that are an essential part of our modern existence. We look to the media to learn about the world and about ourselves. We use it to buy and sell, learn and teach, entertain and inform. But like any other entity that is ubiquitous, the media is subject to abuse and manipulation by anyone who has a stake in it, particularly producers (of news, entertainment programming, marketing material, and so on). As consumers, we are captive to that manipulation. Increasingly, the mainstream media has become a mere money machine telling us what to think, what to buy, what to feel, and how to look. Media

Jeff Shiring

producers, especially marketers, prey on our fears, our compassion, and our vulnerabilities all in the name of profits. Sometimes we become aware of being exploited as consumers and we balk, but generally we are content to blindly let them work their magic on us and we buy into what they are selling.

The paradox of our media is while it is often responsible for the creation of new and popular culture, it is also a reflection of the existing mores and values of our society. A significant number of Americans panicked at the briefest glimpse of a semi-bared breast on television; the backlash resulted in a cloud of censorship that rained on broadcasters across the country. At the same time, the highest rated shows on mainstream television, such as *Law and Order* and *CSI*-full of violence, gore, death, and bare bottoms-continued to air and spawned multiple spin-off series. Cable networks, not subject to the same FCC decency guidelines as the regular broadcasters, have continued to run prime time programming with graphic nudity and sexual content (as well as violence and gore). The internet pornography industry has grown exponentially in the past five years. There is obviously a huge demand in the U.S. for sex as entertainment, but we can't seem to make up our minds about what are acceptable parameters.

As a nation, we are particularly conservative in our attitudes about sex and sexuality. Compared to Europe and Asia, Americans are generally perceived as repressed and puritanical. It doesn't take a psychology degree to know that sexual repression leads to unhealthy behavior. As a result, the situation we find ourselves in is a kind of sexual schizophrenia. We continue to try to prevent our children from accessing practical and realistic sexual education courses in school, which would help them better understand their sexuality and prepare them to be responsible, healthy sexual beings, yet many of us are ill-equipped to honestly and accurately address the subject at home (and so we don't). We rant about the inappropriate dress and behavior of pop icons on television, but then allow our kids to emulate them; we buy the belly shirts and super low-rise jeans for our daughters and let our sons listen to music with lyrics that degrade women and make light of casual and explicit sexual behavior. The result of our mixed messages? Nearly 33 percent of adolescents report having had sex by age fifteen, and the majority of teens believe that oral sex doesn't count. (I think I have heard that somewhere before.)

My first recommendation to improve the inescapable influence of the media is for American adults to begin to mature in their individual and collective thought processes and values. We need to mature in our knowledge and acceptance that not everyone shares the same lifestyle, race, religion, sexuality, and language. We need to broaden our viewpoint just enough to rid ourselves of intolerance and hatred. We should be comfortable enough with ourselves to be secure in our own opinions and attitudes, while respecting those of others. Our leaders, social and political, need to begin addressing our maturity, or lack of it, for what it is and begin to promote respect for differing opinions. We need to promote acceptance and tolerance without being compelled to discard our own core values.

My second recommendation is to provide our youth with the fundamentals of healthy knowledge regarding the human body, human nature, and sexuality. Regardless of our religious leanings or upbringing, we need to provide information to our children both inside and outside the home. We need to teach our youth about their bodies: how they work; how to respect their own and other people's; and how to protect themselves and stay healthy. As parents and educators, we have a responsibility to openly address the biology, beauty, and risks of sex. (This recommendation echoes an earlier one about spending formal classroom time learning about virtues, integrity, honor, who we are, and how we want to live our lives.)

Parents need to watch what their kids are watching and discuss what they see, or better yet, turn off the TV in favor of healthier parent and child interaction. We need to listen to their music and talk about what messages they are getting. We need to face the fact that sexuality comes in many forms, and responsible expression of it is a natural part of the human condition. If kids don't learn about sex and sexuality at home, in an accepting, open environment, they are surely going to go looking for information-any information-elsewhere: on the internet, at school, and among peers. Giving them the tools and information required to make responsible and informed decisions about their bodies doesn't promote sexual activity; but not giving them the tools is negligence. Time and again studies show that high-risk behavior is born out of ignorance. Parents have the ultimate responsibility to provide the information their kids need: if they are unable or unwilling to do so, then there should be appropriate sources available to direct them to find answers, including early exposure and education in the public school system. The media and the regulatory bodies that guide it have an important role to play in promoting positive and consistent messages about sex and sexuality. Censoring that information and pushing it underground because it might offend someone is irresponsible.

In terms of how Americans are manipulated by our media, news reporting is of particular concern. The United States has one of the most powerful propaganda machines in the world. (Witness the demonstration of masses of Muslims around the world after a snippet in the May 9, 2005, issue of *Newsweek* reported that prison guards at Guantánamo Bay had desecrated copies of the Qu'ran as an interrogation tactic: violence in Afghanistan alone resulted in seventeen deaths.) Our deeply cherished freedom of speech exposes us to bias, misinformation, indoctrination,

Jeff Shiring

and outright lies. Controlling interests of the media machine naturally have their own agendas and viewpoints, but freedom of the press in news reporting has reached a point where truth no longer has an objective meaning. Rather than having an independent media that objectively reports the news, facts and events are diluted and twisted to best reflect the political bent of the news outlet. The press is free to present its own truth in whatever way will draw the biggest viewership. More and more of these news outlets are owned by fewer and fewer controlling interests, further limiting public access to true, unsensationalized information. The FCC (or a similar body) needs to institute further restrictions on media monopolies to maintain a truly free and independent press. The government and the people need to prevent limited control, production, distribution, and reporting of news, while protecting and ensuring the open environment of a multitude of divergent news sources. Journalists need to be protected from corporate edicts that force them to change or kill their stories because the information, while in the public's interest, may affect someone's bottom line.

In keeping with the need for an independent and plural press, I recommend that the government create an independent twenty-four-hour-a-day news agency. NPR was established with this intent but has been increasingly criticized for reporting biased news and opinions, including those of reporters from other networks. An independent, unaffiliated group-possibly another branch of the Government Accountability Office-should be granted equal (or first) access to government information over privately held, for-profit media networks. This group should be the media instrument that accomplishes the objectives outlined earlier in the democracy section, providing the public with "truth-in-running" disclosures from all political candidates. This media body would be held under public scrutiny with a strict system of checks and balances to ensure it reports unbiased facts rather than partisan lines. It would be accountable to Congress and the electorate, but its policies and directives would not be set by the government (to avoid conflict of interest issues).

Commercial advertising in the media is another concern, particularly when it is directed at children. I recommend truth-in-lending-style rules for marketers, so that companies must include factual information, based on solid research and market testing, in their advertising. That is not to say that creative license should be banned, but false advertising should be. Disclosure of research sources, statistics, and proof of any claims regarding effectiveness or benefit should be mandatory and not limited to small print.

I recommend that predatory and misleading marketing practices that target children under twelve years of age, adults over sixty-five, and disadvantaged citizens-those who are most vulnerable to advertising-be eliminated. There is something terribly wrong when eight-year-olds are recruited by large companies to test market new products and trends in order to maximize corporate profits. There is something terribly wrong when seniors on fixed incomes are lured by false advertising into spending large sums of money on "miracle" health products.

Corporate branding is an enormously lucrative part of marketing, especially in the toy and clothing industries, but it should be subject to stricter controls when directed at youngsters. For example, beta testing of products aimed at children up to age twelve should be strictly controlled or eliminated. It should be illegal to solicit marketing information from children. Marketing in schools should be prohibited, especially corporate sponsorship and advertising at athletic events. Media awareness courses should be a mandatory part of the school curriculum, starting at the elementary level. We as consumers can exert our own pressure on these companies to change their practices simply by boycotting (loudly) their products and brands and the media outlets that advertise them, and by not giving in to the "pester factor" that advertisers count on when marketing to children. Stricter controls on media marketing will not halt the evolution of trends or the creation of new products and services, but they will change the "in your face" nature of the marketplace for the better.

It's time to start demanding fundamental changes in our media by enacting laws that restrict media ownership, predatory marketing, and false advertising. The media needs to be held more accountable to higher standards of publication and broadcast journalism. Those standards should be fair and firm, not based on a slide rule of ratings and profit potential. The public needs to have access to factual and complete information about products and services in the marketplace, as well as news and current events, to be able to make informed decisions about our lives. To think independently, we need to have a truly free and independent press that is unconstrained by corporate interests.

It is also time to exercise that independent thinking and demonstrate some personal maturity. We should be relieved we do not live in a society constrained by excessive censorship and a state-run press. While watching *Big Brother* on television may be entertaining for millions of people, the difference between reality and reality television still exists. It is up to us to separate ourselves from or ignore material we find offensive, not to dictate what is acceptable to others. As in most aspects of our lives as Americans, consumers who carefully exercise their economic (and parental) control, making mindful choices and teaching their children to do the same, can elicit significant change.

Today's media readily thinks for us. It dictates what to think, how to vote, what styles are in and what to watch. In this very influential area, we need to mature as a culture, while better managing the media outlets. Many of my proposals contain dual solutions for change. In the media section this is very clear: we cannot effect change simply or just on one side of the equation. Yes, the media realm needs to change, but simultaneously our individual values need to be strengthened so we are not so easily moved by the media. The less influence the media has, the more we as individuals of this great country will learn to stand on our own two feet; in turn, this will better enable us to solicit the type of changes necessary to continue moving forward.

Conclusion

We as a country need to clearly define our priorities for our future based on the foundations of our past while recognizing the necessity of progress, change, and evolution. Today's priorities are all too often defined by extreme positions. Foundations that were drafted 225 years ago, while brilliant in design, need to constantly be revised and measured against both the progress and limitations of our human nature and spirit. The observations in this book demonstrate that the country is spiraling out of control and immediate change is necessary to stop the momentum. I deeply believe this change needs to begin within ourselves by accepting greater responsibility for our lives and decisions. From there we need to redefine the majority view of our national priorities and bring our leadership back to a system of government of, for, and by the people. We should be addressing and solving critical problems in health care, finance, foreign policy, law, democracy, and family rather than the narrow agendas of the extreme left or right. In my mind, it is not a priority for the entire country to become absorbed for weeks in one family's decision whether or not to disconnect a person's feeding tube. It is a priority to solve the challenges that affect everyone in this country every single day. Our past and current governments have not managed to resolve the perennial issues that we face. Millions of Americans are not afforded a quality education or adequate health care. Our deficit is at a record high burdening future generations beyond our lifetime. Our politicians, religious leaders, entrepreneurs, and legal representatives are all regarded with suspicion and derision, which affects not only how we perceive ourselves but how the world perceives us. We need to allow the democratic process to operate without undue influence from the free market, and we need to respect and apply the rules of law consistently and blindly without preference to class distinction, wealth, race, or religion.

Relative to Europe and Asia, we are a young country, and I believe our current maturity at times reflects our age. We are fortunate not to have experienced the trials of many nations such as world wars fought on our lands, devastating famine, plague, etc. Yet we have not always learned from the history of those countries and systems who have experienced devastation. We must be cautious in maintaining our current direction without recourse. Our rapid development and rise to become the world's superpower has caused a global perception of a country that is arrogant and invincible, possessive of our superpower status and entitled to maintain it at all costs. And at times, we have acted carelessly with our economic, political, and military might. It is time for us to step back and examine our values and demonstrate maturity within our own borders and to the rest of the world. It is time to acknowledge our personal and national mistakes and accept responsibility for such. It is time to return to our senses and embrace our principles of honor, integrity, and accountability for all and not that of entitlement.

It is time for us to take over the wheel and drive this country forward with our active participation in our own lives, our families, and our local, state, and national politics. By taking an interest in what's going on around us, by exercising our right to vote, and by selectively applying our incredible purchasing power, we can effect change in the election system and its outcomes as well as in policy governing social justice and integrity. By exerting public pressure on corrupt and uncontrolled institutions-corporations, religious organizations, media conglomerates, professional athletes, and the entertainment machine-we can bring justice and integrity back into these highly influential social structures. We can and must demand this of ourselves and our social influences, particularly the democratic processes of the United States, and lead this process of change. If a person who has struggled so in transitioning from a young man into adulthood can make these changes, I submit that anyone can.

It is our right to enjoy the benefits of freedom provided by the United States, but it is our responsibility to ensure that the beacon of freedom and liberty is not lost while under our stewardship. Let us begin today this revolution of personal accountability and growth, democratic reform, free-market accountability, spiritual accountability, media reform, and celebrity responsibility. Let us begin this revolution today before it is simply too late.

---

[402] Chris Seper and John Funk. "Era of cheap oil over: Worldwide scramble on to avert a crisis," Newhouse News Service, *The Chronicle Herald*, June 19, 2005, p. 4.

[403] "Study Shows Rift Between Public Opinion and American Foreign Policy." Citizens for Global Solutions, February 7, 2005, http://www.globalsolutions.org/programs/glob_engage/news/foreign_policy_gap.html (retrieved April 12, 2005).

Jeff Shiring